This book is the first full-length analytical study of the music of Ruth Crawford Seeger. Crawford was a pivotal figure in the American avant-garde, the so-called 'ultra-modern' movement of the 1920s and 1930s. In addition to her historical significance, as part of the first generation of American composers to step out from the shadow of European models, her music deserves attention for its original and compelling structures and its expressive power. Crawford created new ways of writing melodies, of combining them in heterogeneous juxtaposition, of projecting musical ideas over the largest spans of time, and of structuring rhythm and dynamics alongside pitch. In her innovative musical language, Crawford wrote a small handful of works that should now take their rightful place in the musical modernist canon.

Music in the Twentieth Century

GENERAL EDITOR Arnold Whittall

The music of Ruth Crawford Seeger

Music in the Twentieth Century

GENERAL EDITOR Arnold Whittall

This series offers a wide perspective on music and musical life in the twentieth century.

Books included will range from historical and biographical studies concentrating particularly on the context and circumstances in which composers were writing, to analytical and critical studies concerned with the nature of musical language and questions of compositional process. The importance given to context will also be reflected in studies dealing with, for example, the patronage, publishing, and promotion of new music, and in accounts of the musical life of particular countries.

PUBLISHED TITLES

Robert Orledge *Satie the composer*
Kathryn Bailey *The twelve-note music of Anton Webern*
Silvina Milstein *Arnold Schoenberg: notes, sets, forms*
Christopher Hailey *Franz Schreker, 1878–1934: a cultural biography*
James Pritchett *The music of John Cage*

The music of
Ruth Crawford Seeger

JOSEPH N. STRAUS

CAMBRIDGE
UNIVERSITY PRESS

Published by the Press Syndicate of the University of Cambridge
The Pitt Building, Trumpington Street, Cambridge CB2 1RP
40 West 20th Street, New York, NY 10011–4211, USA
10 Stamford Road, Oakleigh, Melbourne 3166, Australia

First published 1995

Printed in Great Britain at the University Press, Cambridge

A catalogue record for this book is available from the British Library

Library of Congress cataloguing in publication data

Straus, Joseph Nathan.
The music of Ruth Crawford Seeger / Joseph N. Straus.
        p.   cm. – (Music in the twentieth century)
Includes bibliographical references.
ISBN 0 521 41646 9 hardback
1. Seeger, Ruth Crawford, 1901–1953 – Criticism and interpretation.
I. Title. II. Series.
ML410.S4446S77   1995
780'. 92–dc20   94–21135   CIP   MN

ISBN 0 521 41646 9 hardback

To my parents

Contents

Acknowledgments

My work on this book was supported by a fellowship from the American Council of Learned Societies and, in its later stages, by a Presidential Research Award at Queens College. The musical examples were expertly prepared by Frank Samarotto, with financial support from the Research Foundation of the City University of New York and the Sonneck Society. John Holzaepfel meticulously prepared the index. Many friends and colleagues read part or all of the manuscript and made helpful suggestions, including Michael Cherlin, Javier Gonzalez, Ellie Hisama, Carol Oja, Anne Shreffler, Stephen Slottow, Arnold Whittall, and Paul Wilson. I am deeply indebted to them. At Cambridge University Press, Arnold Whittall and Penny Souster supported the project from its inception and, with the expert copyediting of Kathryn Bailey, shepherded it through to completion with their characteristic kindness and grace. Closer to home, Sally Goldfarb provided her customary assistance in matters legal, editorial, and otherwise. Michael Straus-Goldfarb helped too.

Acknowledgment of Sources

Permission to reprint the following is gratefully acknowledged:

Examples 2.69–70 and 2.78 from *Music for Small Orchestra* and Suite No. 2 for Four Strings and Piano © by American Musicological Society. Reproduced by permission.

Examples 2.56–58, 2.69, and 2.99 from Sonata for Violin and Piano © 1984 Merion Music, Inc. Used by permission.

Examples 2.2, 2.40, 2.59, and 2.114 from *Piano Study in Mixed Accents* © 1932 Merion Music, Inc. Used by permission.

Examples 2.4, 2.5, 2.43, 2.55, 2.71, and 2.102–104 from "Chinaman, Laundryman" and "Sacco, Vanzetti" © 1973 Merion Music, Inc. Used by permission.

Examples 2.8, 2.9, 2.14, 2.18–19, 2.29–31, 2.35, 2.46–47, 2.62, 2.72–74, 2.77, 2.83–84, 2.87, 2.88, 2.91, 2.96–97, 2.100, 2.106, 2.109, 3.24–25, 3.28–30, 3.33–35, 3.37–38, 3.40–41, 3.43, and 3.45–47 from Four Preludes (Nos. 6–9) and String Quartet © 1941 Merion Music, Inc. Used by permission.

Examples 2.38, 2.41–42, 2.81, 2.105, 2.107, 3.1–10, 3.14–20, and 3.22–23 from "In Tall Grass," "Rat Riddles," and "Prayers of Steel" from Three Songs © Theodore Presser Co. Used by permission.

Examples 2.3, 2.6, 2.7, 2.11, 2.13, 2.20, 2.23–26, 2.32–34, 2.36–37, 2.39, 2.44–45, 2.48–53, 2.60, 2.63–64, 2.69, 2.75–76, 2.79–80, 2.89–90, 2.93–95, 2.108, 2.110–111, 2.115, 3.48–66, and 3.68–70 from Chant (1930), *Diaphonic Suites* Nos. 1–4, and Suite for Wind Quintet © Tetra/Continuo Music Group, Inc. Used by permission.

Examples 2.1, 2.12, 2.15–17, and 2.21 from Charles Seeger, *Tradition and Experiment in the New Music* used by permission of Michael Seeger.

Examples 2.10, 2.27–28, 2.54, 2.61, 2.69, 2.82, 2.88, and 2.92 from Five Preludes (Nos. 1–5), Suite No. 1 for Five Wind Instruments and Piano, Chants (Nos. 1 and 3) used by permission of Michael Seeger.

Examples 2.85–86, and 2.98 from "Home Thoughts" and "Loam" from Five Sandburg Songs © 1990. Used by permission of C. F. Peters Corporation.

"Rat Riddles," GOOD MORNING, AMERICA, copyright 1928 and renewed 1956 by Carl Sandburg, reprinted by permission of Harcourt Brace & Company. "Prayers of Steel," and excerpts from "In Tall Grass" and "Loam" in CORNHUSKERS by Carl Sandburg, reprinted by permission of Harcourt Brace & Company.

1

Introduction

Ruth Crawford was a pivotal figure in American avant-garde music of the 1920s and 1930s.[1] She was a friend and protégé of Henry Cowell, a student and later the wife of Charles Seeger, and a close associate of Carl Ruggles, Edgard Varèse, Dane Rudhyar, and other important figures in the circle of composers whose music was described, by themselves and others, as "ultra-modern." The ultra-modern composers, including Crawford, are of the utmost importance for a history of American music.[2] They represent the first generation of American composers to step out from the shadow of European models, to create a self-consciously independent American music.[3] Their music rejected the forms and sonorities of traditional European art music, including its triadic basis, and created a new musical language, one that elevated formerly dissonant intervals to structural status, promoted the radical independence of the parts in a polyphonic texture, explored new sound combinations and means of sound production, and sought new ways of structuring rhythm and timbre, and of integrating those dimensions with pitch structure. In each of these aspects, the ultra-modern music of the 1920s and 1930s, and Crawford's music in particular, anticipated, and opened the way for, the achievements of subsequent generations of American composers.

In addition to its historic importance, Crawford's music has the greatest intrinsic interest, not only for its original and compelling structures, but for its expressive power. Crawford's early musical training was traditional, but in the late 1920s, when she was in her own twenties, she came under the influence of Cowell and Rudhyar, a contact that marked the first of two crucial turning points in her compositional career, and ushered her into the world of dissonant, ultra-modern music. During the mid and late 1920s, she composed a small number of adventurous and innovative works, including the Nine Piano Preludes, the Suite No. 2 for Piano and Strings, and the Five Songs to poems by Carl Sandburg. In 1929, she began to study composition with Charles Seeger. That experience marked a second turning point, and led to the production of her finest and most characteristic work, including her *Four Diaphonic Suites*, String Quartet, Three Songs to poems by Carl Sandburg, and Suite for Wind Quintet. It is on these works that her reputation must ultimately rest, and on which this book will place particular emphasis. In the early 1930s, Crawford abandoned her compositional career and turned her professional energies to the collection and publication of American folk music. A brief return to her own music, in the early 1950s, was cut short by her premature death in 1953.

A complete picture of Crawford's music, of course, will require placing it in its relevant biographical, cultural, and historical contexts. I attempt this broader contextualization in Chapter Four of this book.[4] For the most part, however, I will be concerned with discussing this music in its relevant theoretical contexts, including theories of musical structure that Crawford would have known, and more recent theories that have emerged to explain the music of her contemporaries.[5]

The more recent theories I have in mind are those of Milton Babbitt, Allen Forte, David Lewin, John Rahn, Robert Morris, George Perle, and others, theories that go by names like "set theory," or "transformation theory," or "twelve-tone theory."[6] I will describe relevant aspects of these theories in the following chapters, and suggest my own emendations and extensions, as Crawford's music seems to require. Like any theory, these have their own cultural history. They emerged in elite American universities in the 1960s and 1970s, initially as an adjunct to composition, to help composers imagine ways of organizing the twelve tones, and then increasingly as a way of explaining the structure of canonical twentieth-century music, particularly music by Schoenberg and Webern, but also by Stravinsky and others. More recently, these theories have branched out in a number of different directions, and their range of reference has expanded to include a variety of twentieth-century composers, although with the continued exclusion of composers who organize their works largely on the basis of traditional tonality.

By employing these theories to analyze Crawford's music, I place her in the context of what has come to be seen as the European modernist mainstream, in the company particularly of the composers of the second Viennese School and, to a lesser extent, of Stravinsky. While her music is highly original, and strongly inflected by the concerns of the American ultra-moderns, particularly Cowell and Seeger, it does have affinities with contemporaneous European music, and deals with similar compositional problems. In invoking recent theories of atonal music, then, it is my conscious desire and intent to place Crawford among the central figures in early twentieth-century music, in America and Europe.

Of the theories that Crawford would have known, by far the most important is the one enshrined in Seeger's treatise, *Tradition and Experiment in the New Music* (1930–31).[7] The treatise is in two parts: the first consists of abstract speculations about the history and structure of music; the second comprises a "Manual of Dissonant Counterpoint," a reasonably detailed guide for composers. Indeed, it served as a guide for Crawford's music, and will also help to guide the analytical approach taken in this book.

I have referred to the treatise as Seeger's, but its authorship is not so starkly individual as that might imply. Seeger is best known today as a musicologist and ethnomusicologist, but he was known in ultra-modern circles primarily as a composer and teacher of composers. His work with two students in particular, Cowell in the 1910s and Crawford in 1929–30, left an indelible mark on the treatise, which took shape during that long period. Among the three of them, the influences intertwine in the treatise and are hard to disentangle. Cowell's own treatise, *New Musical Resources*, is strikingly similar to Seeger's in many ways, including particularly its commitment to "dissonant counterpoint," a term and concept to which we will return.[8] Later, Crawford actively assisted in preparing the treatise for eventual publication, although that did not take place in her, or his, lifetime. She acted as a sounding board for Seeger's voice, and as such shaped the treatise, amplifying some aspects and muting others. Indeed, Crawford was so immersed in the preparation of the treatise that Seeger offered to name her as its coauthor, an honor she declined.[9] Instead, Seeger dedicated the treatise "to Ruth Crawford, of whose studies these pages are a record and without whose collaboration and inspiration they would not have been written."[10] For convenience, I will name Seeger throughout this book as the author of the treatise, but it should be clearly understood from the outset that it embodies Crawford's ideas as well, and that it would not have taken its present form and, indeed, might not have been written at all, without her.

Crawford's contact with Seeger, and her immersion in his theoretical approach, had a powerful effect on her music. Although she retained many elements of her earlier style, she forged a new, consistent, and powerful musical language which will be described in detail in these pages. Seeger's theories thus provide a crucial context for understanding Crawford's music. Indeed, many of Crawford's works from this period had their origins in composition assignments from Seeger, including not only the four *Diaphonic Suites* and the *Piano Study in Mixed Accents*, but even the celebrated last two movements of the String Quartet.[11]

The compositional categories Seeger provided to Crawford will thus become indispensable analytical categories in this book. In Chapter Two, I will describe Crawford's mature style, showing how she wrote melodies, how she combined them to create counterpoint and harmony, and identifying her original approach to register, rhythm, and dynamics. I will proceed element by element, drawing examples from virtually all of her music, and often linking her music explicitly to recommendations in Seeger's treatise. In Chapter Three, I undertake integral analyses of some of Crawford's most important works, including two of the Three Songs, and two movements each of the String Quartet and the Suite for Wind Quintet, and, again, my analytical approach will have some of its roots in Seeger's treatise.

The danger of this approach is in incorrectly suggesting that Seeger was Pygmalion to Crawford's Galatea, that the ideas were his and their embodiment in notes was hers, that she simply did what he told her to do. Nothing could be further from the truth. By the time she met Seeger, Crawford was already a mature composer, reasonably well known in ultra-modern circles, with her works receiving regular performances. Her studies with Seeger shaped her music in far-reaching ways, but that should not be seen to detract from her compositional autonomy and originality, any more than Copland's studies with Boulanger, or Beethoven's with Albrechtsberger. Seeger provided her with a framework for her own musical pursuits, a scaffolding within which she constructed her most distinctive, personal, and original works.

One of Seeger's core ideas, and one which he imparted to Crawford right at the beginning of their work together, was the primacy of melody. In response to what they perceived as the over-reliance of nineteenth-century romantic music on vertically conceived chordal harmony, Seeger urged her, and Crawford sought, to write music that consisted of one or more independent, self-contained melodies. Such melodies, carefully structured to avoid triadic references, as Seeger recommended, and to project compelling original designs, in ways that Crawford discovered on her own, are the essential building blocks of Crawford's mature music. My description of her style, therefore, begins with them.

2

Elements of a style

Melody

Non-repetition and equal distribution of notes

Crawford's melodies, particularly in the period following her work with Seeger, generally avoid emphasizing any note through repetition. Notes rarely recur before several others, usually six or more, have intervened, thus following an explicit recommendation in Seeger's treatise: "Avoid repetition of any tone until at least six progressions have been made. A greater separation is better, but much depends upon the character and leading of the intervening tones. The ear must be the judge."[1] Seeger's music illustration is reproduced here as Example 2.1.[2]

Example 2.1 Avoiding repetition of pitches (Seeger, *Tradition and Experiment in the New Music*, Example 74)

In (a), (c), and (e), two occurrences of a single pitch are insufficiently separated, and Seeger marks the offending repetition with an X. He judges (b) and (f) "better" because more tones now intervene, and (d) the "best" because it contains no pitch repetition whatsoever. The example is not perfectly consistent – both (c) and (f), one "bad" and one "better," have only five intervening tones – but the general principle is clear, and applies not only to actual pitches but also, although with somewhat less force, to their octave duplications.

> Avoid octave repetition of any tone until at least six progressions have been made. In dissonant writing octave reduplication is not such an important factor as it is in consonant writing. So that after a comparatively small number of well

5

dissonated progressions, the repetition of a tone in the octave is not so objectionable as repetition in the unison. The double octave is to an even smaller extent a repetition.[3]

Stated in general terms, Seeger's principle holds that no note should receive special emphasis through repetition, and that therefore a variety and rapid turnover of notes is to be encouraged.

Crawford's melodies subscribe to this principle, but not with absolute fidelity. The first section of the *Piano Study in Mixed Accents* (1930) is a case in point – in Example 2.2, pitch repetitions are marked with a solid, and octave repetitions with a dotted, line.[4] This work consists of a single angular melody, played in octaves, which works its way gradually, in fits and starts, to a registral high point half way through, and then retraces its steps back to its starting point. A steady, virtually uninterrupted stream of sixteenth notes is punctuated by irregular accents. In the first phrase, there are only seven instances of the kinds of repetitions that Seeger condemns, and fully five of those involve the less objectionable octave duplication. Over the course of the work as a whole, an average of eleven notes intervene between repetitions.[5] Despite fluctuations, then, this work avoids repetitions as thoroughly as a strictly twelve-tone composition.

Example 2.2   Pitch and pitch-class repetition in *Piano Study in Mixed Accents*, first section

One likely consequence of non-repetition is that each note will tend to occur roughly the same number of times. The notes of this melody, and of many of Crawford's melodies, tend to be dispersed throughout the available pitch space (from the lowest note to the highest) and pitch-class space (the twelve notes of the equal-tempered scale), ensuring that each pitch, and each pitch class, receives roughly equal emphasis.[6] This melody consists of fifty-four notes and, with three exceptions, states every pitch between its low point (D2) and its high point (C#4) at least once but no more than four times.[7] The twelve pitch classes are even more precisely balanced: each is heard no fewer than three and no more than five times.[8]

The *Diaphonic Suite No. 1* (1930), first movement, shows a similar interest in avoiding repetitions and dispersing its notes throughout the available space (see Example 2.3). This *Suite* is one of a set of four for various instrumental combinations. Three of them, including No. 1, were written during the period of Crawford's study with Seeger and had their origins in his composition assignments.[9] The term "diaphonic" is a coinage of Seeger's and refers to his interest in the radical independence of polyphonic parts and of musical elements within a single part. He speaks of the necessity for modern music "to cultivate 'sounding apart' rather than 'sounding together' – diaphony rather than symphony."[10]

Example 2.3   Pitch and pitch-class repetition in *Diaphonic Suite No. 1* (for oboe or flute), first movement, mm. 1–9

Unlike the relentless, unvaried sixteenth notes of the *Piano Study in Mixed Accents,* this brief piece for solo flute or oboe deploys a melody rich in rhythmic and motivic repetitions. Indeed, these two melodies may be taken to represent the two principal types of melodies that Crawford writes: on the one hand, melodies that are rhapsodic, free, rhythmically flexible, and motivically charged, and on the other, melodies that are strictly regimented, rhythmically uniform, often constrained by some kind of precompositional scheme. The two kinds of melodies, however, despite their often radically contrasting characters, share many features, including the pitch and pitch-class dispersion under discussion here.

The first phrase of *Diaphonic Suite No. 1* contains no forbidden pitch repetitions, and only two pitch-class repetitions. Each of the twelve pitch classes occurs at least once, but no more than four times in the passage and, in the movement as a whole, each pitch class occurs between seven and thirteen times.

That pitches and pitch classes are evenly distributed throughout the available space, however, does not make them functionally equivalent or musically undifferentiated. Frequently, individual pitches or pitch classes take on special roles, as part of the motivic organization of the melody, as registral boundaries, or as centers of inversional balance. At the same time, Crawford's melodies, whether rhythmically uniform or varied, generally conform to Seeger's principle of non-repetition and its likely corollary, the roughly equal number of occurrences of each pitch class and of each pitch between the lowest and highest heard.

Chromatic completion

The tendency of Crawford's melodies to fill whatever musical space is made available to them acts as a dynamic force – they move toward a state of "chromatic plenitude."[11] When gaps appear, they tend to be filled promptly. Indeed, gaps seem to be opened precisely in order to be filled. By the end of a typical melody or melodic phrase, every tone will be connected to the rest by semitone, with no gaps left unfilled and no notes left dangling and unattached.[12] Each note seeks, and usually finds, its chromatic neighbors. I can find no comment by Seeger relevant to the topic of chromatic or aggregate completion. Rather, it seems to have been a deep aspect of Crawford's individual style, one that predates her contact with Seeger, and persists beyond it.

The integrity, the self enclosure, of individual melodic phrases stems, in part, from their achievement of chromatic completion. Each phrase or unit tends to occupy a single chromatic zone, either in pitch or pitch-class space.[13] Crawford's melodies seek to saturate completely whatever space they have opened up for themselves.

"Chinaman, Laundryman" (1932) is a song about the exploitation of a Chinese immigrant in the sweatshops of New York. The piano accompaniment depicts the brutish repetitiveness of the immigrant's work in two ways. First, it consists of only a single-line melody doubled at the double octave and uses a restricted range of rhythmic values. Like the *Piano Study in Mixed Accents*, which it strongly resembles, it is thus stripped of contrapuntal interest and rhythmic variety, and creates a kind of mechanistic clattering and banging that is clearly evocative of repetitious manual labor. Second, its pitch organization is similarly restricted by a systematic fixation on the nine-note melody shown in Example 2.4, which becomes the series for its strict serial organization.[14]

The melody is a self-contained unit, with each of its gaps filled by a subsequent note or spanned by a previous one. F–E♭, the first gap in the line, is filled by the subsequent E just as E♭–C is filled by the subsequent D and C♯. That final C♯ also fills the gap between D and B, already partially bridged by C. By the end of the melody, the notes form a continuous chromatic cluster, from B up to G. Because of their tendency to fill gaps and form semitone links, Crawford's melodies can generally be grouped into chromatic zones of this

Example 2.4   Filling a chromatic zone in "Chinaman, Laundryman," piano accompaniment, m. 4

kind. Later in the piece, the same melody is heard with some of its notes transposed up or down by one or more octaves. In that case, these fills and links still operate, but in pitch class rather than pitch space. In either case, they ensure the self enclosure of the nine-note melody.

Crawford also uses chromatic completion to create a sense of connection across sectional boundaries, as in "Sacco, Vanzetti," a vocal lament for the execution of those well-known anarchists that forms a pair with "Chinaman, Laundryman." These works were written in 1932, when Crawford was a member, along with Seeger, Cowell, Marc Blitzstein, Wallingford Riegger, Aaron Copland, and others, of a radical group known as the Composers' Collective. This group, allied with the American Communist Party, sought musical responses to the ravages of the Great Depression. The texts for both of Crawford's songs had been published in August 1928 in a newspaper called the *Daily Worker* and, in further confirmation of their political origins, Crawford's original manuscript provides Russian singing translations.[15] In Seeger's words,

> These are the two songs which reflected [Crawford's] shock at the depression in 1932 and '33. The words are by an obscure Chinese anarchist, socialist, communist – Lord knows how you characterize him – and they're very much dated in the verbiage of the so-called workers' movement of those days, which was very literary and naive. But the songs really are two declamations of tremendous dramatic power accompanied by piano ostinati that pay no attention whatsoever to the song; they go right ahead on their remorseless course. The singer doesn't even have to be very much with the piano except just to end together.[16]

In the first stanza of "Sacco, Vanzetti," the melody ends with the pitches D–F–D♭–E♭, or, given in registral order, D♭–D–E♭– –F (see Example 2.5).[17] The second stanza begins in measure 41 with the missing E, filling in the gap and creating a musical bridge across the point of articulation. Notice also the subtle motivic statements in this passage. The highest three notes, shown with upward stems, describe the intervallic succession <–2, +1>.[18] Motives of this type, combining a whole tone and a semitone in opposite directions, are extraordinarily pervasive shapes in her music.[19] The whole tone F–E♭ that begins the motive opens up a space which is immediately filled by the semitone in the opposite direction. In that sense, this motive is a microcosmic emblem of the

Example 2.5   Chromatic and motivic completion in "Sacco, Vanzetti," mm. 34–48

gap-filling tendencies of Crawford's music, its urge toward chromatic completion. In this passage, the motive is overlapped with its own ordered retrograde, described by the lowest three notes in the passage, shown with downward stems.[20] Taken together, the two motive statements create a continuous chromatic zone from D♭ up through F.

Similar strategies of gapping and filling shape the soprano solo in Chant No. 2 ("To an Angel"), given in its entirety in Example 2.6. The notes of the melody are sustained at great length and move within a narrow range, in the manner of the chant suggested by the work's title. As it creeps about chromatically, the melody creates numerous statements of Crawford's favorite motive, indicated with beams in Example 2.6. The melody is intoned on meaningless phonemes, and is accompanied by a four-part chorus that hums throughout.

This work is one of a set of three chants written in 1930 in Berlin, where Crawford was spending her year on a Guggenheim Fellowship. The other two, "To an Unkind God" and "To a Kind God," are as yet unpublished. All three chants use invented syllables formed from phonemes. Crawford had originally planned to use Sanskrit text from the Bhagavad Gita, but when she could not locate an English translation in Berlin, she decided to do what she "had wanted to do for years – invent my own syllables."[21] She collated sounds from both English and German, describing the result as "a language of my own – consonants and vowels in a kind of chant which sounds quite Eastern."[22]

Example 2.6   Chromatic and motivic completion in Chant No. 2 ("To an Angel"), soprano solo

The urge toward chromatic completion is particularly evident in the third phrase (measure 26), which begins by opening two gaps, between G and B♭ and between B♭ and C. The second of these gaps is immediately filled by B♮, creating <+2, −1>, and the subsequent C♯ is chromatically connected to the line. After a return to B♭ (A♯), the melody concludes with another statement of Crawford's motive, now inverted to <−2, +1>.[23] The final A not only completes this motive and closes the local gap between A♯ and G♯, but also closes the initial gap between G and B♭, and creates of the phrase a contiguous chromatic zone, from G4 up to C♯5.

The same sense of chromatic completion operates across the entire melody. The melody culminates on E5 at the end of the fourth phrase. That note is the last of the twelve pitch classes to be heard, and thus completes the pitch-class aggregate. Furthermore, it completes an actual pitch aggregate of all the chromatic notes between G4 and G♭5. More locally, it fills a smaller chromatic zone created by the four immediately previous notes: D–E♭– –F–G♭ filled in by the missing E. These chromatic completions, of a small zone and the larger pitch and pitch-class aggregates, help create a sense of cadential arrival on the E. That sense of arrival is reinforced by the motivic organization of the passage: the E completes two overlapped statements of versions of Crawford's motive.

Chromatic saturation operates on two levels in the first movement of *Diaphonic Suite No. 2*, which ends with an increasingly rapid cello melody heard against a sustained and trilled D4 in the bassoon (see Example 2.7).[24] As the cello moves from its lowest register to its highest, its notes come closer and closer together both in time and pitch. While a few gaps are left over toward the start, when the cello reaches F♯4 (measure 65), it begins to fill the pitch space methodically and, with one striking exception, entirely. It states every pitch between F♯4 and C6, its final note, except for D5. It thus avoids duplicating the pitch class sustained in the bassoon. The contrast between rhythm and shape of the two parts is reinforced by their lack of pitch-class intersection. They have no notes in common, but together they comprise the entire chromatic.

This tendency toward chromatic saturation operates also over the shorter spans within the cello melody. Beginning again on F♯4, the melody states Crawford's motive, rising two semitones, then filling in the gap by falling one semitone. A small chromatic zone is thus saturated. That three-note figure is overlapped with its own retrograde inversion, and the resulting RI-pair fills in a slightly larger chromatic zone.[25] Similar RI-pairs are heard at five different pitch levels in the melody, filling in all the available pitches in the registral span,

Example 2.7   Chromatic and motivic completion in *Diaphonic Suite No. 2* (bassoon and cello), first movement, mm. 62–end

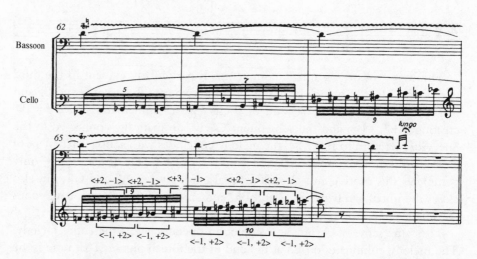

except, of course, the D5. Avoiding that pitch causes the motive to expand slightly at that point to <+3, −1>. The otherwise evenly divided pitch space of the cello melody thus has a slight warp in it.

In Crawford's melodies, the notes that fill the gaps are sometimes displaced by one or more octaves. In that sense, the chromatic zone must be thought of as a pitch-class zone, and the gaps and fills must be understood in pitch-class space. Consider, again, the opening of the *Piano Study in Mixed Accents*, shown above in Example 2.2. The first six-note group describes a chromatic cluster: C♯–D–D♯–E–F–F♯. The second group introduces five new notes, which include a chromatic gap: G– –A–A♯–B–C. The third group fills that gap by supplying, almost immediately, the missing G♯, which also completes the entire pitch-class aggregate. The third group itself has gaps (D– –E–F– –G♯–A), which are filled by the fourth group, and so on.

As in pitch space, chromatic saturation in pitch-class space may have a cadential effect, as in the final three measures of the Piano Prelude No. 6 (see Example 2.8). This Prelude, like the other eight with which it forms a set, was written before Crawford's contact with Seeger, and thus is not conceived in terms of independent melodies, in the manner of her later work.[26] Indeed, the final cadence is clearly harmonic in its conception. Nonetheless, a drive toward chromatic completion may be said to shape both the more harmonically-conceived music pre-Seeger and the melodically-conceived music post-Seeger.

The sustained notes in the bass register comprise a chromatic tetrachord, B–C–C♯–D. The right hand enters with A–B♭, expanding the chromatic zone downward, then adds E and D♯, expanding it upward. The resulting chromatic octachord, A–B♭–B–C–C♯–D–D♯–E, is sustained into the second measure of the example. When the right hand resumes in the final measure, it provides A♭ (one semitone below the bottom of the octachord) and F (one semitone above the top of the octachord). The final three measures of the piece thus comprise a chromatic decachord, built up symmetrically from the chromatic tetrachord at its center. The symmetry of the design, which contributes to the sense of

Example 2.8   Chromatic completion and inversional symmetry in Piano Prelude No. 6, mm. 21–end cadential stasis, is reflected also in the registration of the chords – notice the pitch symmetry of the chromatic tetrachord in the bass.

In the opening measures of the same Prelude, the drive toward chromatic completion expands to include the entire twelve-note aggregate (see Example 2.9). The music begins with a rapid ostinato in the highest registers and lugubrious repeated chords in the bass, which together comprise eleven of the twelve pitch classes. The twelfth, D, is the first note in a melodic line that emerges, in measure 5, in the middle of the texture.

Crawford's awareness of the complete pitch-class aggregate as an integral harmonic unit is strikingly realized in Chant No. 3 ("To a Kind God"), which consists of dense chromatic chords sung by up to twelve choral parts through which alto and soprano solos weave. Seeger suggested the basic layout of the piece to Crawford by describing a crowd of worshippers in a monastery intoning OM "at the pitch most suited to the individual voice regardless of any harmonic relation with the other pitches of other voices sounding at the same time (it is done in a crowd in all the monasteries)," while a single voice declaims the texted chant, adding that "If you wanted to make a complex dissonant veil of sound for the chanting voice to cut through, this idea would be suited."[27] In

Example 2.9   Completing the twelve-note aggregate in Piano Prelude No. 6, mm. 1–6

Crawford's own description of the piece, she sought a "'complex veil of sound,' half-intangible, out of which the chanting voice rises . . . I use the half steps to effect a kind of new composite mass-pitch."[28]

The Chant begins with six choral voices intoning, in close position, a chord consisting of A–B♭– –C–D♭–D–E♭ (see Example 2.10). That chord is sustained at length, and then, as new choral voices enter, notes begin to pile on atop the cluster: E, F, F♯, and G. That larger cluster, now spanning a minor seventh from A up to G, but always with the B missing, is sustained through the end of the first section of the piece. After a contrasting middle section, to be discussed in just a moment, the opening music returns, still of course with the B missing. Finally, at virtually the end of the piece, the alto solo brings in the missing B, and the resulting complete cluster is sustained until the end. A gap created in the opening section of the work is thus filled in the concluding section.

Example 2.10 Creating a chromatic gap in Chant No. 3 ("To a Kind God"), mm. 1–3

15

The middle section of the work is organized in a similar way. It also begins with a gapped chord (B–C–D♭– –E♭–E–F), and it also is gradually expanded upward as new voices enter: F♯, G, G♯, A, and B♭.[29] That creates a complete chromatic span of a major seventh from B up to B♭, but with D still missing. Later, the missing D enters in dramatic fashion an octave higher than expected. The resulting twelve-note chord is sustained for several measures and defines the climax of the piece.

It is one thing to take the aggregate of all twelve pitch classes as a harmonic or melodic norm. That idea was a commonplace of post-tonal music going back to the first decades of the century, with clear historical roots going back still earlier. It is quite another, however, to have all twelve pitch classes sounding simultaneously in a sustained harmony. This is a radical idea, one that would appear to have as much in common with post-war experiments in sound masses by Ligeti and others as it does with any earlier examples, such as Cowell's tone clusters.

Despite the remarkable twelve-note chord of Chant No. 3, however, it would be wrong to characterize Crawford's music as aggregate-based in any consistent way. Instead, it would be more accurate to say that her music moves toward a state in which the available musical space is filled, that is, where gaps are closed and all notes are linked chromatically. That space may be either a pitch or pitch-class space and, in the case of the latter, may comprise fewer than all twelve pitch classes. Aggregate completion in Crawford's music is best understood as a special case of a more general preference for saturating the available musical space. Her melodies and, indeed, all of her music, seek a state of chromatic plenitude.

Non-repetition and equal distribution of intervals

In her most characteristic music, Crawford treats the intervals of her melodies as she does the notes: she avoids repeating them, she seeks to vary them, and she ends up with melodies reasonably evenly distributed among the possibilities. It is rare in her melodies to hear the same class of interval (eg. the class containing minor seconds, major sevenths, and minor ninths), and even rarer to hear the same pitch interval two times in succession.[30] Usually one or more intervals intervene. As Seeger urges: "Not more than two consonant intervals of the same degree should be used in line successions . . . Not more than three dissonances of the same degree should be used in line succession, except rarely in a fast tempo, or for special effect."[31]

As a result of avoiding intervallic repetitions, Crawford's melodies tend to use the intervals with a rough equality of emphasis, although the semitone, its complement (the major seventh), and their compounds occur more than any other. If instead of looking at the intervals formed by pairs of notes, we consider the three intervals formed by the three-note groups, we will again find a rough dispersion among the possible types.[32]

16

Example 2.11 Intervallic repetition in *Diaphonic Suite No. 3* (for two clarinets), first movement, second clarinet, mm. 1–13

In the first phrase of the *Piano Study in Mixed Accents*, for example (see Example 2.2 above), there are only two places in the melody where an interval is immediately repeated (involving a semitone in both cases). The intervals are used with roughly equal emphasis, although there is a preference for the smaller intervals, particularly 1s and 3s.[33] Of the twelve trichord-types, all are represented at least once except the augmented triad.[34] In short, the melody presents an intervallic surface of extreme variety.

In the first two phrases of the second clarinet part in *Diaphonic Suite No. 3*, first movement, there are four instances of direct intervallic repetition, including three successive semitones to end the passage (see Example 2.11). Nonetheless, the intervals are still distributed with rough equality among the six different interval classes, with an emphasis on the smaller intervals. As with the melody from the *Piano Study*, the melodic trichords are also varied – only (037) (the major or minor triad), (048) (the augmented triad), and (026) (the incomplete dominant seventh chord) are missing. As a general matter, Crawford's melodies are varied intervallically and they avoid arpeggiating familiar chord types.

Dissonation

Crawford's preference for intervallic variety, and her persistent avoidance of intervallic repetition or traditional groupings correspond to Seeger's insistence that melodies be "dissonated," that is, rendered dissonant in certain prescribed ways. The concept of dissonance underpins his entire treatise and approach to composition. His basic insight is that if the old music can be understood as a consonant framework within which dissonances occur incidentally and under certain conditions, then the new, experimental music should be built upon a dissonant framework within which consonances occur incidentally and under certain conditions. The kind of music he advocates "is not only popularly known as dissonant, but is actually founded upon a principle of dissonance, just as music prior to 1900 was founded upon a principle of consonance."[35] As we will see later, Seeger attempts to extend the concepts of consonance and dissonance from intervals to other musical domains, including rhythm, tempo, accent, dynamics, timbre, and form, but, for him, dissonance refers primarily and essentially to the intervals in a melody.

Seeger is fully aware of the long and vexed history of attempts to find a physiological or acoustical basis for the distinction between consonance and dissonance. He is also aware of the constant historical evolution in the definition of consonance and dissonance – one era's dissonances may become a subsequent era's consonances, and vice versa. He nonetheless acknowledges the continuing power of traditional tonality to shape our hearing, and is thus content when talking about intervals to adopt the conventional, common-practice classification: major and minor thirds and sixths and perfect fourths and fifths are consonant; seconds, sevenths, and tritones are dissonant.[36]

Melodies, Seeger urges, should be systematically "dissonated," that is, organized to suppress any traditional tonal or triadic implications. Since any consonant interval might be heard to suggest a major or minor triad, it will normally be followed by a dissonant interval, to undermine that implication. If two consonant intervals occur in succession, thus usually arpeggiating a triad, the next interval will usually be dissonant, and the next note must be related by semitone (or tritone) to one of the notes of the triad (see Example 2.12).[37]

> After a progression of two consonant intervals it is advisable to make dissonation. Roots of triads, if present, usually must be dissonated. The situation at (d) in the above example is interesting: dissonation is made of the third degree of the major scale instead of the root. At (f) both accented tones and the root are dissonated. At (g) an exceptional case may be noted in that the accented tones and the root are not dissonated but the major third of the triad is. Generally speaking, many of the prohibitions made on the basis of interval can be disregarded when a clear and strong accentual, modal, or "tonalitous" clash can be effected.[38]

"Dissonation," as Seeger uses the term here, thus refers specifically to the requirement that the notes of any triad or triadic interval be followed immediately by a note a semitone (or tritone) away. More generally, it refers to the ability of a melody to resist a traditional, tonal interpretation. Regular or traditional combinations are to be systematically avoided. The compositional guidelines Seeger

Example 2.12 "Dissonating" a melodic line (from Seeger, *Tradition and Experiment in the New Music*, Example 72)

18

Example 2.13 Avoiding triadic implications in *Diaphonic Suite No. 1* (flute or oboe), second movement, mm. 1–13

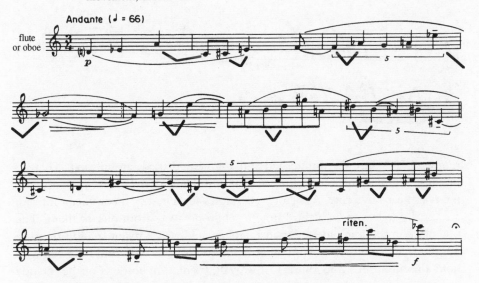

provides are designed precisely to deny traditional implications.

The first melodic phrase from the *Diaphonic Suite No. 1*, second movement, adheres closely to those guidelines (see Example 2.13). Semitones (and major sevenths and minor ninths) predominate, particularly in combination with minor thirds and tritones. Apart from the ascending semitones toward the end of the phrase, no single interval or interval class is heard two times in a row. Furthermore, at no point in the phrase are there two consonant intervals of any size in a row (the consonant intervals are identified on the example). As a result, there are no arpeggiations of major or minor triads, and any incipient triadic implications are immediately and ruthlessly crushed. In virtually every case, two notes separated by a consonant interval are followed immediately by a third note a semitone away from one of them. In most of the exceptions to this general rule, the third note is a tritone away from one of the two consonant notes.

The florid first violin melody from the fourth movement of the String Quartet is virtually an essay in dissonant melodic writing. This melody and the entire movement will be discussed in detail in Chapter Three, but for now let us take a close look at the two short phrases shown in Example 2.14.[39] Each phrase contains all twelve pitch classes and, taking the two phrases together, virtually every available pitch between the lowest and highest is heard at least once. Within each phrase, no pitch or pitch class is repeated before at least four other notes have intervened. In its pitch distribution, then, the melody follows Crawford's usual preference for variety, non-repetition, and saturation of the available musical space.

All the types of intervals are represented, although semitones and whole tones are heard more than the others. Virtually all of the trichord types are also

Example 2.14 Avoiding triadic implications in String Quartet, fourth movement, first violin, mm. 38–43

represented – only the diminished and augmented triads are missing. There is no direct intervallic repetition, and at only one point are two consonant intervals heard in a row. As before, two notes separated by a consonant interval are usually followed by a third note a semitone away from one of them. The one place in the line where a triad is arpeggiated, a D♭-major triad in measure 42, the triad is preceded by a note a semitone from its root, and followed by a note a semitone from its third. In this way, triadic implications of the melody are quashed and its dissonant character assured.

Thus far, we can summarize Crawford's melodic practice as a series of strategies of avoidance. Her melodies avoid repeating or emphasizing any single pitch or pitch class and any single interval or interval class. They also avoid arpeggiating familiar chord types, including particularly the major or minor triad. These preferences, taken together, comprise a definition of "dissonance." Dissonance, however, is largely a negative concept: it describes what not to do and how not to do it. To understand what Crawford's melodies actually do within the boundaries defined by dissonance, we will have to turn our attention to their motivic organization.

Neumes

Seeger's concept of the "neume" must play a central role in any discussion of the motivic organization of Crawford's music. For Seeger, the neume, a succession of at least three "tone-beats" (melodic notes), is the basic structural unit in music.

> A single tone or beat may constitute data for physics, psychology, etc., or may be the subject of mystical rhapsody, but it is not *musical* material. Granted a context it may have musical significance, but even then cannot be regarded as an independent unit of musical technique. Similarly, two tone-beats may have musical significance provided a musical context, but may not be regarded as forming an independent unit. Two tone-beats cannot give tonal or rhythmic centricity, establish a metrical pattern, or perform any of the essential musical functions such as the preparation and resolution of dissonances, modulation,

etc., rubato, accent, crescendo, diminuendo, etc. Three tone-beats, however, can form an independent musical unit or motive and perform all these functions, though in miniature. There is no accepted term at hand to designate this *smallest melodic unit* as a unit, so we may perhaps be justified in resurrecting the term *neume* which was commonly used in ancient times to denote this very thing. The neume was written as a single stenographic symbol which signified to the performer both tonal and rhythmic progress, but conveying it in such a way that the *progress* rather than the *points departed from and arrived at* was emphasized. There is a tendency at the present time to think in terms of the raw materials of music (beats, notes, chords, etc.) rather than in terms of progression of phrases and melodic continuity. The latter is more musical and should be encouraged by the use of a term which by its very nature emphasizes it.[40]

Seeger's "neume" is akin to a traditional "motive" in many ways – it is a musical shape from which other shapes may be derived. A neume is different from a motive, however, in at least three important respects. First, a neume must consist of at least three events because that is the smallest size compatible with performing essential musical functions including, as we shall see, sustaining the standard serial operations of inversion, retrograde, and retrograde inversion.[41] The most important neumes consist of three or four tone-beats – longer neumes are normally understood as combinations of shorter ones. Three-note neumes Seeger calls "binary," because they consist of two "progressions," from the first event to the second and from the second to the third. Similarly, four-note neumes are called "ternary." Second, while a motive is defined by its content, a neume is defined by its internal progressions, by the motions among its elements. This focus on process rather than content is a persistent feature of Seeger's theory and Crawford's music, and will thus be an essential element of the analytical approach taken here. Third, neumes need not consist exclusively of pitches. A neume is simply a shape, a contour, and as such could be realized in a variety of musical spaces (see Example 2.15).[42]

Seeger identifies six basic shapes, named on the right side of the chart as "line neumes," in which progressions are in the same direction, "twist neumes," in which progressions are in different directions, or some combination of the two. Each of the six basic kinds of neumes, numbered 1 through 6 on the left side of the chart, has two possible representations, denoted by the letters a and b, that are related to each other by contour inversion. Seeger also recognizes the possibility of contour retrograde and retrograde inversion. Neumes 1a and 1b may be thought of as related by either inversion (which Seeger calls "contrary") or retrograde. The same is true of 2a and 2b, 3a and 3b, and 6a and 6b. 4a, 4b, 5a, and 5b form a group in which each is related to the others by inversion, retrograde, or retrograde inversion, and thus "constitute really one basic form."[43] These contours can be realized in any of six musical spaces, or what Seeger identifies as the six basic musical functions – pitch, dynamics, timbre, tempo, accent, and proportion.

Example 2.15 Seeger's chart of neume forms (*Tradition and Experiment in the New Music*)

		TONAL			RHYTHMIC			
		Pitch	Dynamics	Timbre	Tempo	Accent	Proportion	
Binary	1a		< ‾		accel-accel	/ /	— —	"Line"
	b		‾ >		rall-rall	U U	U U	
	2a		< >		accel-rall	/ U	— U	"Twist"
	b		> <		rall-accel	U /	U —	
Ternary	3a		< ‾ ‾		acc-acc-acc	/ / /	— — — —	"Line-Line"
	b		‾ ‾ >		rall-rall-rall	U U U	U U U	
	4a		< ‾ >		acc-acc-rall	/ / U	— — —U	"Line-Twist"
	b		‾ > <		rall-rall-acc	U U /	U U —	
	5a		< ‾ >		acc-rall-rall	/ U U	— U U	"Twist-Line"
	b		> < ‾		rall-acc-acc	U / /	U — —	
	6a		< > <		acc-rall-acc	/ U /	— U —	"Twist-Twist"
	b		> < >		rall-acc-rall	U / U	U — U	

Seeger was certainly aware of the relative difficulty of creating meaningful contours in the different spaces. Pitch is the least problematic. Pitches are readily scalable – it is easy to ascertain their relative height – and thus easily arranged into perceivable shapes. Proportions, or relative durations, and tempo also form perceivable shapes – just as notes get higher or lower, durations get shorter or longer, and speeds get faster or slower. In the same manner, dynamic levels can get louder or softer, but dynamics are not as readily scalable as pitch or duration. For example, a C♯ played by a trombone or a flute is the same note, but a pianissimo played by the two instruments would not necessarily be perceived as the same dynamic. Shapes formed from accent are problematic at best – it is hard to imagine how one would go about creating a scale of relative accentuation – and shapes formed from timbres are even more so. Seeger leaves this column blank in testimony to the theoretical difficulties.[44]

Despite the problems associated with creating neumes from some of the musical functions, Seeger imagined the contents of this chart as "stuff from which

Example 2.16   Preserving contour <+, −> while changing intervals and avoiding triads (Seeger, *Tradition and Experiment in the New Music*, Example 63a)

any logic of music must be derived."[45] Seeger has, indeed, adumbrated a general theory of musical contour, one whose implications have only recently begun to be explored.[46] It is a theory that works best for single musical lines, and thus reflects the melodic orientation of Seeger's theoretical work, and of Crawford's compositions. It also works best for pitch and, while later we will discuss neumes and contours of durations and dynamics, for now we will focus on pitch.

At the most basic level, a neume is simply a contour, a gross shape, in part because only at that relatively undifferentiated level can pitch, rhythm, and dynamics be meaningfully compared. Any musical figure that ascends twice, for example, defines a binary line neume, irrespective of its actual intervals (see Example 2.16).[47]

To illustrate, Seeger provides an initial binary line neume, D–D♯–E, then gives forty-six transformations of it, each of which is itself a binary line neume. Each neume begins with D and preserves the contour of the original. For the second note in each neume, Seeger systematically considers each of the eleven remaining pitch classes. For the third note in each neume, Seeger seeks one that will make the neume as a whole "tonally dissonant," which, as we have seen, usually requires a note related by a semitone (or its compounds) to either of the first two notes. When the second note is C♯, itself related by semitone to the initial D, the third note may be any of the ten remaining pitch classes.[48] Seeger provides a similar chart to illustrate the same succession of pitch classes, D–D♯–E, arranged as a twist-neume, first ascending and then descending (see Example 2.17).[49] Within a framework of melodic dissonance, then, a neume may be developed by preserving its contour while changing its intervals.

Seeger's theory of neumes imagines a music like Crawford's, where shapes recur amid an intervallic landscape of enormous variety, as in the melodies from

Example 2.17 Preserving contour <+, –> while changing intervals and avoiding triads (Seeger, *Tradition and Experiment in the New Music*, Example 63b)

the opening of the String Quartet, first movement, shown in Example 2.18. The first four notes of the first melody would be characterized by Seeger as a ternary twist-line neume conforming to model 5b on his chart. For the sake of simplicity, I will instead describe it as <–, +, +>, that is, a descending motion followed by two ascents.[50] The same shape occurs once more in the first melody, and three times in the second melody, comprising all but one of its notes. The inversion of this shape, conforming to model 5a on Seeger's chart and described here as <+, –, –>, can be found twice in each of the melodies. The two melodies contrast sharply in intervallic content and in character (the first is marked *cantando*, the second *marcato bruscamente*), but they can both be understood in their entirety with reference to a single ternary neume.

By confining ourselves just to patterns of upward and downward motion, however, we get only a crude picture of the organization of Crawford's melodies. We will do better if we refine Seeger's concept of contour, taking into account not merely the ups and downs of the melody, but identifying the position of each note in relation to the others (see Example 2.19). For example, instead of thinking of the first four notes of the first melody as a down followed by two ups, we can imagine them more specifically as a four-note figure that begins on its highest note, jumps down to its lowest note, then ascends twice, but never reattains the height of its starting point. We can represent that shape numerically

Example 2.18 A single ternary neume, <–, +, +> and its inversion <+, –, –>, in two contrasting melodies from String Quartet, first movement, first violin, mm. 1–4 and second violin, mm. 6–7

Example 2.19 Recurring contours in two melodies from String Quartet, first movement, first
violin, mm. 1–4 and second violin, mm. 6–7

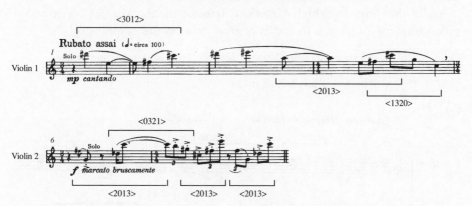

as <3012>, where the notes range in registral order from 0, the lowest, up to 3, the highest.[51] The same shape is inverted in the second melody to become <0321>, that is, a fragment that begins on its lowest note, jumps up to its highest, then descends twice, but never reaches its initial low point.[52]

The first four notes of the second melody describe a different shape, <2013>, which is repeated twice more in the melody, with different actual intervals each time. The same shape also occurs in the first melody, once in its original form and once inverted. I have now described the two melodies in relation to two different shapes, <3012> and <2013>, and their inversions, <0321> and <1320>, which represent the more basic, crude shape <−, +, +> and its inversion, <+, −, −>.

Example 2.20 describes a melody from the third movement of *Diaphonic Suite No. 4* in the same way, but now admitting retrograde and retrograde inversion as well as inversion. The melody begins with a four–note figure describing CSEG <0132>, beginning on its lowest note, moving then to its second-lowest, then its highest, then its second-highest. That same shape occurs three more times in the melody, usually, but not always, with similar intervals and rhythms, and its inversion, <3201> occurs twice (see Example 2.20A). The retrograde of the original shape, <2310>, occurs three times in the melody and its inversion, <1023>, which is the retrograde inversion of the original shape, occurs twice (see Example 2.20B). The entire melody has thus been described in terms of its neumes, its shapes, its contours, without regard to interval, and understood in relation to "one basic form," in Seeger's expression.[53] Indeed, every note in the melody is part of this scheme, except the octave leap in measure 3. The octave, the traditional melodic connector, is thus understood here as an interruption in an otherwise continuous process, one that sweeps through the remainder of the melody.

Even with this refinement of Seeger's notion of contour, however, we will still be able to gain only a crude picture of Crawford's melodies. To know more, we will have to see how contour and interval interact in specific melodic contexts. We will undertake this further refinement and synthesis when we consider the ways in which Crawford transforms her neumes in extended progressions, spinning out melodies of great richness and complexity.

Example 2.20 Recurring contours in *Diaphonic Suite No. 4* (for oboe and cello), third movement, mm. 1–7: A) CSEG <0132> and its inversion, <3201>; B) CSEG <2310> and its inversion, <1023>

Motive M1

While Seeger often conceives of a neume as simply a musical shape, he is also able to discuss it as a succession of specific pitches or pitch classes, susceptible to presentation in the canonical twelve-tone orderings: prime, inversion, retrograde,

Example 2.21 The twelve-tone operations (inversion, retrograde, retrograde inversion) and contour inversion applied to a five-note neume (Seeger, *Tradition and Experiment in the New Music*, Example 89)

and retrograde inversion, which he calls "conversions" (see Example 2.21).[54] I have translated Seeger's terms into more familiar nomenclature: his "contrary," "retrograde," and "contrary of retrograde," are the now the customary inversion, retrograde, and retrograde inversion.

In this example these operations apply to lines of pitches, and the exact pitch intervals are preserved or reversed. Each conversion is then associated with its contour inversion (which Seeger labels simply "inversion"). I think it is safe to assume, however, that if one or more of the notes in the resulting transformation were transferred by one or more octaves, Seeger would still acknowledge it as a conversion of the original. In that sense, his conversions may be understood as operations either on pitch or on pitch class. As a practical matter, Crawford does in fact apply the canonical twelve-tone operators (or TTOs) to pitches and to pitch classes.

While these conversions may be applied to any neume, there is one in particular that recurs persistently in virtually all of Crawford's compositions. It is a three-note fragment consisting of a semitone and a whole tone in opposite directions, what Seeger would call a binary twist-neume. The four forms of this motive are shown in Example 2.22, all beginning on D for the sake of comparison.[55] Usually in Crawford's music, these motive forms are stated in close registral disposition, but any of the intervals may be expanded by an octave or replaced

Example 2.22 The four forms of Motive M1

Prime   Inversion   Retrograde   Retrograde inversion

< +2, –1 >   < –2, +1 >   < +1, –2 >   < –1, +2 >

Example 2.23 Motive M1 in *Diaphonic Suite No. 1* (for flute or oboe), first movement, mm. 1–3

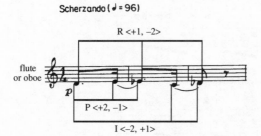

by its complement. In other words, while the intervals of Example 2.22 are usually realized as pitch intervals, they should be understood more broadly as pitch-class intervals.

This motive, which I will refer to as Motive M1 in any of its four orderings, is extraordinarily prevalent in Crawford's melodic lines, with a variety of musical functions. At the most obvious level, it acts simply as a marker, a fingerprint, a point of departure and return for chains of evolving neumes. In the first movement of the *Diaphonic Suite No. 1*, for example, the initial five-note gesture contains three forms of M1 (see Example 2.23). The first three notes, D–E–E♭, present the motive in its prime ordering. It opens a space a whole tone above the D, then immediately fills it with E♭, creating a small chromatic zone. An inverted form of the same motive begins on D and concludes with C and D♭ at the end of the figure. This inverted form has the same rhythmic shape as the prime form (long-short-long), but with a space between its first and second notes. It contains the lowest three notes of the five-note gesture, just as the prime ordering contains the highest three notes of the gesture. And just as the prime ordering opened a space above the D, then filled it in, the inverted ordering opens a space below the D and immediately fills it in. As a result, the phrase as a whole creates a contiguous chromatic zone from C to E. An additional form of the motive, this time in its retrograde ordering, is described by the notes on successive downbeats, D–E♭–D♭. Elsewhere in the movement, Motive M1 in its original rhythmic shape is similarly used to signal beginnings of phrases, often after a rest or other sectional divider.

M1 is also used to end phrases in the *Diaphonic Suite No. 1*. Indeed, it concludes three of the work's four movements (see Example 2.24). The last two notes of the first movement, C♯–D♯, lead *attacca* into the first note of the

Example 2.24 Motive M1 used at cadential points in *Diaphonic Suite No. 1* (for flute or oboe):
A) end of first movement and beginning of second; B) end of second movement;
C) end of fourth movement

A)

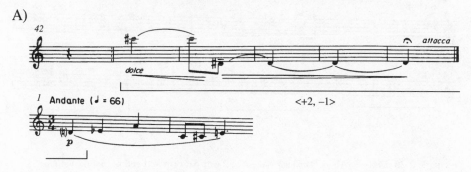

B)

C)

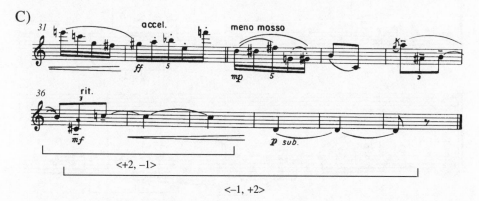

second movement, D. The second and fourth movements end with pitch–class identical M1s. The M1s that end the first and second movements, and the overlapped M1-pair that ends the fourth, culminate on the same pitch, D4, which plays a pivotal role throughout the piece.

M1 is frequently used to create a link across a phrase boundary (see Example 2.25). Amid a profusion of M1s, accounting for virtually every note in the passage, the one that begins in measure 29 spans across a phrase ending, indicated by the

Example 2.25 Motive M1 used to bridge across a phrase boundary in *Diaphonic Suite No. 1* (for flute or oboe), first movement, mm. 20-32

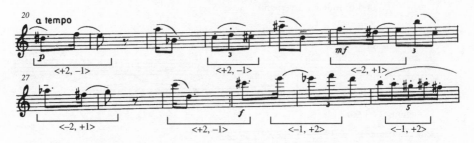

Example 2.26 Motive M1 in *Diaphonic Suite No. 2* (for bassoon and cello), first movement, mm. 1–20

Example 2.27 Intensive use of Motive M1 at the climax of Chant No. 1 ("To an Unkind
God"), mm. 17–18

Example 2.28 Motive M1 in Piano Prelude No. 1, mm. 1–3

dotted double bar at the end of the measure.[56] This bridging M1 is pitch-class identical to the M1 in measure 23. An additional M1 is immediately adjoined to create the opening gesture of the next phrase.

Motive M1 is similarly prevalent in the opening cello melody from the first movement of *Diaphonic Suite No. 2* (see Example 2.26). The melody begins on the favored pitch class D and presents M1 in its prime ordering, emphasized by accents on each note and separated from what follows by an elongated third note. In subsequent occurrences, one or both intervals may be expanded by an octave (mm. 3–4, 8–9) or replaced by their complements (mm. 13–14). The melody follows the general contour of an arch, and ends with an M1 in the register, but not the ordering, of the initial one. Between the first and last statements, M1 occurs with such frequency that it even overlaps with itself in two places (measures 9 and 13–14). Motivic overlaps of this kind are a persistent feature of Crawford's melodies.[57]

The climactic measures of Chant No. 1 ("To an Unkind God") compress numerous statements of Motive M1 into a dense contrapuntal web (see Example 2.27). While the highest voice slowly presents two overlapped forms, the lower voices rapidly present many more. On the second beat of measure 18, the accompanying parts present three forms simultaneously, in a rare moment of rhythmic homophony.[58]

Motive M1 is extraordinarily prevalent in Crawford's post-Seeger music, but it occurs unmistakably in her earlier music as well. The opening melody of her Piano Prelude No. 1 (1924), for example, is highly chromatic, consisting for the most part of pairs of notes related by semitone (see Example 2.28). It contains eleven of the twelve pitch classes – only C♯ is absent – and introduces the first ten of these with no repetitions at all. As the melody approaches its high point in measure 2, Motive M1 comes in for intensive development. Two direct statements of it, G♯–B♭–A and A–C♭–B♭, are embedded within a larger statement defined by contour high points, C–B♭–C♭. In Crawford's pre-Seeger music, occurrences of M1 are not as sharply etched as they later become. Nonetheless, they are an unmistakable presence there, and create a significant link that spans Crawford's change of musical style.

Transformation of neumes

M1 is such a persistent feature of Crawford's melodies that I will occasionally want to discuss other motives as variants of it. All of the hypothetical variants listed in the chart below (and their serial order permutations) preserve at least one of the intervals of M1.

Chart 2.1

name	notes	prime ordering	set class
M2	<D, E♭, D>	<+1, −1>	(01)
M3	<D, E♭, E>	<+1, +1>	(012)
M4	<D, E♭, F>	<+1, +2>	(013)
M5	<D, E♭, C>	<+1, −3>	(013)
M6	<D, E♭, F♯>	<+1, +3>	(014)
M7	<D, E♭, B>	<+1, −4>	(014)
M8	<D, E♭, G>	<+1, +4>	(015)
M9	<D, E♭, B♭>	<+1, −5>	(015)
M10	<D, E♭, A♭>	<+1, +5>	(016)
M11	<D, E♭, A>	<+1, −6>	(016)
M12	<D, E, D>	<+2, −2>	(02)
M13	<D, E, F♯>	<+2, +2>	(024)
M14	<D, E, C♯>	<+2, −3>	(013)
M15	<D, E, G>	<+2, +3>	(025)
M16	<D, E, C>	<+2, −4>	(024)
M17	<D, E, G♯>	<+2, +4>	(026)
M18	<D, E, B>	<+2, −5>	(025)
M19	<D, E, A>	<+2, +5>	(027)
M20	<D, E, B♭>	<+2, −6>	(026)

Each motive is identified by its name (analogous to the familiar M1), its prime ordering beginning on D (Crawford's favored pitch class for beginning and ending neumes and longer melodies), the intervals described by the prime ordering, and the set class that results from considering the notes of the motive as an unordered collection.

The problem with such a scheme is the profusion of apparent variants, including nineteen on the list above representing all but three of the trichord types (only the diminished, minor/major, and augmented triads are excluded). It would be easy to account for most of the notes in Crawford's melodies in terms of these hypothetical variants. Indeed, it would be altogether too easy. Ultimately, we would have shown only that her melodies never go for very long without either a semitone or a whole tone. So, while I will continue to refer casually to the notion of motivic variants, taxonomies of this kind have a limited use. In

Crawford's music, apart from the omnipresent Motive M1, the musical surface is intervallically and motivically varied. M1 gives a measure of consistency and identity to Crawford's melodies, which are otherwise better understood in terms of motivic transformation, the process by which one motive metamorphoses into another. Instead of relating all forms to a single progenitor, we will cut ourselves loose from our analytical moorings and follow the melodies wherever the transformations lead us. Instead of worrying about where we are, we will enjoy the pleasures of the voyage.

Seeger proposes many ways for transforming one neume into another. We have already discussed the possibilities of preserving contour while changing intervals and applying the canonical twelve-tone operations (Seeger's "conversions"). Seeger also proposes a number of more *ad hoc* transformations, including "extension" (adding tones at the beginning, middle, or end of the neume) and "intension" (subtracting tones from the beginning, middle, or end of the neume).[59] In describing each transformation, Seeger's concern is with creating larger shapes (particularly extended melodies) from short structural units (neumes).

> Any neume can be changed into any other provided the change is gradual. This fact has been made use of in composition and may be termed a kind of modulation – a moving from neume to neume in a manner similar to movement from key to key. Neume transformation of this sort is one of the commonest and most important means of building the organic phrase.[60]

The principal neume transformations envisioned by Seeger are sufficiently flexible to move in rapid order from a given neume to pretty much any other neume one could imagine.[61] The music that would result from this conception would most likely present a neumatic surface of great variety. Its coherence would derive not from the identity of the neumes themselves, but from the transformations that link them into a connected network.

What follows is a list of Crawford's most commonly used neumatic transformations with a brief description of each. Some are drawn directly or indirectly from Seeger; I have devised others observing the spirit, if not the letter, of Seeger's enterprise. Each transformation is illustrated by a melody from the first movement of the String Quartet (see Example 2.29).[62] In these analyses, it is not the neumes themselves that receive a descriptive label, but rather the transformation in question.[63]

INT
An interval is replaced by its complement or its compound (see Example 2.29A).[64]

The first bracketed neume in Example 2.29A describes the ordered pitch intervals $<+2, +8>$; the second replaces $<+8>$ with its complement, $<-4>$. This transformation is so common in Crawford's music that normally I will not bother labeling it. Two neumes related by INT will simply be treated as equivalent.

Example 2.29 Neumatic transformations in String Quartet, first movement, Violin 1, mm.
16–20: A) INT; B) the twelve-tone operations; C) MULT; D) EXP; E) PE

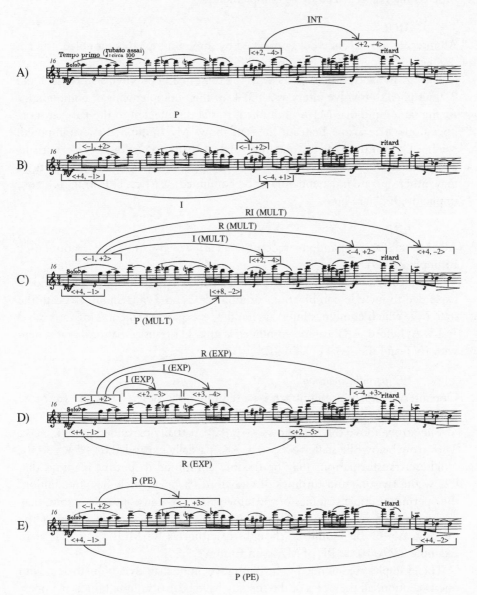

P, I, R, and RI

The neume is treated as a brief series of pitches or pitch classes, and subjected to
the traditional serial operations: prime, inversion, retrograde, and retrograde
inversion (see Example 2.29B).[65]

The arrow above the staff shows a neume, Crawford's familiar M1,
transformed by P (its ordered intervals preserved). The arrow below the staff

shows another neume, M7 on my list, transformed by I, which is inverted (each ordered interval replaced by its complement).

MULT

All intervals are expanded or contracted by some multiple (eg. doubled, tripled, divided in half, etc.) (see Example 2.29C).

The arrows above the staff show M1, a twist neume involving intervals 1 and 2, multiplied to involve intervals 2 and 4 (or their complements or compounds). At the same time that M1 is multiplied, it is also subjected to the familiar serial operations. The arrow beneath the staff shows M7 multiplied and transposed: <+4, −1> is multiplied to become <+8, −2> or, replacing <+8> with its complement, <−4, −2>. As this example suggests, Crawford's transformations may either operate independently or be combined, as MULT, P, I, R, RI, and, implicitly, INT are here.

EXP

All intervals are expanded or contracted in size by the same amount (see Example 2.29D).[66]

The arrows above the staff show M1, which combines intervals 1 and 2, expanded to include combinations of intervals 2 and 3 or 3 and 4. Beneath the staff, M7, which combines intervals 1 and 4, is expanded to combine intervals 2 and 5. As before, EXP can be combined with other transformations, as it is here with INT and the serial operations.

PE (partial expansion)

One interval expands or contracts by a semitone, the other(s) stay the same (see Example 2.29E).

The arrow above the staff shows <−1, +2> partially expanded to <−1, +3>. The arrow below the staff shows <+4, −1> partially expanded to <+4, −2>.

These transformations may be flexibly combined to permit readings that follow the twisting and turnings of Crawford's slippery melodies. In addition, they permit multiple readings of the same passage, because a single gesture may be interpreted in different ways. For example, the last three notes of the melody, A♭–C–B♭, could be thought of either as RI(MULT) of M1, as in Example 2.29C, or as PE of M7, as in Example 2.29E.

The examples are intended to be illustrative, not exhaustive. Nonetheless, with one exception, all the notes of the melody have been accounted for as members of neumes that are transformations of the two initial three-note figures. In readings of this kind, the initial figure is seen as a source for what happens later, and everything that happens later is seen as a development of the initial figure. The same transformations, however, permit a different kind of reading, one in which each neume is connected only to the neumes that come right before or after it. In readings of this kind, we cut ourselves off from a fixed mooring and follow the flow of the melody wherever it leads us, as in Example 2.30.

Example 2.31 combines the two kinds of readings, tracing the melody step by step, but also pulling back to hear it as a whole. In the first half of the melody, A♭–G–A moves through a series of expansions and contractions, finally returning to its original shape, transposed down one semitone, on G–F♯–G♯. That neume is overlapped with its inverted multiple, to become F♯–G♯–E. From this point on, this new neume is developed, culminating in its own transposed retrograde at the end of the melody. That final neume can also be related back to the first one, as its RI(MULT).

CONT
The contour of the neume is preserved, or inversion, retrograde, or retrograde inversion is applied without respect to the intervals.

This transformation, as noted earlier, gives only a crude picture of Crawford's melodies, even when Seeger's understanding of contour is refined to the more precise CSEGs. Furthermore, this transformation, by itself, is analytically promiscuous – it establishes connections among neumes so freely and so widely as to be of dubious value. It will be more effective if we conjoin CONT with other transformations that act directly on intervals.

In a melody from the first movement of *Diaphonic Suite No. 2*, brackets above the staff identify all of the binary twist-neumes in the passage, that is, all those three-note groups that involve a change of direction (see Example 2.32). Segmented in this way, in terms of contour but in ignorance of interval, the

Example 2.30 Neumatic transformations in String Quartet, first movement, Violin 1, mm. 16–20

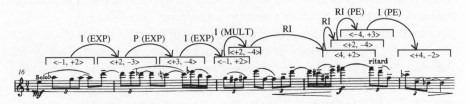

Example 2.31 Neumatic transformations in String Quartet, first movement, Violin 1, mm. 16–20

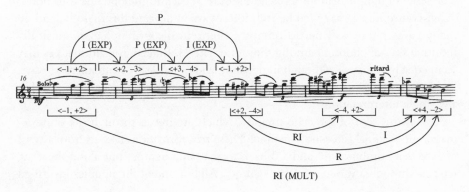

Example 2.32 Two transformational paths through a melody from *Diaphonic Suite No. 2* (for bassoon and cello), first movement, cello, mm. 1-4

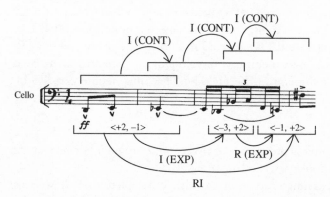

melody can be understood in terms of a chain of contour inversions, alternating <+, −> with <−, +>. Brackets below the staff simply divide the melody into three segments and analyze it in terms of its intervals, irrespective of contour. The motion from the first neume to the last is understood in terms of two intervallic expansions, combined first with inversion and then with retrograde. As a result of those two moves, the first three notes and the last three are related by retrograde inversion.[67] Both readings, one based on contour without regard to interval and the other based on interval without regard to contour, strike me as plausible, although neither seems compelling on its own.

Readings that consider both contour and interval, and that follow the various transformations in a flexible way stand the best chance of mapping the shifting, evasive structure of Crawford's melodies. *Diaphonic Suite No. 4* is a duet for oboe and cello. The third movement pits two contrasting melodies against each other, a free, angular melody in the oboe and a relentless, motoric melody in the cello. Both melodies can be described, independently, in terms of neumatic transformation (see Example 2.33). In the oboe melody, brackets identify four statements of CSEG <0132>. The progress among these neumes usually involves partial expansion, that is, the alteration of one constituent interval by semitone. The series of transformations leads, in measure 5, back to the opening four notes.

Of course, there may well be still other ways of hearing this melody, and, in many cases, there will be no obvious, theoretically principled or musically intuitive way of choosing among these alternatives. Indeed, the alternatives may seem equally attractive, although in different, and occasionally contradictory, ways. In general, Crawford's melodies are multivalent, slippery, and elusive, resisting any single interpretation.

This is true also of the cello melody, which progresses through the transformation of its initial three-note neume. These transformations take us from a twist neume that combines a 1 and a 3 back to the same neume, but along the way, we pass through a variety of other neumes. All but one of the neumes identified

Example 2.33 Neumatic transformation in *Diaphonic Suite No. 4* (for oboe and cello), third movement, mm. 1–5

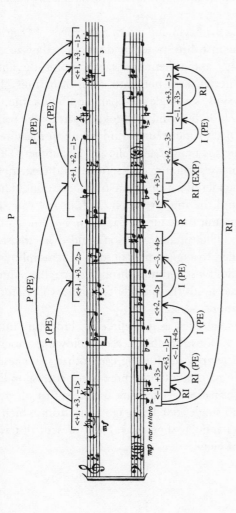

Example 2.34 A transformational path through *Diaphonic Suite No. 2* (for bassoon and cello), first movement, cello, mm. 1–10

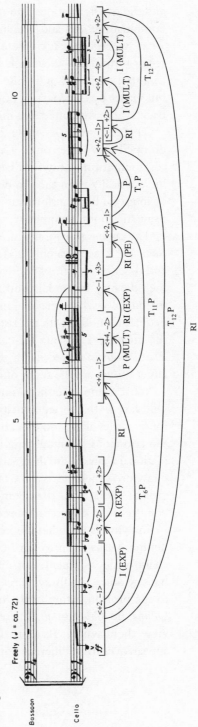

with brackets are twist neumes, that is, with the contour <+, –> or <–, +>, and the transformations lead us from a combination of intervals 1 and 3 through combinations of 1 and 4, 2 and 4, 3 and 4, 2 and 3, and finally back to 1 and 3. That we end up back where we started in both the oboe and cello melodies seems fortuitous – they are held together not by a sense of directed motion back to a starting point, or a sense of ineluctable motion toward any particular goal, but rather by the cogency of each step along the way. When we find ourselves back where we started, we may be pleased, but we will certainly be surprised.

The analyses in Example 2.33 appear hierarchical, with the smaller motions grouped into larger ones. That, however, is an illusion fostered by this visual representation. Crawford's melodies should not be conceived as generated hierarchically from the top down. Rather, they are better understood in terms of intertwining transformational paths, none of which is hierarchically superior to or subsumes the other.

The same is true for the melody at the beginning of first movement of *Diaphonic Suite No. 2* (see Example 2.34). The first three notes are distinguished by accents and describe a form of Motive M1. Taking them as a starting point, the entire melody may be understood as a network of neumatic transformations. The melody as a whole may be understood as a single RI-chain combining the first neume, D–E–Eb, with the last, E–Eb–F, but which is broken apart by the rest of the melody. The same RI-chain, occurs intact and in miniature in measure 9. That RI-chain is preceded by one octave transfer and followed by another. These larger moves are the result of the many small moves described on the example.

What is important here is not the identification of the transformations. These will vary with the segmentation and the interpretation, and, in any case, the music rattles along too quickly to permit these identifications to become part of the conscious listening experience. These transformations, and these transformational analyses, are designed, rather, to suggest the constant metamorphosis of Crawford's melodies. As the melodies twist and turn through space, the neumes change. What links the neumes, and holds the melody together, is Crawford's consistent use of certain transformations.

Crawford's melodies are not generally felt as goal-directed. From any initial neume, paths seem to fan out in various directions, each following a logical chain of development, but not necessarily reinforcing each other. As a result, her melodies are always susceptible to multiple interpretations, corresponding to the protean nature of the transformations. These are melodies that obey no *Urlinie*, no *Grundgestalt*. There is no single, fixed vantage point from which to view them whole. Rather, they change as they move, and present different appearances from different points of view.

Melodic process

Crawford's melodies often give the impression of living organisms, like amoebas that change shape as they move. They expand and contract, surge forward and hold back, twist and turn, move forward and shrink back, and, all the while, their intervallic identity shifts and changes. Inevitably, then, whatever coherence they may be heard to possess derives not from their content, which is constantly in flux, as from the processes of melodic formation. In the previous section, we tried to trace these processes at the level of the neume, by identifying musical units at least three notes long and pursuing them through their often slippery transformations. It is also possible to trace the melodic process at the level of the single note.

Crawford employs a small group of strategies for generating the notes of her melodies, including the following:

ASSERT

The first note of a movement, or a section, is simply asserted, to become the initial tone in a chain of development. This note may become a center of inversional balance, or function in some other way as a focal point.

OPEN

Once an initial note has been asserted, a second note can be added to open a musical space that then becomes the locus of the ensuing action.

CENTER

Melodies often move toward the note lying symmetrically at the center of a previously opened space. In the second movement of the String Quartet, there is a melody that is punctuated by four large leaps (see Example 2.35). The notes

Example 2.35 Moving to the symmetrical center of a previously opened musical space in String Quartet, second movement, first violin, mm. 57–61

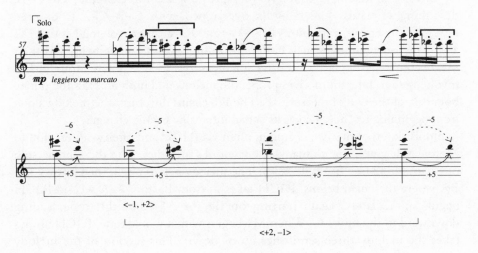

following each leap move toward the symmetrical center of the leap, either nearly so, as in the first leap, or exactly, as in the rest. The melody can thus be understood as four related gestures, each involving a leap and a symmetrical filling in. The leaps themselves are arranged to create two overlapping RI-related statements of M1, reflecting the frequent M1s of the musical surface, which are indicated with brackets above the music.

FILL

A previously opened space (either pitch or pitch-class space) is often filled in chromatically. This strategy is closely related to the drive of Crawford's melodies toward chromatic completion, as discussed earlier. Her melodies usually move promptly to fill any gaps. The ubiquitous Motive M1, when it begins with a whole tone, epitomizes this strategy in microcosm: after an initial whole tone, the melody reverses direction to fill in the open space.

ADJOIN

A new melodic note is often adjoined at the top or bottom of a chromatic cluster. Like FILL, ADJOIN is an aspect of Crawford's interest in chromatic completion. New notes in a melody tend to be related by semitone to some previous note. Motive M1, when it begins with a semitone, epitomizes this strategy: after two notes a semitone apart, the melody adjoins an additional note adjacent to that pair.

RICH

Melodies often work to continue or conclude RI-chains. An RI-chain results when the last two notes of a motive become the first two notes of its retrograde inversion.[68] RI-chains involving Motive M1 are particularly prevalent in Crawford's music, as in the first movement of *Diaphonic Suite No. 1*, shown in its entirety in Example 2.36. In measures 34–35, for example, B♭–C–B, describing intervals <+2, –1> is overlapped with C–B–C♯, its ordered retrograde inversion, with intervals <–1, +2>. RI-chains involving Motive M1 and many other motives may be found throughout the movement, and their use becomes particularly intensive in measures 15–19. There, four chains involving four different motives propel the melody and push it across the phrase boundary at the end of measure 18. The RI-chains thus carry the melody along from beginning to end, even as its actual intervallic profile changes.

Similar kinds of motivic chaining, often via RICH and often with relation to Motive M1, give shape to many of Crawford's melodies, as in the soprano solo of Chant No. 2 (see Example 2.37). The melody begins on G, then leaps +3 to B♭, where the chain begins. RICH takes us from B♭ to C♯. A second RICH begins immediately, again starting on B♭ (or A♯), but this time leading downward to the initial G. When M1 begins with a whole tone, RICH always takes the melody three semitones up or down. This section of the melody

Example 2.36 RI-chains in *Diaphonic Suite No. 1* (for flute or oboe), first movement

Example 2.37 RI-chains in Chant No. 2 ("To an Angel"), soprano solo, mm. 26–40

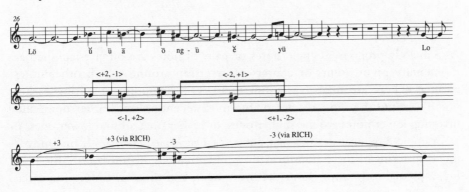

contains two leaps of ip3, and two instances of ip3 spanned by RICH, the second of which leads the melody back to its starting point.

In the third phrase from "In Tall Grass," one of the Three Sandburg Songs, virtually every note in the vocal melody participates in at least one RI-pair (see Example 2.38). The poet Carl Sandburg was a friend and neighbor of Crawford's during her years in Chicago, and she frequently set his poems to music.[69] The song consists of a central group of instruments, in which the vocal melody is accompanied by oboe, piano, and mixed percussion, and an optional secondary group of winds and strings that contribute various kinds of interjections. The vocal melody in Example 2.38 contains four RI-pairs, each involving different intervals. The intervallic content of the melody thus varies, but the process of melodic generation is consistent throughout. The oboe countermelody also contains RI-pairs, as well as several freestanding statements of the ubiquitous Motive M1.

Example 2.38 RI-chains in "In Tall Grass," from Three Sandburg Songs, vocal melody and oboe countermelody, mm. 21–32

PIVOT

As a melody progresses, single notes or pairs of notes are often established as momentary pivot points or centers of inversion around which other notes balance. There are many variations of PIVOT, including inverting earlier note(s) around the most recent, or the most recent around earlier ones, and inverting lower notes around higher ones, or higher ones around lower ones.[70]

Example 2.39 analyzes the first phrase of *Diaphonic Suite No. 1*, first movement, in terms of these transformations. The melody begins by ASSERTing D4, a pivotal tone throughout the movement, and then OPENing the space

Example 2.39 Melodic transformations in *Diaphonic Suite No. 1* (for flute or oboe), first
movement, mm. 1–9

between D4 and E4. E♭4 FILLs the space and, at the same time, occupies the
symmetrical CENTER between the two previous notes. The E♭, like many other
notes throughout this and other melodies, can thus be accounted for in more
than one way. Here, the conjunction of FILL and CENTER creates the familiar
Motive M1, <+2, –1>. The C4 and D♭4 that follow result from PIVOTing the
recent E and E♭ around the earliest note in the line, D. For each PIVOT, the
specific inversional operation is identified following Lewin's notational
convention.[71] Here, the notation says that the C and D♭ in the melody result
from inverting E and E♭ around D. The progress of the entire melody could be
narrated in this way and, indeed, such a continuous narration is embodied in the
analytical abbreviations above the music.[72]

Example 2.40 tells a similar story about the first section of the *Piano Study in
Mixed Accents*. FILLs and ADJOINS are so common that I have not bothered
identifying them, concentrating instead on the PIVOTs. This melody contains
many symmetrical sets representing many different set types. Of the fourteen
symmetrical tetrachord types, for example, nine appear in this short melody, all
as by-products of the inversional pivots. These tetrachords are intervallically distinct
from each other, sharing only their common source in the inversional moves.
The melodic organism changes shape, but is consistent in the way it moves. The
identity of the musical objects changes, but the transformations remain the same.
The melodic unity is one of process, not content.

Example 2.40 Melodic transformations in *Piano Study in Mixed Accents*, first section

Inversional symmetry

Most of Crawford's melodies play a rapid game of leap-frog, with new notes balancing old ones around constantly shifting pivots. In some melodies, however, a single pivot remains in place for a longer time, and organizes an entire phrase or section. Inversional symmetry around some central tone was for Crawford, and for Seeger, a kind of substitute for the organizing power of the tonic in classical tonality, but with two obvious differences. First, the central tone will be a single pitch, not a pitch class with its octave reduplications. Second, its centrality results not from repetition or functional progression, but from inversional balance. The pitch center will be literally the center of a pitch-inversional structure; it will be an axis of pitch inversion.

> Since the old tonality and modality have weakened to such an extent that they have no use in dissonant writing except to be negated, we have nothing left but *pitch center*. Instead, however, of regarding pitch center as being reduplicated in each octave as in the old tonality, we can regard pitch center as something absolute – there being only one in the whole gamut for a piece or passage in one tonality. As to the subordinate centers whose relationship to the tonal center increase its strength, a balancing to either side is recommended. For instance, if the first movement away from the adopted tonal center is to a major seventh above, the second movement could be to a major seventh below, a return to the main pitch center being made afterward.[73]

It is significant that Seeger disallows the octave as a source of reinforcement and simultaneously promotes the major seventh. As we will see in the following section, when Crawford's melodies move through pitch space, they often find points of articulation separated not by octaves, but by major sevenths or minor ninths, and frequently these intervals are flanked symmetrically around some central tone. Crawford herself emphasized the importance of pitch centers, listing them among the central components of her compositional credo:

> As for a "credo" typifying my music of the type of *String Quartet* and Three Songs, I could mention a few points about which I felt strongly. And I still feel strongly about them. I believe when I write more music these elements will be there, or at least striven for:
>
> Clarity of melodic line
> Avoidance of rhythmic stickiness
> Rhythmic independence between parts
> Feeling of tonal and rhythmic center
> Experiment with various means of obtaining at the same time organic unity and various sorts of dissonance.[74]

Despite these comments, however, the sense of tonal center in Crawford's music is always fleeting at best. Occasionally, pitches will persist throughout an extended passage as points of departure and arrival. More commonly, however, the centricity is evanescent, changing or vanishing almost as soon as it is established.

The first melodic phrase of "In Tall Grass," for example, begins with an explicit wedge, a higher part and a lower converging on a central G♯4–A4 (see Example 2.41). Part of the same wedge is reasserted at the end of the phrase, which concludes with the axial notes, A–G♯. In the middle of the phrase, the inversional balance is not so explicit, but the central A–G♯ continue to play a pivotal role. The A at the end of the opening wedge begins a registrally-defined statement of Motive M1, which begins on A and ends on G♯. That G♯ then begins another statement of M1, inversionally related to the first, which thus begins on G♯ and ends on A. These two forms of M1 balance around G♯–A, just as the rest of the phrase does.

In an extended melody, each phrase may be symmetrical around some axis. The opening section of a piano melody, also from "In Tall Grass," is shown in Example 2.42. The longer melody of which this fragment is part is repeated several times in its entirety and dominates the middle section of the song. It involves a single line doubled at the octave in the manner of the *Piano Study in*

Example 2.41 Inversional symmetry in "In Tall Grass" from Three Sandburg Songs, vocal melody, mm. 8–13

Example 2.42 Inversional symmetry in "In Tall Grass" from Three Sandburg Songs, piano, mm. 40–43

Mixed Accents and "Chinaman, Laundryman," although the two hands tend to diverge a bit at the ends of phrases.

I have divided the fragment into seven segments, each of which is symmetrical on some axis. The axes are identified and the inversionally balanced pairs of notes are connected by a slur. In four cases, a retrograde symmetry reinforces the inversional symmetry – these segments proceed by the familiar RICH. Inversional structures of this kind are prevalent in Crawford's melodies, almost an inevitable outgrowth of their constant pivoting.

Register

As Crawford's melodies twist and turn, now surging ahead, now doubling back, they shape the musical space within which they move. Many music theories, including atonal set theory, imagine musical space as a pre-existent grid, marked out into equal semitones and octaves, waiting to be filled. They suggest, apart from any specific musical context, that notes an octave apart will be treated as equivalent and that each octave will be divided up in the same way, into twelve equal semitones. Crawford's music requires a different approach, because her melodies create their own space, one which is frequently unevenly divided, and in which the octave no longer plays its preeminent role. Crawford's melodies often articulate upper and lower registral boundaries, which may remain fixed for extended periods of time, or may rise and fall as the melody unfolds. Often, the upper and lower boundaries are eleven or thirteen semitones apart. These intervals come almost to supplant the octave as the underlying structural frame.

In the first half of "Sacco, Vanzetti" the melody is circumscribed by a gradually ascending registral frame.[75] The melodic activity in the first section of the song, part of which is given in Example 2.43A, lies entirely between C♯4 and C5, and those boundary tones are heavily emphasized. As the piece continues, the registral frame gradually ascends, with boundary tones always eleven semitones apart (see Example 2.43B).

The first movement of *Diaphonic Suite No. 1* creates a fixed underlying registral frame, D♯4–D5–C♯6. D5 is thus the centric tone for the piece, flanked, as recommended by Seeger, by notes a major seventh above and below. The outer extremes of this frame are the last two notes of the movement. The boundaries are pierced on occasion, but still serve to encompass most of the melodic motion. Within this underlying frame, the melodic gestures are normally contained within a series of 11s, that gradually ascend or descend.

The middle section of the movement, which begins in measure 10 and ends in measure 28, consists of one long, ascending gesture (see Example 2.44). The first note (E♭4), the last note (D5), and the first note of the next section (C♯6) define the registral frame of the entire piece, one which is gradually filled by the ascending series of 11s in this passage. Some members of the frame, like the initial E♭4, are missing their 11-related partners, but the frame is generally

Example 2.43 Ascending registral frame in "Sacco, Vanzetti": A) vocal melody, mm. 15–33;
B) analytical summary for entire piece

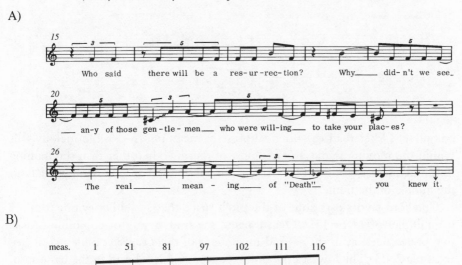

Example 2.44 Ascending registral frame in *Diaphonic Suite No. 1* (for flute or oboe), first
movement: A) mm. 7–31; B) analytical summary

Example 2.45 Partitioning the pitch space in *Diaphonic Suite No. 2* (for bassoon and cello), second movement, mm. 1–12

complete. Other than the brief outburst in measures 15–16, the melody falls within the moving frame. In fact, most of the melody, other than the framing notes themselves, consists of statements of Motive M1 placed symmetrically in the middle of the frame.

Crawford favors partitions of the pitch space that are either symmetrical or in multiples of 11 or 13.[76] Occasionally, she finds a way of conjoining these two preferences, as in the second movement of the *Diaphonic Suite No. 2* (see Example 2.45). The lowest note of the passage, C♯2, is heard in the bassoon in measure 6 and again in measure 12, at the end of the passage. From there to the highest note, the C6 sustained in the cello in measures 9–12, is forty-seven semitones, an enormously compound ip11.[77] That large pitch space is divided up symmetrically, with particular emphasis on simple ip11s. The boundary tones, summarized at the end of the example, are emphasized musically in various ways. In the beginning of the passage, for example, the cello presents the ip11 from F♯4 to G3 melodically, then sustains its G3 as the bassoon enters ip11 lower on A♭2. The remaining notes of the melody tend to move within and around these boundaries.

A similar partitioning scheme, involving both inversional symmetry and an interest in ip11 and ip13, shapes the second movement of the String Quartet. An extended section in the middle of the movement involves sustained notes initially in the first violin and cello, and then in the second violin and viola, amid which a melody shared among all four instruments wanders, twists, and turns (see Example 2.46). Each vertical dyad is a member of ic1. Beginning fifty-nine semitones apart, the two parts of the wedge move toward each other, at first by either eleven or thirteen semitones, and finally by five, converging on F♯4/G4, at the precise midpoint of the pitch space. Leaving aside that point of convergence, the entire pitch space is divided nearly symmetrically and always into intervals of ip11 and ip13. Those dividing points, and the point of convergence, act frequently as melodic boundaries in this section and throughout the movement. Melodies frequently begin or end there, or employ those points as contour highs or lows.

The entire pitch space of the Prelude No. 9 is carved out in an even more consistent and systematic way. The opening section of the piece, repeated exactly as its conclusion, pits long sustained whole tones deep in the bass against

Example 2.46 Partitioning the pitch space in String Quartet, second movement: A) mm. 21–40;
B) analytical summary

more rapidly moving ip11s and 13s high in the treble (see Example 2.47). The passage conveys a sense of an ethereal, other-worldly airy spirit, moving down toward a distant earth, rumbling far below, then returning to its original height. This may have to do with what Crawford referred to as the work's "program from Laotze's Tao," but she does not specify the program, so it is impossible to be sure.[78] For the most part, the two strands seem to occupy separate musical worlds, distinguished by both the vast registral gulf between them and their distinct intervallic concerns. But there are subtle links between them, including the unified pitch space they jointly define.[79]

In the passage shown in Example 2.47A, the entire A-section of an ABA-form, ip13 and ip11 predominate, as does a recurring gesture in which 11 expands to 13, or 13 contracts to 11. In most cases, the 11 is heard on a beat, and one note moves by ip2 to expand the interval to ip13. This idea, of 13 divided into 11 plus 2, is central in the articulation of the musical space.

Among the 11s, a few (marked with an asterisk) seem to have a special role at the beginnings or endings of melodic phrases. The initial move (repeated at the end of the section), arrives on G5–F♯6. That ip11 is transposed down ip13 to F♯4–F5 at the beginning of measure 5. Transposition down another ip13 brings the music to F3–E4, where the second phrase begins in measure 7. At that point, the right hand ascends, retracing its steps.

Example 2.47B summarizes these principal moves, and projects their hypothetical continuation downward into the lowest register. There, the recurring gestures of the right hand hook up with the ostinato C♯1–D♯1 that rumbles in the depths throughout the passage. The entire musical space then, from the G5–F♯6 of the opening down to the ostinato C♯1–D♯1, is systematically carved up into successive 13s. The 13s themselves are divided into an 11 and a 2, reflecting at this deeper level the frequent 11–13 and 13–11 progressions of the surface.

This passage suggests two related notions with general applicability in Crawford's music. First, one should not assume any *a priori* division of the musical space, into octaves or otherwise. Second, the musical motions themselves will shape the space in which they move. The musical space is not already out there, a preexistent grid waiting to be filled; rather, space is something created by the motions of a musical organism.

The persistent division of the pitch space into successive ip13s has potentially radical implications for the musical structure. Normally, musical pitch space is understood as divided into octaves. Any two pitches that lie one or more octaves apart are understood as similar in some fundamental way. In much of Crawford's music, however, there is often a stronger affinity between notes that lie ip11 or ip13 apart. Notes separated by those intervals, and not by the traditional octave, will tend to have a similar function, as points of articulation and repose. The music asserts the intervals traditionally considered most dissonant as structural bases, supplanting the octave in that role. It is in this area that Crawford offers her most profound challenge to the musical tradition.

Example 2.47 Partitioning the pitch space in Piano Prelude No. 9: A) last six measures;
B) analytical summary

A)

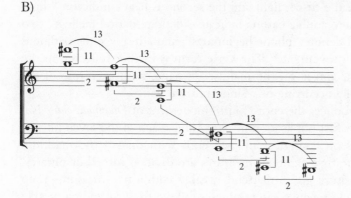

B)

Large-scale designs

Metric form or verse form

Over the course of her compositional career, Crawford organized the larger
structures and forms of her music in a variety of ways. In her music pre-Seeger,
she favored establishing explicit links among the movements in multi-
movement works. In both the Suite No. 1 for Piano and Winds (1927–29) and
the Suite No. 2 for Piano and Strings (1929), the movements share motivic

content, and music from the first movement is recalled in the later ones. In her music post-Seeger, Crawford is less concerned with inter-movement unity and more concerned, within each movement, to "experiment with various means of obtaining at the same time organic unity and various sorts of dissonance."[80]

Thus far we have seen Crawford's melodies as ever-changing organisms wandering through a strange musical space. One of Crawford's experiments in containing and shaping the wanderings, in finding an organic unity amid the threatened aimlessness, involved what Seeger called "metric form" or "verse form."

> Music may have a form which can be likened to prose, as can much of the vocal polyphony of the 16th century; or it can be sectionalized as dance music; or it can be given what may be called "verse-form." The prose form is well suited to the soaring and sostenuto cantilena − which should be very much sought after in dissonant melody. The verse-form, however, is perhaps the easiest to work in . . . With [verse-form], many devices of musical assonance and rhyme can be combined. For instance, a repeated tone, a characteristic interval, some particular neume, or rhythmical figure, a distinctive slurring or dotting, can recur at symmetrical intervals at the beginning, middle, or ending of each phrase.[81]

In her music in verse form, Crawford employs a system of single and double barlines to set off the lines and sections of a musical poem. In the four *Diaphonic Suites*, for example, a heavy single barline indicates "slight phrase feeling"; a double barline where the first is light and the second is heavy indicates "slight period feeling"; a heavy double barline indicates "definite period feeling;" two slashes above the staff denote "phrase beginnings"; and a heavy triple barline is used at the end of a movement.[82] The verse form is further reflected in the physical layout of the music on the manuscript page, with each line of the musical poem generally occurring on a single musical staff.[83]

Example 2.48 reproduces the entire fourth movement of *Diaphonic Suite No. 1*, as it appeared in its first publication in *New Music*. Each of the seven lines of the musical poem is on a single staff, and ends with one of the markings described above. The first eighteen measures are divided into four phrases, alternating a four-measure group that ends weakly with a five-measure group that ends strongly. Two seven-measure phrases follow, the first ending weakly and the second strongly, and the movement ends with a single nine-measure phrase, elongated by sustained notes at the end. A clear sense of formal balance and proportion is conveyed by these divisions.

The divisions are made audible by, among other things, the changes in dynamics, articulation, and tempo that generally accompany the beginning of each new phrase, and are further reinforced by the use of a distinctive musical figure, or its variants, to begin each phrase. The rhymes at the beginning of each line, defined musically by Crawford's usual neume transformations and one less usual one, namely reordering, are summarized in Example 2.49.

54

Example 2.48 "Verse form" in *Diaphonic Suite No. 1* (for flute or oboe), fourth movement

Example 2.49 Musical rhymes at the beginning of each phrase in *Diaphonic Suite No. 1* (for flute or oboe), fourth movement

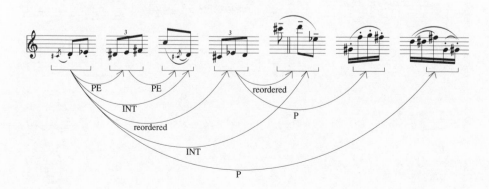

Crawford employs a similar design in the first movement of the same piece. That movement contains nine poetic lines arranged into four periods. The melody reinforces this basic design, although it also creates independent shapes (see Example 2.50, where I have realigned the first six lines to reflect their internal structure). The first two lines and the next two (measures 1–9 and 10–18) are exactly equal in length and have extremely similar melodic and rhythmic profiles, measure-by-measure. The fifth and sixth lines, however, (measures 19–28), have a more complex inner structure, one that is not well captured by Crawford's formal designations. They break down into three sub-phrases, which I have written out on separate staves, each of which is articulated by musical rhyme, beginning and ending with distinctive figures. Within the sub-phrases, however, there is progressively less material between the beginning and the end. The melodic organization is one of progressive liquidation or decomposition, a process that minimizes the phrase boundary at the end of measure 23, and creates a new demarcation at the end of measure 25. The melodic process is partly articulated, but not entirely constrained, by the verse form. Verse form must thus be understood as providing a formal outline, but not as foreclosing alternative interpretations.

Apart from the four *Diaphonic Suites*, Crawford uses verse form, with its attendant articulative markings, in only two other pieces. The first movement of the String Quartet includes internal rhymes in the opening section and a larger rhyme when the opening music returns at the end of the movement.[84] The manuscript of "Sacco, Vanzetti" uses double bars to "mark the separation of the recurring ostinato sections," but these appear only as commas in the published

Example 2.50 *Diaphonic Suite No. 1* (for flute or oboe), first movement, mm. 1–28, realigned to show internal phrase structure

score.[85] Musical rhyme, as an aspect of Crawford's interest in neumatic transformation, is a ubiquitous feature of her musical style. Verse form, however,
with its articulative marks and striking visual layout, was an experiment of
limited scope and implication.

Phrase-neume (motivic projection)

A second strategy of large-scale organization, one that unlike verse form is a
virtually universal feature of Crawford's music, involves what Seeger calls a
phrase-neume or a *form-neume*. The idea here is that a motive may be projected
over a large musical span, through the association of salient surface events. In
any melody, notes might become marked for special attention in various ways,
as, for example, the highest, loudest, or longest notes in the line. Those salient
notes might combine to form larger shapes – spanning phrases, sections, or
entire pieces – that are identical to, or closely related to, the motives of the
musical surface.

> Important tones in the phrase form among themselves what may be called the
> *phrase-neume.* It is not unusual to find the initial neume and the phrase-neume
> the same. Longer phrases are made up of several phrase-neumes which can be
> put together by the same technical means mentioned above [i.e. the neumatic
> conversions] . . . It is possible to envisage the flow of the whole composition as
> a long line or a network of long lines with a definite contour limned by the
> salient points in it . . . In this way a kind of *form-neume* evolves which assists in
> the organization of even the largest masses.[86]

Motive M1, so prevalent on the musical surface, is often projected over larger
spans, with its notes associated by register, as in the second movement of
Diaphonic Suite No. 2 (see Example 2.51). In the cello, it occurs twice right on
the musical surface, although with one of its intervals expanded by an octave in

Example 2.51 Motive M1 projected in register in *Diaphonic Suite No. 2* (for bassoon and cello),
second movement, mm. 12–16

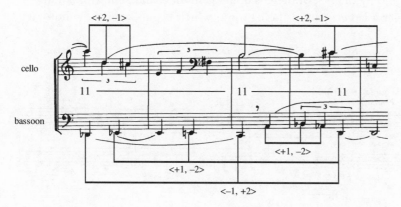

each case. In the bassoon, it occurs once right on the surface, among the three highest notes of the melody. It also occurs in a more concealed, elongated way, among the three notes in the middle register and among the three lowest notes. The lower two M1s are related by inversion and converge on a shared D, their axis of inversional symmetry, and a familiar goal or point of departure in Crawford's melodies. Each of the bassoon's principal notes, Db–C–D, is supported by a cello note eleven semitones (or a compound) higher. That rough parallelism links together the otherwise quite independent parts.

Something similar happens in the second clarinet melody from the beginning of *Diaphonic Suite No. 3*, first movement (see Example 2.52).[87] The melody rises and falls in irregular curves, and projects four direct occurrences of M1, identified with brackets. The four highest notes, each lying atop a melodic curve, project two elongated statements of M1, D–E–Eb overlapped with its retrograde inversion, E–Eb–F.

The second movement of *Diaphonic Suite No. 3* projects Motive M1 at various levels of structure (see Example 2.53). Motive M1 is formed right on the musical surface, by pairs of grace notes and the notes they embellish, and by longer rhythmic values. It is also formed over the entire melody by the association of Bb, the first note, C, the note that begins the second phrase, and B, the note that ends it. In addition to their prominence at phrase beginnings and endings, these three notes are also similar in articulation, each preceded by one or two grace notes and by small-scale forms of M1. One final surface statement connects the last note of the second clarinet with the first two notes of the first clarinet.

"Phrase-neume" and "form-neume" are coinages of Seeger's, but well before she met Seeger, Crawford's procedure was the same, and involved projecting surface motives over larger musical spans. In the slow opening measures of the Suite No. 1 for Piano and Winds, the bassoon plays a melody over accompanying countermelodies in piano and horn (see Example 2.54). The horn and the right hand of the piano generally play in unison while the left hand of the piano follows them fourteen semitones lower. The horn plays two forms of Motive M1, although only the first of these is doubled in the piano. The same motive is projected over a larger span in the bassoon, which begins with the whole step

Example 2.52 Motive M1 projected in register in *Diaphonic Suite No. 3* (for two clarinets), first movement, mm. 1–6

E♭–D♭, then abandons that register, only to return to it at the end of the phrase with the D that completes M1. I have not found examples of true "form-neumes," motivic statements that span entire works, but motivic projections of smaller scale are a universal feature of Crawford's music throughout her compositional career.

Example 2.53 Motive M1 projected over a the span of a phrase in *Diaphonic Suite No. 3* (for two clarinets), second movement, mm. 1–11

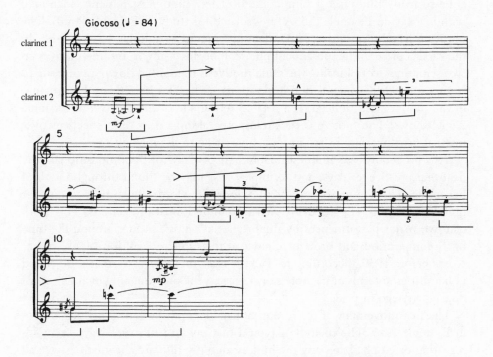

Example 2.54 Motive M1 projected in register in Suite No. 1 for Piano and Winds, first movement, mm. 1–4

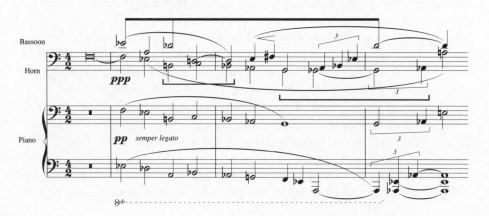

59

Transpositional projection

A third strategy of large-scale organization, one closely related to the phrase-neume or form-neume, involves what I will call *transpositional projection*: the transposition of distinctive bits of melodic material along paths that reflect either their own intervallic profile or some other significant shape. The resulting transpositional schemes may extend over large musical spans.

In "Sacco, Vanzetti," a recurring figure describing the intervals <–2, –1, +2> is heard many times (see Example 2.55). These motivic statements, identified with brackets in Example 2.55A, are isolated for study in Example 2.55B. The motive is heard first starting on D, then moving up a semitone to start on E♭. In the parallel place in the subsequent phrase, it begins again on E♭, then moves up two semitones to F. Finally, the same motive is transposed down a semitone to begin on E. That sequence of transpositions <+1, +2, –1> reflects the structure of the motive itself, indeed, is a rotated retrograde of the motive, as Example 2.55C shows. The motive is thus transposed along a path that reflects its own internal structure, and its recurrences give shape to the melody.

This procedure was unquestionably part of Crawford's compositional style from her pre-Seeger days, and examples of it may be found throughout all of her music. The Violin Sonata (1926), which Crawford valued most among her pre-Seeger works, is particularly rich in transpositional projections. This work had two major performances by important new music groups around the time of its composition and brought Crawford the most recognition of any of her works before 1930. According to Tick, it was "the only work that is described in her diaries in terms of its professional success, the only one in which Crawford displays any ego or pride."[88]

The first movement of the Violin Sonata features the lyrical melody shown in Example 2.56. The melody is typical of Crawford in many ways. It avoids repeating or emphasizing any pitch; it assiduously fills any chromatic gaps, and thus forms itself into discrete chromatic zones; it contains all twelve pitch classes; it is intervallically varied, although punctuated by the usual large leaps of ten, eleven, and thirteen semitones. The melody begins with an RI-chain of a motive that contains pitch intervals 1, 3, and 4 (I am ignoring the third note, D5, which is in a different register). The melody is divided into smaller sub-phrases by means of legato slurs. Toward the end of the melody, those slurs connect pairs of notes that lie eleven semitones apart. That recurring figure is transposed at this higher level by the same intervals: 1, 3, and 4.

The second movement of the Violin Sonata features a brief ostinato figure in the piano (see Example 2.57). Ostinati are extremely common elements in Crawford's music from the early *Music for Small Orchestra* (1926) through the Suite for Wind Quintet (1952).[89] The ostinato from the Violin Sonata is a typical, if brief, Crawford melody: it begins and ends with statements of Motive M1; its first five notes form an inversional wedge; and it concludes with a segment of

Example 2.55 A distinctive melodic fragment transposed by intervals it contains, in
"Sacco, Vanzetti": A) mm. 86–129; B) the fragment transposed by intervals
<+1, +2, −1>; C) the fragment analyzed in terms of the same intervals

one of the whole-tone scales (see Example 2.57A).[90] It can also be thought of as
in Example 2.57B, in terms of a lower component that ascends two semitones
and an upper component that moves down four then up six, to create another
ascending two, in parallel with the lower at the distance of eleven semitones.

Example 2.56   The intervals of a motive replicated at a higher structural level in the Violin
Sonata, first movement, mm. 12–14

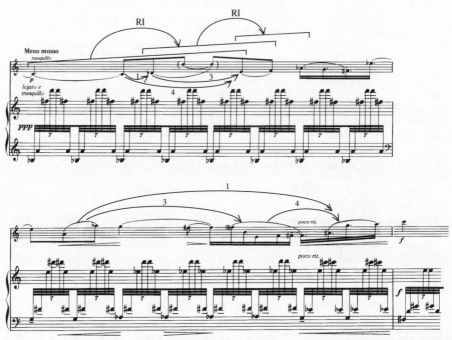

Over the course of the movement, this ostinato figure is transposed to many
different levels, often with one or more of its notes out of position by one or
two semitones. Three transpositions of it beginning in measure 20 are shown in
Example 2.57C. Like the melody itself, those transpositions involve movement
down four semitones followed by movement up six, thus replicating the shape
of the melody at this higher level.

The fourth movement of the Violin Sonata begins with, and is preoccupied
with, the short tune shown in Example 2.58A. The triplet figure at the center
of the melody is a characteristic gesture, partitioning ip11 into 4+7. Over the
course of the movement, this melodic fragment is manipulated in a variety of
ways. As the movement approaches a climax, a slightly altered version of the
fragment is presented three times in quick succession (see Example 2.58B). The
three presentations describe an ascending ip11 partitioned into 4+7. The
transpositional progression thus mirrors, in inverted order, the intervallic
succession within the original motive. The transposed tunes are not intervallically identical to the prototype, nor to each other, but the overall pattern is
clear. This tendency for intervals within a tune to come back later as intervals of
transposition is a permanent and central aspect of Crawford's musical style.

As we have seen, the *Piano Study in Mixed Accents* is a long, single-line
melody whose second half is the retrograde of the first. Each half consists of

continuous sixteenth notes divided into three sections by brief rests. Example 2.59A shows the six-note group that begins each of the three sections in the first half, and gives one possible interpretation of the relationships among them. The first group is transposed at T_1 onto the second, and inverted around D/E onto the third. The transposition at T_1 is actually a pitch transposition (each note in the second group is exactly one semitone higher than some note in the first group) and the inversion around D/E is a pitch inversion – each note is inverted, in order, and the pitch intervals are simply reversed, a procedure that continues well beyond the six notes shown. The third group and the second are related at T_2.

The initial six-note group itself can be understood in virtually the same way (see Example 2.59B). Its first dyad inverts onto the second around D/E and is transposed onto the third at T_1. The second and third dyads are related at T_2. The six-note figure is thus projected along a path that reflects its own internal shape.

In the third movement of *Diaphonic Suite No. 2*, descending leaps of ip11 provide structural markers in the bassoon melody (see Example 2.60). It occurs there at five different transpositional levels, which project two overlapping forms of M1: the first three, C♯–D, D♯–E, and D–E♭, describe <+2, −1> while the last three, sharing the D–E♭ in the middle, describe its inversion, <−2, +1>. That intervallic sequence returns the music to C♯–D, where the passage began and where the movement ends. Many of Crawford's melodic lines are similarly punctuated with large leaps of ten, eleven, or thirteen semitones (octave leaps are virtually nonexistent). Frequently, those large leaps, understood as transpositions of each other, trace a motivic path.

The sort of "near transposition" that shaped the climactic passage in the fourth movement of the Violin Sonata, where notes were moved out of position by one or two semitones amid an otherwise unambiguous progression, also shapes the structure of Prelude No. 6. There, the opening musical figure is gradually and freely transposed over the course of the piece in a way that roughly reflects its internal organization (see Example 2.61A). The first four notes of the top line can be understood as a single note transposed at T_1, T_5, and T_8. The entire figure can be similarly understood as the free transposition of that four-note fragment at T_1, T_5, and T_4 (see Example 2.61B). These are free, not exact, transpositions – there is a single "wrong note" in each – but they are close enough to be unmistakable. Except for the substitution of T_4 for its complement, T_8, the four-note figure generates the entire excerpt in the same way that it is itself generated from its first note. The same process also applies, at least in a general way, at the highest structural level, where the entire contrapuntal excerpt is transposed (see Example 2.61C). Toward the beginning of the piece, it is transposed at T_1 and T_8, reflecting again its internal structure. The transpositions are not exact – that is why I have qualified them with an asterisk – but are still identifiable. The entire transpositional plan of the piece cannot be accounted for in this way (indeed, I have trouble accounting for it in any way), but it does seem reasonable to speak, even in regard to this relatively early work, of a

Example 2.57   Ostinato transposed according to its own internal shape, in the Violin Sonata, second movement: A) ostinato in relation to Motive M1; B) ostinato in relation to intervals +2, −4, and +6; C) mm. 19–33

A)

B)

C)

Example 2.58 A transpositional progression that mirrors the intervals within the motive transposed, in the Violin Sonata, fourth movement: A) the motive, with 11 partitioned
into 4+7; B) the same intervals used to transpose the motive in mm. 39–41

A)

B)

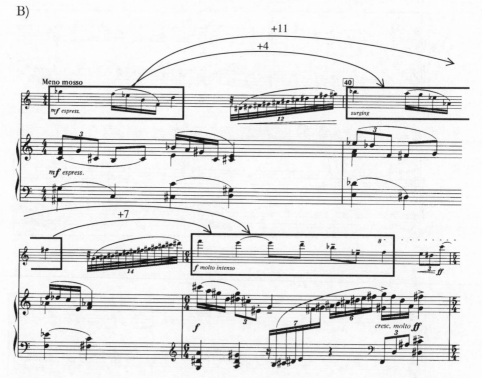

preference for transposing musical material in purposeful ways, often reflecting
the internal structure of the material being transposed.

The first movement of the String Quartet is an essay in vigorous polyphony.
It contains six distinctive melodies, two or three of which are sounding at any
given moment in the work.[91] Each melody has its own character and its own
developmental life, as it is spun out or transformed through transposition,
inversion, or retrograde. Some of the melodies are quite lengthy and give the
impression of spontaneous improvisation that characterizes so many of
Crawford's melodies. That impression may nonetheless belie a surprising degree
of motivic concentration. A long, seemingly improvisatory melody may result
from the structured transformation, in multiple levels, of a single motivic idea.

Example 2.59   Opening figure transposed and inverted to reflect its internal structure in *Piano Study in Mixed Accents*: A) initial figure in three formal sections; B) initial figure analyzed

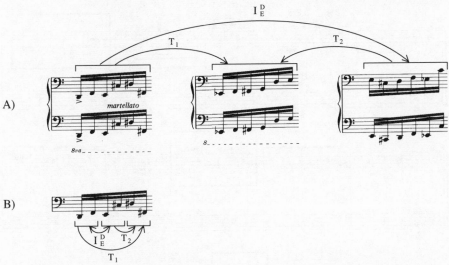

One such melody is shared by the cello and viola in the first section of the movement (see Example 2.62). The melody wanders through a wide range, moving usually by small intervals and in rapid rhythmic values. Despite its improvisatory character, most of it can be accounted for in relation to its first eight notes, which are heard most often at their original transposition level or at T_4 or T_8, either in their original order or in retrograde, and with notes occasionally omitted or interjected.

Those first eight notes themselves can be understood in a way that suggests their eventual transposition by T_4 or T_8 (see Example 2.62B). The melody begins with a whole tone, E–G♭, which is expanded, via RICH, into two overlapping statements of Motive M1. Two additional whole tones follow, A♭–B♭ (which is T_4 of E–G♭) and C–D (which is T_8 of E–G♭). This eight-note segment thus does to its initial whole tone pretty much what the rest of the melody then does with the eight-note segment. As in other Crawford works, the transformations of the musical material dramatize and realize its internal structure.

Precompositional plans

Retrograde symmetry

A large class of Crawford's melodies are organized around some explicit, systematic precompositional plan. Several are constituted as palindromes, the same from end to beginning as they are from beginning to end. These works – the *Piano Study in Mixed Accents*, *Diaphonic Suite No. 4* (first movement), and the

Example 2.60   Leaps of 11 semitones transposed to compose–out two statements of Motive M1, in *Diaphonic Suite No. 2* (for bassoon and cello), third movement, bassoon, mm. 24– end

Example 2.61   Opening figure transposed by intervals it contains, in Piano Prelude No. 6:
                A) first four notes; B) entire opening figure; C) mm. 1–7 (asterisks indicate that
                the transpositions involved are not exact)

Example 2.62   Opening figure transposed by intervals it contains, in String Quartet, first
movement, cello and viola: A) mm. 1–15; B) analysis of opening figure

String Quartet (fourth movement) – all had their origins as composition assignments from Seeger, who recommended the procedure: "The more rigorously
the dissonant fabric is sustained, the better it will be in retrograde motion.
Whole sections and whole compositions can be performed backward with
either exact or modified relation. This is a form of 'repeat.'"[92] Usually, Crawford
finds some way of enlivening their otherwise mechanical workings, as in the
long, single-line melody of the *Piano Study in Mixed Accents*, which gradually

works its way from the lowest register of the piano to the highest, then retraces its steps in reverse, ending where it began.[93] The first half of the piece presents not only a certain succession of pitches, but also a rhythmic pattern that articulates the steady flow of sixteenth notes into groups of two, three, four, five, or six notes, with an accent at the beginning of each group. At the midpoint of the movement, Crawford adds eighteen free notes which do not participate in the palindrome, and these result in a realignment of pitch and rhythm. In the second half of the piece, both the pitches and rhythms are heard in retrograde, but the rhythmic groupings are shifted over by three sixteenth notes. As a result of this shift, new groups of pitches are created in the second half of the piece. This slight independence of pitch and rhythm charges the palindrome with an unexpected dynamism.

The first movement of *Diaphonic Suite No. 4* (for oboe and cello) combines retrograde symmetry with a precompositional plan that operates on the smaller segments of a melody. Crawford described the movement as "in the form of a much-disguised canon."[94] The two instruments play the same pitch-class line – they create a canon at the unison – but are rhythmically different from each other and free from any apparent rhythmic scheme. That shared pitch-class line is retrograde-symmetrical – someplace in the middle of the movement (a different place for each of the instruments) the pitch classes simply run backwards, ending where they began.[95]

The shared pitch-class line has a remarkable internal structure (see Example 2.63A). It consists of a seven-note segment which is progressively altered in each appearance. In its first appearance, marked with a 1 in both instruments, the seven-note segment is F♯–G–E♭–A–A♭–F–E. In its second appearance, marked with a 2 in both instruments, Crawford retains the first note, transposes the second and seventh notes down two semitones, and transposes the rest down a semitone. She does the same to the second seven-note segment to produce the third, and so on. Each seven-note segment begins with F♯. The second and seventh notes cycle down by whole step, returning to their opening pitch classes in the sixth and twelfth segments. The remaining notes cycle down by semitone, returning to their opening notes in the twelfth segment. The twelfth segment thus marks a return to the first, and an entire cycle of transformations is complete. Seeger seems to have had a plan like this one in mind when he writes: "While the theme and variation plan is not recommended at present, various forms of ostinato (passacaglia, chaconne) are possible. The ostinato can be modulated by changing one tone in it at symmetrical intervals until a new ostinato is formed (a return to the original can be similarly managed)."[96] At the end of that cycle of transformations, when the series returns to its original state, the entire thing is repeated in pitch-class, but not rhythmic, retrograde.[97]

The process is entirely consistent and systematic, but the seven-note segments that result are intervallically different. There are interesting patterns of recurrence due to the cyclical nature of the motions, but each seven-note segment has a

Example 2.63   A progressively altered seven–note segment in *Diaphonic Suite No. 4* (for oboe and cello), first movement: A) mm. 1–22; B) the seven–note segment analyzed in terms of the same transpositions to which its notes are subjected

distinct intervallic profile. As we have seen in other aspects of Crawford's music, the coherence here is one of process, not object. The means of getting from place to place are the same, but the places are constantly changing. The result is a movement in which the surface is constantly varied, but coherence is assured by the consistency of the transformations.

The seven-note segment itself is a typical, if brief, Crawford melody. It comprises a chromatic cluster, showing the drive toward chromatic completion we have seen elsewhere, and it shows some of the intervallic variety and inversional pivoting we have come to expect. In relation to the large-scale design of this movement, it can also be understood in terms of the same pattern of transformations to which it is subjected (see Example 2.63B). To get from segment to segment, we saw that one note was transformed by T_0, two by T_{10}, and four by T_1. Leaving aside the T_0, the series itself can be exhaustively described in the same way, as the application of those transformations to individual tones. Beneath the obvious retrograde symmetry of the surface, then, lurks a highly structured proto-serial organization in which all aspects of the pitch organization can be related to the internal structure of a short line of pitch classes.

Rotational serialism

Five of Crawford's melodies follow rigid, mechanistic serial plans of rotation and transposition, as in the third movement of *Diaphonic Suite No. 1* (see Example 2.64). Its first measure presents a seven-note series: G–A–G♯–B–C–F–C♯. In the seven measures that follow, the series is systematically rotated so that the second measure begins on the second note of the series (A), the third measure on the third note (G♯), and so on, until the original ordering is restored in measure 8. The series is thus stated on the successive downbeats, an effect that is enhanced by *sforzando* accents.

Example 2.64 A seven-note series and a complete set of rotations in *Diaphonic Suite No. 1* (for flute or oboe), third movement, mm. 1–8

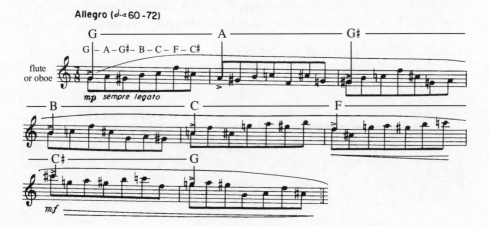

When the rotations have been completed, the series is transposed up two semitones, and that new series-form is rotated in the same manner. If we call the original series P_0, then its transposition up two semitones is P_2, which, of course, begins with A, the second note of the original series.[98] As the movement continues, the series is subjected to inversion, retrograde, and retrograde inversion, with each new series-form rotated in the original manner. Each new series-form begins in turn with the next note of the series, thus projecting, on this highest structural level, the pitch-class succession of the original series (see Example 2.65). When the seven notes of the series have been stated at this level, the first note is repeated, and so is the second, creating the impression of a large-scale rotation. Each of the orderings (P, R, I, and RI) is heard at two levels, and the original series is projected at three different structural levels: in eighth notes within each measure of the piece, from downbeat to downbeat, and from section to section. Crawford referred to this piece as a "triple passacaglia perpetuo mobile," its tripleness defined by the three structural levels.[99]

Like the motives and transpositional schemes discussed above, the series is thus transformed in accordance with its own internal content. All of the transpositions and inversions of the series are by intervals and indexes found in the series, either formed between G and some other note (in the case of P and I forms) or between C$\sharp$ and some other note (in the case of R and RI forms) (see Example 2.66).[100] The series can thus be described in terms of the transformations to which it is later subjected.

Despite its brevity, the series is contructed like most of Crawford's melodies. It contains no pitch-class repetition and is intervallically varied – its adjacent notes form six different ordered pitch-class intervals and its five trichords are of five different types. It begins with a statement of M1, <+2, −1>, then continues Crawford's typical process of growth and change via inversional pivoting (see Example 2.67).

Of course, that process of growth and change is suddenly arrested at the end of measure 1. A short melody, emblematic of freedom and variety, suddenly finds itself in the grip of an entirely mechanical system. Its evolution is arrested, its freedom to change suddenly taken away. Crawford seems to equate her melodies with growth, evolution, spontaneity, change, and freedom and the serial operations

Example 2.65   The series projected at the highest level through transposition, inversion, retrograde, and retrograde inversion, in *Diaphonic Suite No. 1* (for flute or oboe), third movement

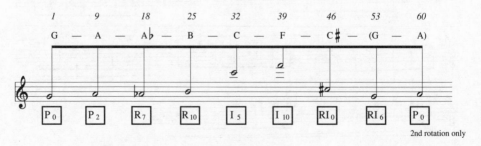

2nd rotation only

Example 2.66   The series analyzed in terms of the same transformations to which it is later
                subjected, in *Diaphonic Suite No. 1* (for flute or oboe), third movement

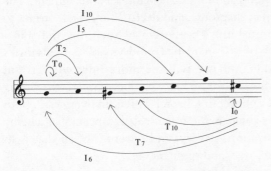

Example 2.67   The series for *Diaphonic Suite No. 1* (for flute or oboe), third movement,
                described as a typical Crawford melody, in terms of filling chromatic space and
                inversional pivoting

Example 2.68   Serial-rotational plan in *Chinaman, Laundryman*, piano accompaniment

with stasis, planning, and a kind of mechanized slavery. This dichotomy is fundamental to her music. In the *Diaphonic Suite No. 1*, that dichotomy is felt between the movements – the mechanical third movement is contrasted with the rhapsodic others. In other pieces, the dichotomy is felt within a single movement, as a serialized melody is heard in counterpoint with a free one.

In "Chinaman, Laundryman" that dichotomy takes on an obvious dramatic significance. The piano accompaniment follows a three-level serial plan like the one in the third movement of *Diaphonic Suite No. 1*. A nine-note series is systematically rotated to begin in turn on each of its notes, then it is transposed to begin in turn on each of its notes, and each transposition is systematically rotated (see Example 2.68).[101] There is also a rhythmic series that corresponds to, but is not perfectly aligned with, the pitch series.[102] The serialization of pitch and rhythm is undoubtedly what Crawford has in mind when she designates this song a "Ricercar," the traditional term for a work employing learned contrapuntal devices.

The text of this vocal work concerns the exploitation, low wages, poor working conditions, indeed, the virtual slavery of an immigrant Chinese laundryman toiling in a big city sweatshop. The cruel, unyielding world in which he is trapped is symbolized musically by the relentless and inflexible piano accompaniment. The melody he sings, in contrast, is free, rhapsodic, and declamatory, as he strives to break free of the chains that bind him. The system of rotations and transpositions in the accompaniment of "Chinaman, Laundryman" is Crawford's usual way of serializing a melody, and we will see more fully worked out applications of it in "Prayers of Steel" from Three Sandburg Songs, the String Quartet, and the Suite for Wind Quintet in Chapter Three. In every case, both in the presence of a text and in its absence, the rotational/transpositional scheme embodies the values of mechanization, slavery, and restraint, of all that is in starkest contrast to what is human, free, and spontaneous.

In addition, there are many melodies that are serialized only in part, where extended segments are transposed, inverted, retrograded, or retrograde-inverted. These include *Diaphonic Suite No. 3*, first movement (the opening figure of which bears a remarkable resemblance to the series for the fourth movement of the String Quartet – they share the same first six notes), *Diaphonic Suite No. 4*, third movement, *Diaphonic Suite No. 3*, third movement, and the String Quartet, first movement. In these cases, however, the serial operations are woven into the melodic fabric, merging with other kinds of melodic and motivic processes. In the rotational pieces, on the other hand, the serial manipulations shape every aspect of the melody.

Ostinato

In Crawford's rotational plans, the series acts as a kind of ostinato, a recurring figure found in every measure. Many other Crawford works involve ostinati that are not treated so systematically. Indeed, the ostinati, which are confined for the most part to the earlier works, may be understood as the progenitors of the later serial melodies. Like the serial melodies, the ostinati often serve to partition the musical texture into at least two layers, with the ostinato heard in contrast to free music. Also like the serial melodies, the ostinati in textures like this come to represent dramatically a sense of strictly enforced musical limits, of an almost mechanistic repetitiveness, of musical system pushed to its limits.

Crawford wrote six movements built on ostinati. Five of these involve short, characteristic figures (shown in Example 2.69) while the sixth, the first movement of *Music for Small Orchestra*, combines numerous ostinati in a dense polyphonic veil, and will be discussed separately. As a general matter, Crawford's ostinati have a light, scherzando character. The first two, from the Suite No. 1 for Piano and Winds, second movement, and the *Music for Small Orchestra*, second movement, are rhythmically square, with regular beat divisions within a 4/4 or 4/8 measure. The others are much more flexible rhythmically, with syncopations, changing meters, and unusual beat divisions to assist in the "avoidance of rhythmic stickiness," one of Crawford's compositional goals.[103]

All of the ostinati involve a sense of inversional symmetry, although the symmetry is rarely exact and is usually skewed in some way. In the Suite No. 1 for Piano and Winds (Example 2.69A), the ostinato wedges outward from an implicit center of F/F♯, but the E in the left hand, the inversional partner of G in the right, comes a beat too late, and the G♯ with which it sounds has no partner. In the *Music for Small Orchestra* (Example 2.69B), the cellos and bassoon wedge inward, although inexactly, from their initial interval. The piano doubles and embellishes this melody two semitones higher. In the Suite for Piano and Strings (Example 2.69C), the opening figure flanks E♭ symmetrically with notes eleven semitones above and below, creating the kind of division of pitch space that is

Example 2.69   Ostinato figures: A) Suite No. 1 for Piano and Winds, second movement;
                 B) Music for Small Orchestra, second movement; C) Suite No. 2 for Piano and
                 Strings, second movement; D) Violin Sonata, second movement; E) Suite for
                 Wind Quintet, first movement

familiar to us from many of Crawford's melodies. The second figure in the ostinato preserves the contour, but not the intervals or the symmetry, of the first. The two figures together fill a chromatic zone in pitch-class space, D–E♭–E–F–G♭, just as the ostinato from the *Music for Small Orchestra* fills in a chromatic zone in pitch space, B–C–C♯–D–D♯–E–F–F♯. The ostinati from the Violin Sonata and the Suite for Wind Quintet (Examples 2.69D and E) are remarkably similar in every way. Among other resemblances, both begin with a leap of eleven semitones, and then wedge inward toward the center of that interval.

Each ostinato is subjected to a purposeful, directed series of transpositions over the course of the movement in which it occurs. In most cases, those transpositions traverse intervals, or patterns of intervals, within the ostinati themselves. The melodies against which the ostinati are opposed are also transposed in purposeful ways, but not necessarily in parallel with the ostinati. Rather, each layer of the stratified texture pursues its own path. Thus the basic musical distinction between ostinato and free is reinforced by the independent development of the contrasting musics.

In *Music for Small Orchestra*, first movement, there is a similar contrast of ostinato and free music, but here the ostinato consists in fact of many different layers, each with its own recurring figure and distinctive rhythm. The different layers are transposed over the course of the piece, but not always in parallel with each other. The result is an extreme polyrhythmic density, a thick veil of sound reminiscent of many works by Ives, although Crawford did not know his music at this time.[104]

In the characteristic passage cited in Example 2.70, solo melodies in clarinet and flute are heard within, through, and finally above a dense network of ostinati in the strings and piano. The four-note chord in the left hand of the piano changes or is reattacked every ten beats while the interval in cello 2, which is part of the chord, changes or is reattacked every five beats. Cello 1 plays a pattern in quarter notes, piano right hand a pattern in quintuplets, and violins 1 and 2 a duet in sextuplets. These individual lines coalesce into a shimmering wall of sound, an insulated musical block that plays the role in this movement played by single-line ostinati in the others.

As we observed earlier, Crawford writes two kinds of melodies. The first kind, the free, rhapsodic melodies, the melodies held together loosely by chains of transformation, test the limits of musical freedom. They seem to ask, "How independent of system or constraint is it possible for music to be without fatally compromising its coherence?" The second kind, the restricted, repetitive melodies, the retrograde-symmetrical, ostinato, and the serial rotation melodies, test the limits of musical control. They seem to ask, "How strictly can system or constraint be applied to music without fatally compromising its expressive power or degenerating into mere machine?" Crawford's music, in a deep sense, is concerned with exploring the traditional, interrelated dualisms of freedom/ slavery, independence/constraint, and human/machine. Her most characteristic and profound explorations take place in works where two melodies are combined, each representing one pole in this network of opposites.

Example 2.70   Multiple ostinati in *Music For Small Orchestra*, first movement, mm. 29–36

Counterpoint

Heterophony

While melody is the basis of Crawford's style, it is when two or more melodies are combined, when they interact contrapuntally, that her music becomes most distinctive and interesting. It is also in a contrapuntal framework that Seeger's idea of "heterophony" can be most fully realized.[105] Heterophony is a term Seeger uses to describe a particularly intense polyphony in which the individual parts are concerned only with their own internal organization, not with the content or behavior of their neighbors.

> By *complete* heterophony we understand a polyphony in which there is no relation between the parts except mere proximity in time-space, beginning and ending, within hearing of each other, at more or less the same time: each should have its own tonal and rhythmic system and these should be mutually exclusive, while the forms should be utterly diverse. Heterophony may be accidental, as, for instance, a radio-reception of Beethoven's "Eroica" intruded upon by a phonograph record of a Javanese gamelan. But from an artistic point of view, a high degree of organization is necessary (1) to assure perfect non-coincidence and (2) to make the undertaking as a whole worth while.[106]

Dissonance is crucial in this enterprise, because it guarantees the independence of the parts, their mutual repulsion. When individual lines are bound to each other by consonance, the result is traditional polyphony; when individual lines have exclusively dissonant relations to each other, the result is Seeger's heterophony.

> We have had a great deal of homophony. The impulse and the logic point toward a new polyphony, "heterophony." And since this means real independence of parts, it follows that the parts must be so different in themselves and the relation between them (which makes their simultaneous sounding agreeable) must perforce be such that their difference rather than their likeness is emphasized. This is possible upon a basis of dissonance; but with the slightest error in the handling of consonance, our homophonically over-educated ears will infer chordal structures not intended and the polyphony will be lost. So it becomes necessary to cultivate "sounding apart" rather than "sounding together" – diaphony rather than symphony.[107]

To practice the art of heterophony, of sounding apart, Seeger recommends the combination of two independent melodies, and many of Crawford's works take just that form.

> While a single melodic line may be characterized as heterophonic in that the mood in which it started has given place to an opposite or different mood, it is obvious that the scope of heterophony is vastly enlarged by the undertaking of two-line counterpoint . . . It is in the two-line composition as a whole that

true dissonance of mood – actual 'other-soundingness' and 'sounding-apart' can be appreciated . . . Either line of a well constructed composition in dissonant counterpoint should be capable of solo performance as an entirely adequate and self-contained whole. The composition should be such, however, that when the two are combined as indicated the effect will justify the combination and give the listener something he did not find in the lines separately.[108]

Although Crawford explores the possibility of heterophony more thoroughly and systematically in the aftermath of her studies with Seeger, her earlier music also shows a clear interest in maximizing the independence of the parts. In the ostinato pieces discussed earlier, for example, the distinction between the repetitive ostinati, chugging along in regular periods, and the free melodies around them is absolutely clear. The two layers go their own way, largely ignoring each other.

The Five Songs to poems by Carl Sandburg date from the summer of 1929, just before Crawford's move to New York and her first contact with Seeger. While they are certainly thicker textured, more harmonic in conception, than her works were shortly to become, several reveal a striking independence of self-contained musical strata. "Sunsets," for example, the last song in the cycle, begins by setting in motion four independent layers, each with distinctive material and separated from the others by register. Over the course of the opening section of the song, each bit of material is transposed successively only to end up right where it started. Instead of layers moving in tandem, however, each layer moves independently, following its own path. The song is not intensely contrapuntal, but is certainly stratified in a way that recalls Crawford's earlier ostinato works, and suggests her later heterophony.

During and after her work with Seeger, when Crawford combines two or more melodies, the principle of heterophony prevails more strictly. Each line goes pretty much its own way, responding to its own internal imperatives. The melodies are normally distinguished in a variety of ways. They usually have different characters, shaped by differences in articulation, rhythm, register, instrumentation, and contour. Often the contrasting melodies are intervallically and motivically distinct as well. The melodies sound at the same time, but are not regulated to each other in the manner of traditional polyphony. Rather, each maintains a high degree of internal integrity and independence.

It is easy, of course, for a composer to write polyphonic parts of radically contrasting character. What is more difficult, and potentially more rewarding for listeners, is to create subtle links between the disparate parts that might justify their appearance together. These links between the otherwise independent and contrasting parts are what "will justify the combination and give the listener something he did not find in the lines separately," and thus "make the undertaking as a whole worth while."

In the discussion that follows, then, I will focus not so much on what distinguishes the individual lines (this will be readily apparent) as on what binds them. Crawford has three principal ways of coordinating the parts in a heterophonic texture. First, seemingly independent lines may share intervallic or motivic content; they may have common musical concerns beneath their obvious differences. Second, there may be some degree of consistency and control in the intervals formed between the melodies, particularly at those relatively rare moments when they repose at the same time. Third, the principle of inversional pivoting that creates motion within the melodies often governs the relations between them as well. Sustained notes in one part often act as fulcrums around which the notes in the other part balance. While one part holds its note, the other part leaps symmetrically over it. When the parts take turns holding and leaping, the result is a kind of contrapuntal leap-frog.

Shared motivic content

Melodies even of radically contrasting character may nonetheless share motivic content. In "Chinaman, Laundryman," a free declamatory vocal line is heard with a strictly serialized accompaniment, a contrast that is essential to the dramatic effect of the work. At the same time, there are subtle correspondences between melody and accompaniment, one of which is suggested in Example 2.71. A parallel series of questions in the text is set to a single melody, transposed up a semitone each time, and slightly altered in its third appearance. That upward path is the mirror image of the descending trajectory of the first three notes of the series: G–G♭–F. A further connection is suggested on the example: both melodies are organized in part around a framework of descending minor thirds. Thus, while they are sharply differentiated in many obvious ways, the melodies do have subtle affinities with each other.

These affinities raise interesting questions about the dramatic program of the work. Initially, we described an absolute opposition between the free plaint of the narrator and the brutal world embodied in the piano accompaniment. Now it appears that he is bound to that world by subtle ties, that he himself forms part of that world. The dramatic duality between strict and free inherent in the heterophonic program and realized by Crawford in so many different ways may thus admit, if not a higher synthesis, then at least a possibility of mutual recognition and awareness.

The first movement of the String Quartet begins with the simultaneous statement of two contrasting melodies (see Example 2.72). This was the first passage Crawford wrote for this, her most important work. She began by writing the melody assigned to the first violin, which she initially conceived as a "little piano melody . . . a one-voiced little something in metric form." Then she "took the little monody which is lyric and gave it a leggiero pal with a bass voice and it insisted on becoming a string quartet."[109]

Each of the melodies, identified by Crawford in her annotated score of the piece as Melody I and Melody II, undergoes its own independent development

Example 2.71   Affinities between the free melody and the strictly serialized piano
accompaniment of "Chinaman, Laundryman": A) melodic fragments involving
intervals +1 and −3; B) the same intervals in the nine-note series

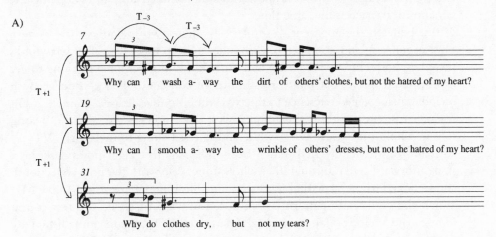

A)

Why can I wash a- way   the   dirt of others' clothes, but not the hatred of my heart?

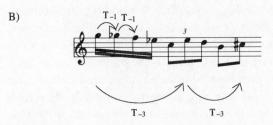

Why can I smooth a- way   the   wrinkle of others' dresses, but not the hatred of my heart?

Why do clothes dry,   but   not my tears?

B)

Example 2.72   Two contrasting melodies in String Quartet, first movement, mm. 1–4

over the course of the movement, including rhythmic and intervallic variation,
transposition, inversion, and retrograde.[110] The melodies are dissimilar in many
obvious ways. Melody I has the *cantando* quality indicated in the score: it features
a slowly moving legato line, with wide, expressive leaps. Melody II, marked *ben
marcato*, scrambles around with rapid twists and turns. It moves generally by the
smallest intervals and its motions are frequently punctuated with irregularly
spaced accents. The shortest rhythmic value in Melody I, the eighth note, is the
longest value in Melody II. The evident contrast between the melodies is
heightened by the rhythmic relationship between them: they never attack at the

same time. In brief, while Melody I sounds lyrical and free, Melody II sounds crabbed and regimented. This would seem, then, to be the embodiment of the heterophonic ideal – two contrasting melodies unified only in occupying the same musical space at the same time.

But beneath the apparent dissimilarities, these two melodies share certain musical concerns and are linked to each other in deep ways. Like all of Crawford's melodies, both employ RI-chains and other kinds of inversional pivoting to get from place to place, but there are affinities of content as well as process. Both melodies make veiled reference to the two whole-tone scales (see Example 2.73). Melody I is registrally partitioned: its lowest three notes (C, E, and F$\sharp$) belong to one whole-tone scale, WT_0, while all the rest belong to the other, WT_1.[111] Virtually all of Melody II is drawn from WT_0. Its first eight notes describe a straightforward ascent through that whole-tone scale, with the non-collection F and G linked to the structural G$\flat$ by an embellishing statement of Motive M1. When the eight-note pattern is transposed upward to create the rest of the phrase, the melody maintains its allegiance to WT_0, again embellished by statements of Motive M1 (indicated by brackets in Example 2.73). Because Melody II generally lies below Melody I, a registral partitioning into complementary whole-tone scales characterizes the entire passage, and links the two melodies: all of the notes higher than F$\sharp$5 belong to one whole-tone collection, and virtually all of the notes lower than G5 belong to the other one.

Both melodies are inversionally symmetrical to some extent, and on the same axis of inversion (see Example 2.74). Melody I begins with a leap of eleven semitones from D$\sharp$ down to E, and the remaining notes frequently fill in that space symmetrically. The first gesture in Melody II moves up eleven semitones from E to D$\sharp$, then concludes with a descending leap retracing that interval. Within that space, as in Melody I, the remaining notes are often arranged in a symmetrical manner.

The apparently heterophonic relationship between the melodies thus conceals deeper connections between them. Despite their contrasting character and the intervallic distinctions between them (such as the exclusive use in Melody I of perfect fourths and fifths and tritones), they do share certain musical concerns, including an interest in whole-tone partitions and inversional balance. Even as they declare their independence from each other, they acknowledge a deeper kinship.

Diaphonic Suite No. 3 involves contrasting melodies that turn out, on closer inspection, not only to have certain intervallic concerns in common, but to be combinable into a single composite melody that shares the same concerns. In the first movement, the melodies have contrasting characters – the second clarinet plods along in even eighth notes while the first uses an enormous variety of rhythmic values to create a sense of maximum flexibility – and they virtually never attack their notes at the same time. Nonetheless, both melodies frequently state and project Motive M1, although the second clarinet is more interested in

Example 2.73   Whole-tone scales used to shape two contrasting melodies in String Quartet, first movement, mm. 1–4

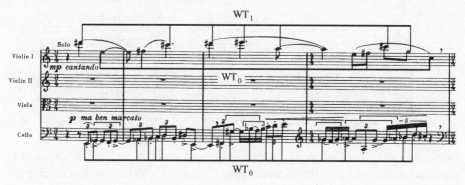

Example 2.74   Both melodies symmetrical on a D♯/E axis, in String Quartet, first movement, mm. 1–4

this motive than the first. What is more significant, the melodies frequently combine to create additional statements of Motive M1 (see Example 2.75). Because the two instruments rarely attack at the same time, one can easily hear a new melody with a hocket-like texture, drawing its notes in irregular alternation between the two individual clarinet melodies. In measures 9–13, this new, composite, melody contains five statements of Motive M1. That motive thus occurs not only within each part, but between the parts as well. It creates a subtle link between otherwise distinct lines.

Intervals formed between the parts

Thus far, we have considered only the internal qualities of individual melodies, or of the composite melody formed by combining them. Now we need to turn our attention to the intervals formed between melodies, the usual subject matter of theories of counterpoint. Such a discussion is made more difficult in Crawford's music precisely by the independence of the parts. The splendid isolation of the melodies results in as much intervallic variety between them as there typically is

Example 2.75   Statements of Motive M1 formed between contrasting melodies in *Diaphonic Suite No. 3* (for two clarinets), first movement, mm. 9–13

within them. Nonetheless, Crawford does show general preference for the traditional dissonant intervals, particularly ip11 and ip13. When both melodies are on the move, maintaining a high degree of rhythmic independence from each other, one is not acutely conscious of the intervals formed between them. When both melodies sustain notes at the same time, and the listener is able to attend to the harmonic intervals, those intervals tend to be the traditionally dissonant ones, particularly ip11 and ip13.

In the music at the end of *Diaphonic Suite No. 2*, second movement, the lines are distinct and rhythmically independent (see Example 2.76A). Each has its own integrity, its own motivic life, and its own transformational progression. Nonetheless, there is a degree of intervallic consistency between them, in particular a recurrence of a movement from ip13 to ip11, recalling the same recurring progression in Piano Prelude No. 9. This motion occurs three times in the passage, in three different ways (see Example 2.76B). First, there is a voice exchange: the lower voice moves up a semitone from G to A♭ while the upper voice descends a semitone from A♭ to G. In the second case, the lower voice holds while the upper voice descends two semitones. There is an inversional pivot here: G moves to F by inversion around the sustained F♯. The third case is the reverse of the second. The top voice now holds while the lower voice ascends two semitones, pivoting around it. The passage as a whole can be thought of as in 2.76C, involving the parallel movement of two ip11s down two semitones.

The analytical reductions in Examples 2.76B and C are designed to evoke Seeger's dissonant species counterpoint, a kind of anti-Fuxian approach he dreamed up and taught to students including Cowell and Crawford. In order to teach students to write free dissonant counterpoint, Seeger wanted them first to master a dissonant species counterpoint in which first species, rhythmically one-against-one, consisted exclusively of dissonances. In second species, rhythmically two-against-one, consonances might be introduced, but only on weak beats, and only if approached and left by leap. The idea was to construct a music that turned the traditional relationship between consonance and dissonance on its head. Now the dissonant intervals would be stable and structural, while consonances could be introduced only under special conditions.[112] Seeger intended his species as a purifying discipline for composers, but they are useful

Example 2.76   Intervallic relations between two voices in *Diaphonic Suite No. 2* (for cello and bassoon), second movement, mm. 43–end

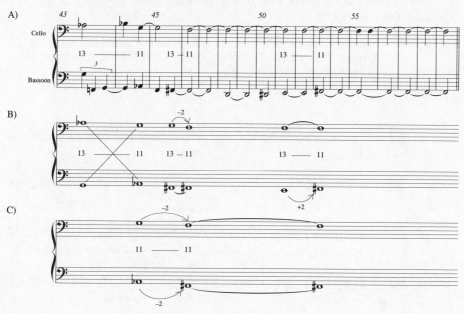

Example 2.77   Intervallic relations between two voices in String Quartet, first movement: A) mm. 1–2, with ten intervals circled; B) arranged as second-species counterpoint; C) arranged as first-species counterpoint

also for listeners and analysts. Beneath the complexity of the musical surface in Crawford's music, one often finds relatively simple, species-counterpoint-like dissonant frameworks.[113]

Example 2.78   Dissonant counterpoint in Suite No. 2 for Piano and Strings, first movement: A) mm. 1–9; B) analytical reduction of violin 1 and violin 2; C) analytical summary of viola, cello, and piano

A)

B)

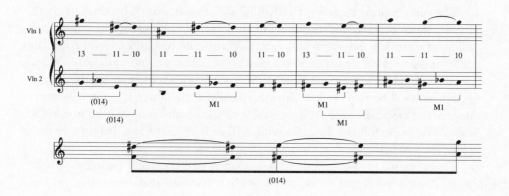

C)

Such a dissonant framework underlies the opening passage in the first movement of the String Quartet, whose contrasting melodies we examined earlier
(see Example 2.77). The ten vertical intervals circled on the score in Example
2.77A are represented as two-against-one in 2.77B and one-against-one in
2.77C. The principal intervals, formed on the downbeats of the measures in my
reduction, are always 10s or 11s; the subsidiary intervals, on the weak beats, are
usually consonances, and are thus subsidiary to the structural 10s and 11s. The
pattern is reasonably consistent, with the traditionally consonant 9s or 8s always
moving back to the traditionally dissonant 10s and 11s.

The preference for 10s and 11s between the parts is equally pronounced in
the pre-Seeger works, and easier to discuss because the parts are not so rigorously independent. Suite No. 2 for Piano and Strings begins with the music
shown in Example 2.78A. There are two relatively independent streams of music
here: a continuous trio between viola, cello, and piano; and five brief interjections
of a duet between the violins. Let us consider the duet first (see Example 2.78B).
The second violin melody begins with an RI-chain involving set class (014),
and contains many statements of Motive M1 thereafter. Against that melody, the
first violin's notes always create ip13 or ip11 vertically, and the five interjections
always end on ip10. The cadential ip10s, taken together, replicate at this higher
level the (014)s of the second violin melody.

The cello melody begins with (014), then wanders around by small intervals,
frequently embedding additional (014)s. It is typical of Crawford in its gradually
filling of the pitch and pitch-class spaces. Within the trio in the lower parts, the
cello acts as a kind of tenor voice, with contratenors *altus* and *bassus* added
above and below it (see Example 2.78C). The cello moves in steady pairs of
eighth notes. The viola follows in strict parallel ip10s above it – virtually every
note in the viola part forms this interval with the second note of each pair in the
cello. The piano follows the cello with ip10 or ip11 below the first note in each
pair. The result is a kind of dissonant *fauxbourdon*.

This texture, in which a melody is shadowed by parallel melodies that lie
some dissonant interval away, or in which a trichord that consists of ip11 or
ip13 with an additional note in the middle is projected through time, is common
in Crawford's music before her studies with Seeger. (Prominent instances occur
in the third movement of the Violin Sonata, and in the first, second, and fourth
movements of the Suite No. 1 for Piano and Winds.) It is accurately described
by Adolf Weidig, Crawford's most important teacher of theory and composition
during her years in Chicago, in a textbook that she doubtless studied:

> A single tone appears to us as such only so long as the mind does not become
> conscious of its overtones. If the overtones are emphasized by actually sounding
> them, a given succession of tones, called a melody, may thus be played along
> with its octaves, or fifths, or thirds, or sevenths, or ninths – in fact, in conjunc-
> tion with any interval, or combination of intervals – creating merely "units of
> sound" which may possibly be moved with the same freedom as the single
> tone . . . A melody consisting of single tones may be likened to a thread in a
> primary color of which a design (melody) is woven. If the different strands in

such a thread are of different colors, the thread still remains a unit, with which designs may be created; so may the melodic strand consist of different sound colors, being used as a "sound unit" in the melodic weave.[114]

Crawford's later works never show the degree of parallel motion implicit in the concept of "sound unit." The individual lines become too independent to submerge their identity in this way. Nonetheless, the preference for ip10, ip11, and ip13 that defines the sound units of her earlier music remains in effect even in the more rigorously contrapuntal framework of her music post-Seeger.

Inversional pivoting

Whatever the intervals formed between them, one melody occasionally exerts a gravitational pull on the other. A single note sustained in one melody can become the fulcrum around which notes in the other melody find themselves balancing. The fulcrum may move from melody to melody as they take turns sustaining and balancing. In a passage from the second movement of the *Diaphonic Suite No. 2*, each part pivots around notes sustained in the other (see Example 2.79). As the passage begins, the sustained E♭ in the bassoon is the fulcrum around which the cello leaps from D to E. The cello's E then itself becomes the fulcrum for a series of motions in the bassoon. In measures 26–27, the two instruments rapidly shift between establishing a fulcrum and leaping around a fulcrum in the other voice.

Example 2.79   Inversional pivoting in *Diaphonic Suite No. 2* (for bassoon and cello), second movement, mm. 23–27

Example 2.80   Inversional pivoting in *Diaphonic Suite No. 4* (for oboe and cello), second movement, mm. 43–end

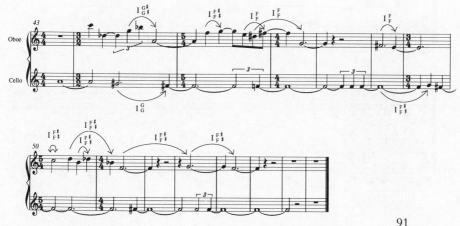

A similar situation prevails in the concluding measures of *Diaphonic Suite No. 4*, second movement (see Example 2.80). In measure 44, G moves to A in the oboe part around the sustained G♯ in the cello. At the same time, the G in the oboe part itself acts as the fulcrum around which the cello moves from G♯ to F♯. A similar contrapuntal leap-frog occurs in measures 48–49: the oboe moves from F♯ to E around the cello's F, which itself moves to G around the oboe's F♯. When the cello comes to rest on F♯ at the end of the passage, all of the oboe's motions balance around it including, most obviously, the final G–F.

At the end of "In Tall Grass," the voice intones the entire last line of the poem on a single note, D4. The supple oboe melody never states that note, but hovers around it, each note above it balanced by a note below it (see Example 2.81). Before the voice enters, the oboe plays A–B♭–B–C♯. After the voice enters, establishing a central pivot, those four notes are answered by four balancing notes, D♯–F♯–G–F, symmetrically on the other side of the D4. The sixth oboe note, E4, does not immediately participate in this balancing scheme, but it finds its partner, C, shortly afterward. Much of the balancing takes place in pitch-class space, but final notes in the oboe melody, C♯4–D♯4, lie a semitone below and above the central voice note. The axial role of the voice's

Example 2.81   Inversional pivoting around a sustained D4 in "In Tall Grass," mm. 67–end

D is enhanced by a basic complementarity between the two parts. The oboe melody excludes not only pitch class D, but also G♯, its axial mate. It contains every other pitch class.

The phrase from Chant No. 1 ("To an Unkind God") shown in Example 2.82 is remarkably similar in organization. Here again a sustained D4 creates a fulcrum around which an active upper part balances. Each note in the upper part seeks, and finds, its inversional partner – the balanced pairs of notes are indicated with slurs on the example. Most dramatically, the final two notes in the upper part lie symmetrically a semitone below and above the still-sustained D. Passages like this one exemplify Seeger's idea of "pitch center," in which a single note is established as central, with other notes "balancing to either side." Here, the balancing takes place between two melodies rather than within one of them.

Example 2.82   Inversional pivoting around a sustained D4 in Chant No. 1 ("To an Unkind God"), mm. 7–9

Harmony

Although Crawford's style is based on melody, there are many passages scattered throughout her works, particularly the early works, that are conceived primarily in harmonic terms. Crawford's music pre-Seeger is relatively homophonic, based more on motivically animated harmony than on genuine contrapuntal independence of the parts. Seeger himself took a somewhat condescending view of her earlier music:

> The style of her work before 1930 is basically homophonic, not too noticeably of the Scriabin school, but embroidered with sudden whirls and whip-snaps of thirty-second notes that give a distinct and characteristic vitality to what is often a languid moodiness in the basic chordal structure. Those vicious little stabs of dissonance remind one of the lion's tails in the movies of the African veldt.[115]

Crawford's later music combines two or more distinct melodies, each of which retains a high degree of independence and integrity. Crawford's comment about her String Quartet, that it is "music which is thought horizontally," applies equally well to most of her music post-Seeger.[116] In music of this kind, the intervals or larger sonorities formed between the melodies are often best understood as mere by-products of the heterophony. But, as we have seen in the previous discussion of counterpoint, the simultaneities formed between the lines can also be subject to compositional control, and thus to analytical understanding. It is possible then, at least in a limited sense, to discuss the harmonic organization of her music, and to identify certain defining characteristics.

Integration of melody and harmony

Crawford's music tends to integrate melody and harmony by projecting the same musical ideas simultaneously in both dimensions. In this respect, her music is similar to that of Schoenberg and others of her European contemporaries in ensuring that "the two-or-more-dimensional space in which musical ideas are presented is a unit."[117] In the Piano Prelude No. 7, for example, both the large chords that punctuate the piece and the melody that floats above, below, and through them are concerned with partitioning an interval of eleven semitones into two smaller intervals of either four and seven semitones, or five and six semitones (see Example 2.83). The brackets on the example indicate instances of ip11,

Example 2.83   Similar musical ideas in melody and harmony in Piano Prelude No. 7, mm. 1–3

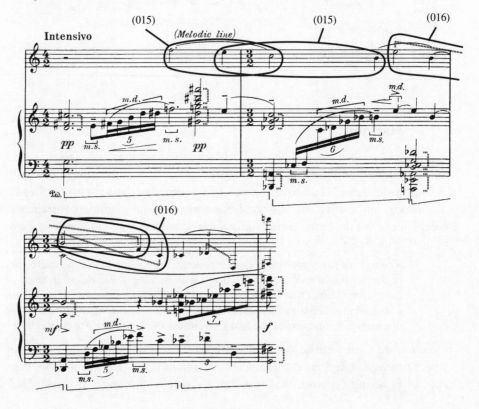

prevalent in both the chords and the melody. The second chord, at the end of measure 1, is typical of the harmonies in this work. In the left hand, an 11 (G♯–G) is divided into 6+5 (G♯–D + D–G), creating trichord type (016), while in the right hand another 11 (B–A♯) is divided into 4+7 (B–D♯ + D♯–A♯), creating trichord-type (015).[118] The melody begins with two RI-chained forms of (015) and continues with two RI-chained forms of (016), both of which divide an 11 into a 5 and a 6. The melody then continues with a statement of Motive M1 and a final descending 11. Similarly, the final chord of the Prelude, consisting almost entirely of 11s divided into 5+6, supports a melody that presents two final statements of (016) and (015) (see Example 2.84).[119] In this way, melody and harmony share the same intervallic and motivic concerns. The unity of musical space remained a feature of Crawford's music, although that space is more rigorously stratified into independent parts in her later work.

Example 2.84   Similar musical ideas in melody and harmony in Piano Prelude No. 7, mm. 17–end

Whole-tone affiliations

In the pre-Seeger music, the harmonies often have a whole-tone affiliation. Often, all, or all but one, of the notes in a given chord or melodic fragment will come from the same whole-tone collection. In a phrase from "Home Thoughts," for example, the melody consists of two notes, F and G, taken from WT_1, while all the notes of the accompaniment, other than the passing G–B, are drawn from WT_0 (see Example 2.85). The first four notes of the accompaniment, E–F$\sharp$–G$\sharp$–A$\sharp$, expressed as two consecutive major thirds, return as the four-note chord that ends the passage.

In the final measures of "Loam," also one of the Five Songs, the vocal melody is drawn, with one exception, from WT_1 (see Example 2.86). The melody notes are [D$\flat$, E$\flat$, F, G, A] from WT_1, and C is the odd man out.[120] The same is true of the final chord. The five notes sustained through the final three measures, [F, G, A, B, C$\sharp$] belong to WT_1; the D that enters in the final measure does not. Both of these harmonies are of the same class as Scriabin's so-called mystic or

Example 2.85 Whole-tone harmonies in "Home Thoughts," from Five Sandburg Songs, mm. 28–35

Example 2.86   Whole-tone and "almost-whole-tone" harmonies in "Loam," from Five
Sandburg Songs, mm. 33–end

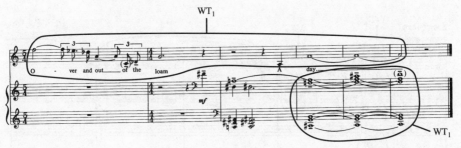

Prometheus chord. In Scriabin's music, however, this chord often has attenuated dominant function, whereas Crawford strips it of any apparent tonal reference.

As a general matter, Crawford, like Scriabin, makes extensive use of harmonies that are "almost-whole-tone" in structure, that is, all of whose members but one are drawn from the same whole-tone collection.[121] Harmonies of that kind would include not only the two "mystic"-type harmonies at the end of "Loam," and the somewhat different hexachord formed between voice and accompaniment at the end of Example 2.85, from "Home Thoughts," but also the ubiquitous (016)s and many other harmonies throughout Crawford's music.

Crawford's music post-Seeger generally takes the aggregate of all twelve notes as its basic referential collection. Still, there are striking occasions where the whole-tone concerns of the earlier music can still be felt. The first movement of the String Quartet, discussed earlier in Example 2.73, is one such instance, and the second movement of the same work is another (see Example 2.87). In the opening chord, the highest five notes come from WT_1, while the lowest five, except for E♭, come from the other WT_0. The melody that follows, shared between the violins, begins with a similar but reversed registral partitioning: its lower notes generally come from WT_1 and its higher from WT_0. The notes that do not belong to the prevailing whole-tone collection are attached to those that do with embellishing statements of Motive M1. After its climax at the end of measure 4, the melody turns around and works its way back down, now shared among three instruments. The entire descending melody is affiliated with WT_1, and as before, the notes that do not belong are related to those that do via embellishing statements of M1. Whole-tone affiliations, however, are more of an occasional strategy than a defining characteristic of Crawford's later music.

Symmetrical harmonies

Symmetrical harmonies, however, do play a special role throughout Crawford's music. Often they result, as we have seen, from a sense of progression that depends heavily on inversional pivoting. If the pivoting is sufficiently prevalent, symmetrical harmonies will inevitably occur as by-products. Symmetrical

Example 2.87   Whole-tone harmonies in String Quartet, second movement, mm. 1–7

harmonies can also take on a life of their own, however, not merely as by-products but as entities in their own right. Frequently in Crawford's music symmetrical harmonies are used to create a sense of balance, sometimes correlated with feelings of stasis, arrival, or cadence. Her music often moves from asymmetry to symmetry, from imbalance to balance, from tension to repose.

Virtually all of the nine Piano Preludes end with a symmetrical, or nearly symmetrical, harmony. We have already discussed the symmetrical ending of Prelude No. 6 (see Example 2.8), and the rest behave in a similar fashion (see Example 2.88, the endings of Nos. 3, 4, and 8). The excerpt from Prelude No. 3 begins with a symmetrical subset of WT_1. A descending melodic figure leads to a non-symmetrical four-note chord: [C, C♯, E♭, F♯]. The symmetry, however, is restored by the addition of the final two notes, A and G♯, creating a cadential hexachord: [C, C♯, E♭, F♯, G♯, A]. The final phrase thus moves from symmetry to non-symmetry and back again, although the symmetry is one of pitch class, not pitch.

Prelude No. 4 ends with two sustained trichords, and a single sustained note between them. The two trichords have an identical structure – both divide ip13 into 7+6. The five notes they contain between them (they share a note) are not symmetrical, but when the sustained F♯ is also included, the result is a symmetrical hexachord, [C, C♯, D, F♯, G, A♭].

98

Prelude No. 8 ends with two descending gestures, each of which consists of two pairs of perfect fifths, a pattern disrupted only by the concluding perfect fourth. If that anomaly were brought into conformance with the pattern, and the final lowest note were G instead of A, each tetrachord and each complete gesture would be entirely symmetrical in register, and the second gesture would contain the same six notes that ended Prelude No. 4.

Example 2.88   Symmetrical harmonies at the final cadences of Piano Preludes: A) No. 3; B) No. 4; C) No. 8

A)

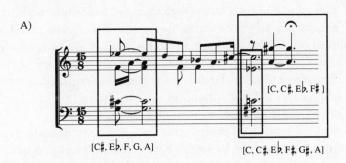

B)

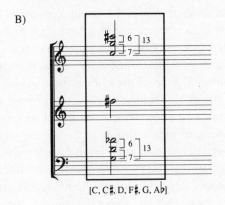

C)

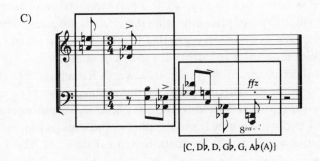

It is superfluous to identify symmetrical harmonies in Crawford's later music, as they are ubiquitous there, left in the wake of each inversional melodic pivot. It is worth pointing out, however, that as in the earlier works, cadences in the later works frequently involve a careful symmetry or near-symmetry, a delicate balancing of elements to suggest an ending.

Harmonic progression

Beyond a preference, particularly in the earlier works, for having the harmonies share the intervallic concerns of the melodies, for harmonies with whole-tone affinities, and, particularly at cadences, for symmetrical harmonies, it is difficult to generalize about Crawford's harmony. This is because, like her melodies, her harmonies are in a constant state of evolution, changing shape as they move. They have little fixed identity. To discuss the harmonic organization of her music, then, we will have to shift our attention from the content of the harmonies to the processes by which they are transformed.

Throughout Crawford's music, the harmonies frequently progress by transposition or inversion, or by somewhat more idiosyncratic operations I will call "near-transposition" and "near-inversion." Progression via inversion is particularly central to her style, recalling as it does the familiar inversional pivoting that drives her melodies forward. As with melodies, a note or notes of a chord may pivot around another note or notes of the same chord to create a new one. A lengthy harmonic progression may result from the successive pivoting moves.

In Chant No. 2, the sopranos and altos of the chorus hum a duet in quarter notes, the tenors and basses of the chorus hum a single slow-moving drone, and a solo soprano sings, using a variety of phonemes, an embellished version of the drone. There is a basic opposition, or heterophony, of the slow-moving voices and the faster duet, each of which makes good sense on its own terms. Crawford's own comment on the work suggests that the parts were conceived independently, without concern for the harmonies formed between them beyond making sure they are "dissonant": "I vary between an objective viewing of it as bad, impressionistic and worthless, and a secret liking for its simplicity and a slightly fascinated interest in the fact that the second part wanders about naively in its own tonality (which was not planned) while the effect is dissonant vertically."[122] The musical evidence, however, suggests that Crawford did pay careful attention to the interplay of the parts, particularly at cadence points.

The second short phrase of the piece is shown in Example 2.89. The basses hum a drone A♭ while the altos and sopranos hum a duet above. The first chord formed between the parts is related to the last chord by inversion around A♭. From the G–F♯ with which they begin the phrase, the altos and sopranos invert themselves around the drone A♭ to attain their final B♭–A.[123] The horizontal and near-horizontal lines in the example are designed to reveal the underlying pitch-class counterpoint: the operation $I_{A\flat}^{A\flat}$ maps F♯ onto B♭, G onto A, and A♭ onto itself.

Example 2.89   Harmonic progression via inversional pivoting in Chant No. 2 ("To an Angel"), mm. 5–7

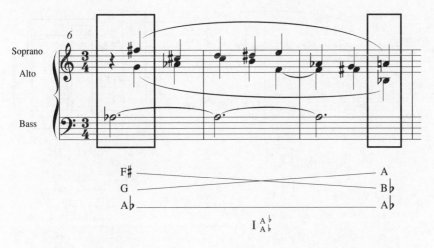

Something similar happens at the end of the piece. Example 2.90 shows the penultimate and final cadences. The two cadential chords are related by inversion around D♯/F♯. This time, the drone note moves, from E to F, by inverting itself around the dyad in the sopranos and altos.

Similar progressions shape the harmonic flow in the Prelude No. 9 (see Example 2.91, the final phrase of the piece). The first chord in the passage moves to the last chord by inversion around the sustained C♯–D♯ in the bass. The inversional relationship between the chords is palpable – E5 moves down

Example 2.90   Harmonic progression via inversional pivoting in Chant No. 2 ("To an Angel"), mm. 46–end

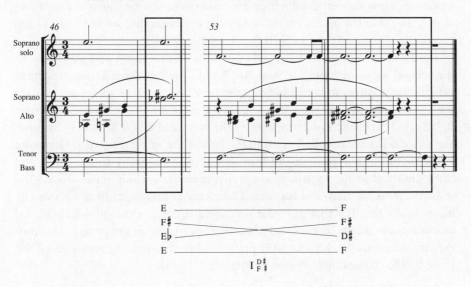

Example 2.91   Harmonic progression via inversional pivoting in Piano Prelude No. 9, mm. 22–end

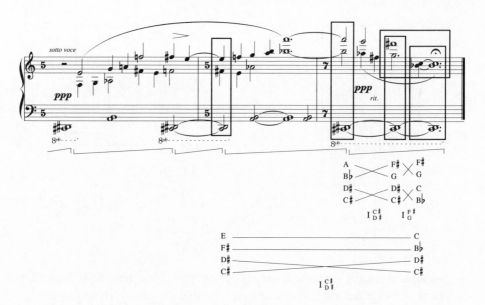

four semitones to C5 while F♯4 moves up four semitones to B♭4. A brief progression of three harmonies also leads to the final chord, or at least to its upper
component, B♭–C. The final chord of the piece is thus the confluence of two
strands of inversional pivoting.

Chant No. 1 ends with two harmonies, the second of which is the inversion
of the first (see Example 2.92). In both harmonies, a sustained whole tone in
the two choral parts accompanies a single melodic note in the alto solo, brought
in both times by a statement of Motive M1. In the first case, the solo note is a
semitone below the sustained whole tone and in the second case it is a semitone
above. The two harmonies are related by the inversion that sends A onto D and
causes B♭–C to invert onto C♯–B (see Example 2.92B).

Harmonic progressions frequently combine transposition and inversion. In
the second movement of the Suite for Wind Quintet, the extended cadential
progression involves sustained notes in the horn and, later, the horn and bassoon
which accompany melodies that feature an ascending whole tone. Example
2.93A labels five different harmonies on the score and 2.93B provides a synopsis
and analysis (I have supplied the B in the bass of the first harmony to clarify the
larger picture). The progression from the second harmony to the third, and
from the third to the fourth, involves inverting the melody notes around the
sustained B♭–C in horn and bassoon. Those central inversions are symmetrically
balanced by the T_{-1} that precedes them and the T_{+1} that follows them and
terminates the movement. Notice that the upper voice in the progression from
the first harmony to the second is prefigured in the opening measures of the
piece by the clarinet melody (see Example 2.93C).

Example 2.92 Harmonies related by inversion in Chant No. 1 ("To an Unkind God"): A) mm. 27–end; B) analytical reduction

A)

B)

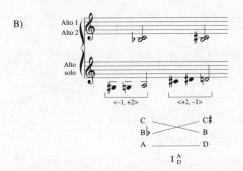

In the third movement of *Diaphonic Suite No. 2*, the cello alternates melodies with chordal passages. Over the course of the movement, the cello plays twelve different four-note chords, representing nine different tetrachord types. Amid their variety of internal structure, the chords are usually connected smoothly as each of the four registral lines, the soprano, alto, tenor, and bass of the chords, moves by small intervals. In some cases, the chords are still more closely connected by the underlying pitch-class counterpoint.

The final three chords of the movement are linked together by transposition or inversion, and by the linear mappings those operations induce (see Example 2.94).

103

Example 2.93   Harmonies related by transposition and inversion in Suite for Wind Quintet, second movement: A) mm. 21–end; B) analytical reduction; C) similar gesture in opening melody, mm. 3–4

A)

B)

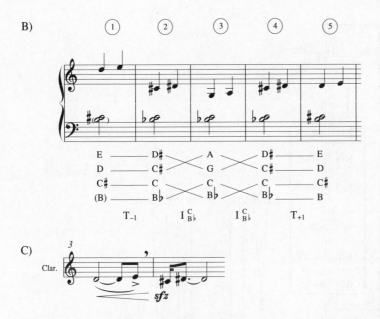

C)

Through all three chords, the C and G, the cello's two lowest open strings, are retained in the lower two voices while the upper two move by small intervals (notice the statement of motive M1 in the alto). Transposition and inversion provide an even more intimate connection among the chords. The inversion that maps the first chord onto the second maps C and G onto each other and A and G♯ onto each other. The final two chords have the same pitch–class content (and are thus related at T_0), but the upper voices exchange places. The progression from the first chord to the third can also be understood as an inversion around C/G. The progression is thus unified by both the harmonic relationships among the chords and the voice leading that connects them.

In the progressions we have discussed so far, the harmonies have been related by either transposition or inversion and are thus, by definition, chords of the same type. More commonly, however, Crawford progresses between chords of different types, as in the opening chords of the same movement (see Example 2.95).[124] None of these chords is related by transposition or inversion, and yet the progression sounds smooth and connected, as one chord melds into, or is transformed into, the next. In part, this is because of common tones, particularly the retained low C. At a deeper level, however, the connection is forged by the transposition of three out of the four notes in each case. From the first chord to the second, three notes are transposed at T_0 while one is not. From the second to the third and the third to the fourth, three notes are transposed at T_2 while one is not. Now the outer voices are paired as are the inner voices. Near-transpositions do not necessarily combine to create a coherent larger motion, although here they do: the first chord and the fourth are related by near-transposition at $*T_3$. In the discussion that follows, I will define near-transposition and near-inversion as the

Example 2.94   Cadential progression in *Diaphonic Suite No. 2* (for bassoon and cello), third movement, mm. 36–end

Example 2.95   Progression involving "near-transposition," in *Diaphonic Suite No. 2* (for bassoon and cello), third movement, mm. 1–10

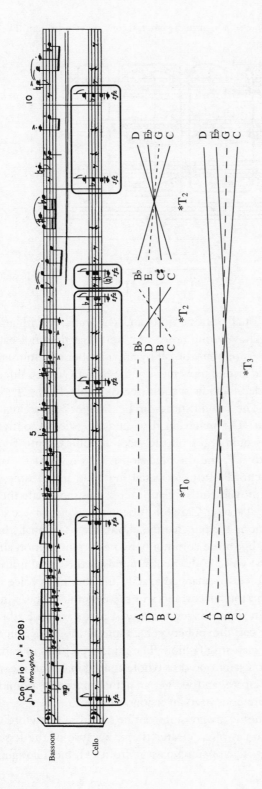

Example 2.96   Harmonic progression in String Quartet, second movement, mm. 11–13

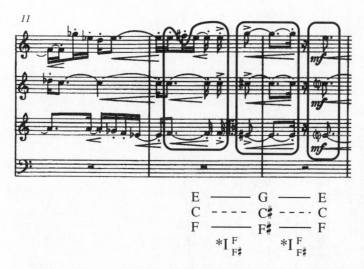

transposition or inversion of all but one note, and will indicate with an asterisk when that has occurred. The "wrong note," the note that does not participate in the transposition or inversion, may be off by any number of semitones.

In measures 12–13 of the second movement of the String Quartet, three chords mark the end of an extended melodic section (see Example 2.96). The first and third chords are the same. The second chord can be thought of as related to both of them by near-inversion. The inversion that sends the viola F onto F♯ and the first violin E onto G would also send the second violin C onto B. Instead, the second violin moves to C♯, and the inversion is thus not exact – one note does not participate. The chord returns to its starting point in the same way.

Elsewhere in the same movement, similar progressions punctuate the occurrences of a melody whose character Crawford designates as *giocoso* (see Example 2.97). The connections among the punctuating chords are occasionally by actual transposition or inversion, but more commonly by near-transposition and near-inversion. In both cases, the voice leading corresponds to the actual instrumental lines. Usually, the outer voices are mapped exactly and the inner voice is off by one or two semitones. The four occurrences in the example of near-inversion around E are instructive. In all four cases, the lowest part stays on E, the axis of inversion, while the upper part moves between E♭ and F, moving symmetrically around the axis in familiar leap-frog fashion. The middle part fails to participate, and is always off by either a semitone or a whole tone. Finally, in measure 93, the middle part does participate, and we get an actual inversion around E as a kind of corrective to the previous near-inversions around E.

The same kinds of harmonic progressions can be found in Crawford's earlier music. Indeed, the situation is often clearer there, because of the less intense nature of the heterophony. The opening passage from "Home Thoughts," one

Example 2.97   Harmonic progression in String Quartet, second movement, mm. 16–21 and
91–95

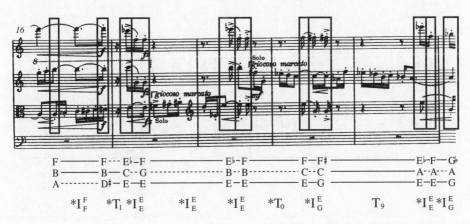

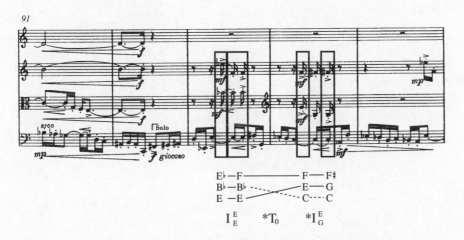

of the Five Sandburg Songs from 1929, contains many familiar elements (see
Example 2.98). Notes are usually related by a semitone to a note already present,
gaps are promptly filled, and the passage as a whole creates a chromatic cluster
containing seven different notes. The note that completes the cluster, A, is
emphasized at the top of a crescendo and further stressed by a *tenuto* mark.
Within the harmonies, notes are often separated by ten, eleven, or thirteen
semitones. Several forms of Motive M1 are embedded in the passage, including
the first three notes, F–G–G♭, which are overlapped with its first three bass
notes, G–G♭–A♭, in an RI-chain.

The passage can be understood as a progression of four tetrachords, circled in
Example 2.98A. The first and fourth chords could be thought of as related by
T_1, but the larger context makes inversion a more plausible interpretation. The
notes in the upper three voices pivot around the sustained G♭ in the bass
(Example 2.98B1). The second and third chords are related in a similar way:

Example 2.98   Harmonic progression in "Home Thoughts" from Five Sandburg Songs:
A) mm. 1–5; B) analytical reductions

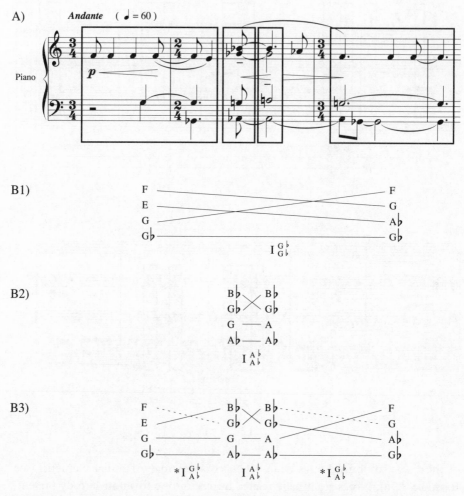

again the notes in the upper three voices pivot around a sustained bass note, now an A♭ (Example 2.98B2). The first and fourth chords are not of the same type as the second and third, but the entire progression can be understood as a series of inversions or near-inversions in which the upper voices always pivot around the bass (Example 2.98B3).

The Violin Sonata, another relatively early piece, contains similar kinds of chord progressions. The passage shown in Example 2.99 involves the traditional texture of a lyrical melody accompanied by arpeggiated chords, of which there are five, all intervallically distinct. The progression can be understood as a motion from the symmetrical first chord, to the asymmetrical and intervallically varied third chord, to the symmetrical fifth chord, a pure whole-tone subset.[125] As the harmony gradually changes shape, connections are forged via near-transposition and near-inversion (see Example 2.99B). Each step in the journey follows logically from the one that precedes it, but we nonetheless end up in a very different place from where we began.

Example 2.99   Harmonic progression in Violin Sonata, first movement: A) mm. 12–14; B) analytical reduction

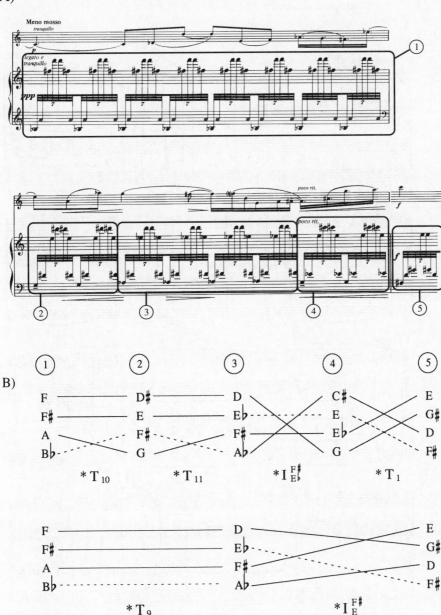

Progressions of this kind can span passages of considerable length, as at the end of the first movement of the String Quartet, where the opening melodies of the movement are recalled amid long, sustained notes (see Example 2.100A). At the beginning of the passage, two four-note chords, numbered 1 and 2, are built up gradually beginning from the solitary A3 in the second violin. In the music that follows, the last note of each of the short melodies is sustained to form four

Example 2.100   Harmonic progression in String Quartet, first movement: A) mm. 59–end; B) analytical reductions

A)

B1)

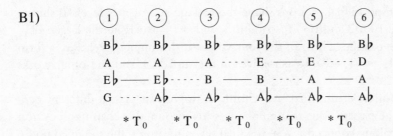

B2)

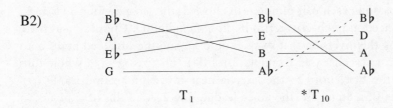

B3)

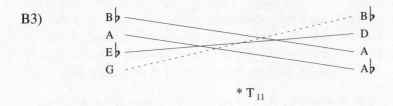

B4)

B5)

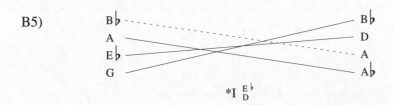

additional four-note harmonies, numbered 3 through 6. Each of the chords retains three notes from the chord right before it, a pattern I describe in terms of successive $*T_0$s in Example 2.100B1. Each of the instrumental voices changes notes at least once, except for the first violin, which sustains its B♭4 throughout the passage.

Larger transpositional motions shape the passage at a deeper level, as shown in Example 2.100B2 and B3. T_1 combines with $*T_{10}$ to create the larger $*T_{11}$ that spans the passage. Three of the four voices at this higher level trace a form of Motive M1, $<+1, -2>$, so pervasive on the surface of this and other works by Crawford.

The disposition of the final two chords, however, suggests a different perspective on the passage, one that emphasizes inversion rather than transposition as a way of making connections. In the final seven measures, the sustained notes, A♭2–A3–B♭4, are arranged symmetrically in pitch space, with thirteen semitones separating each pair of notes. In chord 5, the second violin adds an E, which is balanced in pitch-class terms by its concluding D. Chords 5 and 6 are thus related by the inversion that maps E onto D, and the sustained notes onto themselves or each other (see Example 2.100B4). The passage as a whole thus moves from the first chord to the last via near-inversion around E♭/D (see Example 2.100B5). Strangely, the voice leading involved in this near-inversion is precisely the same as that induced by the near transposition at $*T_{11}$.

In "Sacco, Vanzetti," a single progression spans the entire piano accompaniment, where a single chord is gradually changed, one note at a time. The transformation has five stages, each of which corresponds to a stanza of the text (see Example 2.101).[126] Each chord differs from its immediate predecessor by only one note; the arrival of the new note signals the beginning of the new

Example 2.101 Large-scale harmonic progression in the accompaniment of "Sacco, Vanzetti"

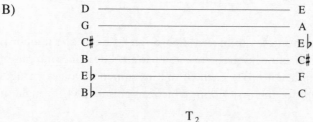

stanza	1	2	3	4	5
meas.	*1–50*	*51–80*	*81–140*	*141–184*	*185–295*

A)

D	—— D	—— D	—— D	⋯$+3$⋯ F
G	—— G	—— G	⋯-3⋯ E	—— E
C♯	—— C♯	—— C♯	—— C♯	—— C♯
B	⋯-2⋯ A	—— A	—— A	—— A
E♭	—— E♭	—— E♭	—— E♭	—— E♭
B♭	—— B♭	⋯$+2$⋯ C	—— C	—— C

$*T_0$ $*T_0$ $*T_0$ $*T_0$

B)

D	——————————————	E
G		A
C♯		E♭
B		C♯
E♭		F
B♭		C

T_2

stanza. Each chord shares five out of six notes with the chord that comes right before it, a relationship that I describe as $*T_0$ (Example 2.101A). The new notes are introduced in a symmetrical way. When the first chord moves to the second, B moves down two semitones to A, and when the second chord moves to the third, that is balanced by B♭ moving up two semitones to C. Similarly, when the third chord moves to the fourth and fifth chords, the motion down three semitones from G to E is balanced by the motion up three semitones from D to F.[127] These four symmetrical transpositions of individual notes have a surprising result: the fifth chord as a whole is the transposition of the first chord at T_2 (Example 2.101B). Of the five chords in the progression, only the first and last are related by actual transposition.

One might imagine this progression as a goal-oriented, directed motion from the first chord to its T_2 with the intervening chords as mere by-products along the way. Alternately, one might imagine the progression rolling along an attractive path but with no apparent destination, with the conclusion at T_2 of the opening coming as a surprise. Either way, there is an obvious dramatic significance to the larger move. That ascending whole tone is clearly associated with the apotheosis, in the text, of Sacco and Vanzetti. The first four stanzas of the poem focus on the injustice of their arrest and execution, but the final stanza imagines them, and their struggle, as living on, just as plant roots live through the winter to produce new blooms in the spring. And just as the large harmonic T_{+2} is buried deep in the structure of the work, the same gesture blossoms at the moment of their apotheosis (see Example 2.102). While the last chord is undergoing its final registral permutations, the vocal line presents a compound melody whose highest and lowest strands are organized around successive ascending whole tones, thus reflecting, right on the musical surface, the piece-spanning harmonic gesture.

Rhythm

Precompositional plans and patterns

Like the pitches, the rhythms of Crawford's melodies are generally organized in either of two contrasting ways: strictly or freely. Usually, but not always, the strict rhythms – characterized by steady streams of equal pulsations (grouped regularly or irregularly by accents or meter) or regular beats (partitioned into recurring patterns of smaller values) – are associated with some sort of rigid precompositional scheme for the pitches.

In the *Piano Study in Mixed Accents*, an uninterrupted procession of sixteenth notes is grouped irregularly by accents, and the pitches follow a strict plan of retrograde symmetry. The rhythmic groups are also heard in reverse order, but by adding some free notes in the middle of the melody, Crawford shifts the rhythmic groups out of their original alignment with the pitches. This sense that

Example 2.102 Large-scale T_{+2} blossoming to the musical surface in the final measures of "Sacco, Vanzetti"

rhythms and pitches may be patterned independently, and that the patterns may shift in and out of alignment with each other, is a persistent feature of Crawford's music, and one to which we shall return.

The first clarinet melody in *Diaphonic Suite No. 3*, third movement, is organized in a similar way. Much of the melody consists of a forty-note pitch series, which is transformed by the transposition, inversion, and retrograde. The series is presented for the most part in a steady stream of eighth notes, partitioned into irregular groups by accents. When the series is transposed, the groupings remain the same, and when it is retrograded, the groupings are too. Only the pitch inversion is not supported by comparable rhythmic organization. The close mutual support of pitch and rhythm is most apparent in the completely serial melodies, like the third movement of *Diaphonic Suite No. 1*. There, a steady stream of eighth notes is punctuated by accents every seven notes, emphasizing the first note in the seven-note series.

The rhythms themselves may be subjected to some kind of systematic treatment. In the piano accompaniment of "Chinaman, Laundryman," for example, each measure contains the nine notes of some series statement. Those nine notes always occur in one of three possible rhythmic arrangements, as in measures 4, 5, and 6 (see Example 2.103A). In measure 4, the nine notes are grouped into

Example 2.103   Rhythmic pattern in "Chinaman, Laundryman": A) mm. 1–6; B) rhythmic organization of entire accompaniment

117

4+3+2, a grouping I will call x; in measure 5, the groupings are 5+2+2 (y); in measure 6, they are 4+2+3 (z). There are six possible ways of ordering these three patterns: xyz, xzy, zxy, zyx, yzx, and yzx. Crawford uses all six possibilities, in just this order, requiring eighteen measures to do so (see Example 2.103B). Over the course of the piece, this eighteen-measure pattern occurs five times, and accounts for the entire accompaniment.[128]

The nine-note pitch series for the piece requires nine measures for a complete set of rotations. Each eighteen-measure rhythmic pattern thus spans two complete series rotations. In the manuscript for this work, Crawford uses a complicated system of markings to indicate formal divisions, none of which appear in the published score. In the manner of "metrical form," she uses double or triple barlines every nine measures, to indicate sets of rotations. Heavy single barlines every three measures identify the components of the eighteen-measure rhythmic pattern (these are omitted when they coincide with a double or triple barline). What is more interesting, the manuscript also contains designations that apparently indicate beginnings of lines and stanzas of the poem. The poem contains seven stanzas with three lines in each. Each line of the poem lasts either four or five measures, and these lengths are also noted. This reasonably regular periodicity in the text declamation cuts across the regular nine-measure and eighteen-measure groups in the accompaniment – the two never coincide. This is a wonderful example of what Seeger and Crawford would have understood as heterophonic form, a sense that there is not one single form for a piece, but rather a multiplicity of forms that contradict and strain against each other. Heterophony, in this sense, is not merely something that happens between parts, but potentially within a single part, when its different dimensions, usually rhythm and pitch, are structured independently.

"Sacco, Vanzetti" presents a similar kind of heterophonic form, in which patterns in various dimensions move in and out of alignment with each other. In the piano accompaniment, the chords discussed earlier are interspersed with single pitch classes heard simultaneously in three octaves. The pattern established in the first ten measures – five chords interspersed with five single pitch classes in the pattern xyxyxxyxyy – is maintained as an ostinato throughout the song (see Example 2.104). In the first two sections of the song (mm. 1–50 and 51–80) and in the final section (mm. 185–95), the rhythm consists exclusively of

Example 2.104 Alternation of chords and single notes in the recurring ostinato accompaniment of "Sacco, Vanzetti"

uniform half notes, one per measure. The ostinato is thus heard once every ten measures – eight times in measures 1–80 and eleven times in measures 185–295.

In the third and fourth sections of the song (mm. 81–140 and 141–84), however, the rhythmic pattern changes while the chord pattern remains the same. In the third section, the rhythmic pattern is ♩♩ | ♩♩ . That pattern is two measures long, and thus aligns with the chord pattern only every two times through. In the fourth section, the rhythmic pattern is ♩.♪ | ♩♩ | ♪♩. , a three-measure pattern that aligns with the chord pattern only every three times through. The chordal ostinati are separated by commas in the published score and by the usual double bars of "metric form" in the manuscripts. The two- and three-measure rhythmic patterns are unremarked in the published score, but indicated with brackets in the manuscript. Both the chordal ostinato and the rhythms are carefully patterned, but the patterns move in and out of alignment with each other.

A similar, but more varied, shifting of alignment of patterns of rhythm and pitch can be found in "In Tall Grass." Toward the middle of that song, the piano plays four statements (the last one truncated) of a seventy-four-note melody (see Example 2.105). Crawford indicates the beginning of each statement, in measures 40, 47, 54, and 60, with brackets above the staff. The melody is generally played in octaves, in the style of *Piano Study in Mixed Accents* and "Chinaman, Laundryman," although at the end of each phrase the left hand diverges somewhat from the right. The melody itself is typical in many ways. It pivots on itself, constantly changing shape as it moves. There is some degree of internal repetition, but for the most part, it is extremely varied intervallically.

The rhythms are also patterned, but independently of the repetitions of the melody notes. The passage consists of nine phrases, each indicated with a slur, and usually arranging the notes into a fixed pattern of 5–6–7–5–4 notes per beat. On two occasions additional groups are inserted in the middle of the pattern, and the final statement is truncated. The rhythmic pattern repeats every twenty-seven notes while the melody repeats every seventy-four notes. Rhythm and pitch are both rigidly patterned, but shift constantly in relation to each other. After the downbeat of measure 40, the beginning of a rhythmic phrase and the beginning of a melodic statement never again coincide.

As their relationship shifts, rhythm and pitch offer changing perspectives on each other. One can imagine, for example, that the rhythmic groups provide a lens that focuses on whatever part of the melody happens to pass beneath it. Consider, for example, the groups of four notes that end the second, fourth, and fifth phrases. These are drawn from various places in the seventy-four-note melody, but all are members of the same tetrachord-type, and these are the only occurrences of that tetrachord-type anywhere in the melody. In other words, the fixed rhythmic pattern, as it shifts in relation to the melody, picks out and associates groups of notes that also have intervallic affinities. The rhythmic pattern offers a segmentation, or, more accurately, a series of shifting segmentations, of

Example 2.105   Independent melodic and rhythmic patterns in "In Tall Grass" from Three
Sandburg Songs, piano, mm. 40–63

the melody. The musical dimensions, melody and rhythm, are organized independently and, in their constantly shifting relationship, offer interesting perspectives on each other.

The relationship between rhythm and pitch shifts in a somewhat different way in the first movement of the String Quartet. That movement begins with a melody marked *cantando* and a contrasting melody marked *marcato bruscamente*, followed by varied repeats of each. The movement ends in a similar way, only now the pitches from the *cantando* melodies are combined with the rhythms from the *marcato bruscamente* melodies, and vice versa (see Example 2.106). The pitches are not retained exactly – they may be off by one or two semitones and notes are occasionally added to or omitted from the line – but the sense of repetition is unmistakable. The rhythms and pitches of Crawford's music may thus be thought of as independently structured with the resulting potential for shifting juxtapositions and combinations.

Returning to "In Tall Grass," shifting alignments characterize not only the relationship between pitches and rhythms within the piano part but the relation-

Example 2.106 Pitches from one melody combined with rhythms from another, and vice versa, in String Quartet, first movement

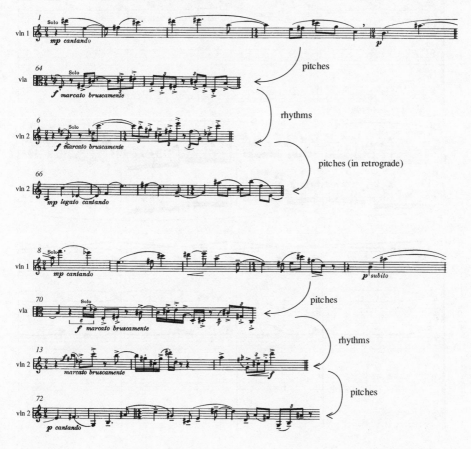

ship between the piano and the other layers in a complex, heterophonic texture. The basic layout of the piece pits a central group of instruments which Crawford calls "concertante" (voice, oboe, piano, and percussion) against an optional

Example 2.107 Pattern of dynamic high points in "In Tall Grass" from Three Sandburg Songs, mm. 40–47

secondary group (massed strings and winds) composed months after the song in its concertante-only version had been completed.[129]

The upper ostinato strings are designed to imitate the buzzing bees described in the song text. They slide up and down in their upper registers, frequently coming to rest on densely packed clusters of notes, and the resulting acoustical beats intensify the poetic description. As they move, they get louder and softer, and in reasonably regular ways. Indeed, Crawford's performance indications tell of her greater interest in the dynamic scheme than in the actual pitches: "The various dynamic ostinati should not stand out as individual tones; the rhythmic pattern made by their crescendi and diminuendi (particularly in the violins and violas) must be distinguishable as unified pulsating masses of sound."

The distances between the dynamic high points in the ostinato strings become entirely regular right at the point where the piano begins its seventy-four-note melody (see Example 2.107). They occur every 1–2–1–2–1 measures, creating a pattern that takes seven measures to complete. The beginnings and ends of this pattern of dynamics, which is repeated exactly three times before being varied, do not, after the downbeat of measure 40, coincide with the patterned repetitions in either the rhythm or melody of the piano. Their alignments are constantly shifting.

Around them, other parts are also sounding, although these are less regular internally. The voice part, for example, declaims the text in irregular phrases and sub-phrases. Its beginnings and endings coincide with neither the rhythms of the piano nor the dynamics of the upper strings.

The lack of coincidence between the parts, their constantly shifting relationship to each other, has radical implications for the form of the song, and for musical form generally. Musical form is traditionally understood to arise from patterns of "dimensionally conjoined repetition."[130] Points of formal articulation are normally marked by melodic arrival and harmonic cadence, and frequently reinforced by changes in melody, harmony, rhythm, register, and instrumentation, all occurring simultaneously. In Crawford's music, however, the dimensions are structured independently; they are not conjoined. Furthermore, no dimension can be taken as primary. Each cuts across the others in an unbounded play of equals. There is no privileged dimension, and thus no single place from which to perceive the whole. There is thus no form at all in the traditional sense. Instead, one should speak of the multiple forms of the piece, each suggested by patterns or articulations in some musical dimension.

Rhythmic contours

Rigid rhythms, with regular pulsations or beats, while common in Crawford's music and often associated with a rigid pitch scheme, are less typical than free rhythms, usually associated with free melodies. Like the pitches in such melodies, the rhythms tend to be dissonant in Seeger's sense. They change rapidly, avoid repetition, and rely heavily on uneven divisions of the beat into threes, fives, and sevens, with frequent use of ties to create a wide range of values.[131]

The melody in Example 2.108, from the second movement of the Suite for Wind Quintet, is typical of Crawford's practice. The durations of the notes are calculated in twelfths of a beat, and written beneath the staff. When the same duration is repeated immediately, only the duration of the first note is indicated. The durations range from 3 to 21 and, in this brief melody, include fully nine different values. Most of the values occur only once, and those that occur more than once, like the sixteenth notes, triplets, and eighth notes, tend to have several other values intervene between the recurrences. Like Crawford's melodies, her rhythms avoid repetition, avoid traditional combinations, and present a highly varied surface.

When melodies are combined, Crawford prefers to keep them rhythmically independent. They will virtually never attack at the same time. They will tend to avoid the simple, or, in Seeger's terms, "consonant", ratios of rhythmic value. Note-against-note counterpoint is extremely rare, and 2:1, 3:1, and 4:1 only a little less so.

> On the whole, our art of music has contented itself for the last three centuries with a comparatively consonant proportional practice. Most of the relations (intervals) have been of the nature of one unit against some whole number of units. These may be called "rhythmic consonances." The type of relationship borne between partial and partial which does not reduce to consonance (as 2:4, which reduces to 1:2) may be called dissonant.[132]

In the contrapuntal relation between melodies, dissonance prevails, and it is hard to characterize the rhythmic relations between the parts any more precisely than that. Within the melodies, however, it is possible to describe their rhythmic organization by returning to Seeger's concept of the neume. As with pitches, rhythms can be described in terms of their contour – pitches go up and down, and durations get longer or shorter. The contour <+, +, –>, for example, might describe either a melody that goes up, then up, then down, or a rhythmic figure that gets longer, then longer, then shorter.[133] The melody in Example 2.108 makes frequent use of a pattern of durations that get shorter, and then immediately longer again, or <–, +>. Durational neumes of this kind are identified with brackets on the example, and they account for virtually the entire melody. Like the pitches, the rhythms of Crawford's melodies are organized with reference to recurring neumes and their transformations.[134]

Example 2.108   Rhythmic contours in Suite for Wind Quintet, second movement, oboe, mm. 5–9

Example 2.109   Rhythmic contours in three melodies from String Quartet, first movement: A)
Violin 1, mm. 1–4; B) Cello, mm. 1–3; C) Violin 2, mm. 6–7

Example 2.109 describes three contrasting melodies from the first movement
of the String Quartet in the same way. The melodies are distinct in their
melodic shapes, but noticeably similar in their rhythmic contour. All begin with
the rhythmic shape <+, −, +, −, +>, although of course that shape is expressed
with different actual durations in each case. A rhythmic "twist," a shape that
alternates lengthening and shortening, thus seems to be a unifying element here.

The rhythmic neumes may be coordinated with the pitch neumes in various
ways. Example 2.110 analyzes the first melodic phrases of the second and fourth
movements of *Diaphonic Suite No. 1* in terms of both rhythmic and melodic

Example 2.110   Coordination of rhythmic and pitch contours in two melodies from *Diaphonic
Suite No. 1* (for flute or oboe): A) second movement, mm. 1–5; B) fourth
movement, mm. 1–4

A)

B)

contours. In both cases, the rhythmic contour is reflected, either directly or in inversion, by the melodic contour.

The rhythmic contour may also be coordinated with a contour of dynamics (see Example 2.111, from the Suite for Wind Quintet, second movement). In this four-note figure, the durations get shorter, then shorter, then longer, while the dynamics invert the shape, getting louder, then louder, then softer. The contour of the pitches, of course, is quite different. This raises necessary cautions about neumatic analysis in the domain of rhythm. It does not appear that neumes and neume transformations will be nearly as revealing for Crawford's rhythms as they are for her pitches. She apparently did not work systematically in this area. Nonetheless striking relationships between pitch and rhythm do emerge on an *ad hoc* basis, and we will discuss them as they do so.

Example 2.111 Coordination of rhythmic and dynamic contours, in Suite for Wind Quintet, second movement, clarinet in B♭, mm. 3–6

Dynamics

Of all the musical parameters other than pitch and rhythm, dynamics is the most susceptible to systematic organization because, like them, it is scalable. Just as pitches and rhythms can be organized into patterns of rising and falling, or lengthening and shortening, dynamics can be organized into patterns of increasing or decreasing volume. General contour patterns like <+, +, –>, or even more specific contour segments like <0132>, could be realized in any of the three domains. One can speak, in Crawford's music, of dynamic neumes, patterns of loud and soft, that can be transformed on their own terms – expanded, inverted, retrograded, etc. – and can furthermore be related to simultaneously occurring pitch or rhythmic neumes.[135]

In the *Piano Study in Mixed Accents*, Crawford offers three possible dynamic schemes, among which the pianist is free to choose. This marks a historically early, if modest, experiment in performer choice. The first possibility is to play the entire work *fortissimo* throughout, an uninflected dynamic level that does not admit any neumatic content or development. The second possibility, however, involves a gradual, inflected crescendo toward a dynamic high point in the middle of the piece, followed by a gradual decrescendo to the end, and the third possibility does just the opposite, growing louder toward the middle and softer toward the end. Both of these schemes show a rudimentary coordination of dynamics with pitch structure, projecting a rough retrograde symmetry in both dimensions. The organization of the dynamics can be more completely understood, however, both on its own terms and in relations to the pitches and rhythms, if its neumatic organization is taken into account.

The performer's second option is represented in various ways in Example 2.112. In level A, the dynamics are written in conventional notation, as they appear in the score. In level B, each dynamic level is assigned a numerical equivalent, ranging from the softest, *pp*, assigned 0, to the loudest, *ff*, assigned 5. Level C calculates the interval from dynamic to dynamic, just as one might calculate the interval from note to note, and identifies some of the neumatic transformations involved. If one imagines <–3, +2> as a basic dynamic neume in this work, then many of the other dynamic shapes can be understood as transformations of it, via either the expansions and partial expansions in the first part of the piece, or the extended RI-chain that concludes it.

Furthermore, the same neume receives expression among both the rhythms and pitches of the piece. Rhythmically, the piece involves a steady stream of sixteenth notes broken up into groups by irregularly spaced accents. Example 2.113 represents the rhythmic organization of the first quarter or so of the piece in several ways. In level A, the groups are given in conventional notation, as they appear in the score. Level B gives the number of notes in each group. Level C calculates some of the durational intervals, that is, the number of notes added to or taken away from the previous group, and identifies some relevant neumatic transformations. As with the dynamics, most of what happens rhythmically can be accounted for in relation to the durational neume <–3, +2>, which is transformed in the usual ways, including two brief RI-chains.

The same neume is expressed in the pitch domain in a variety of ways. Example 2.114 shows the highest note in each of the twelve rhythmic groups

Example 2.112 Neumatic organization of dynamics with reference to <–3, +2> in *Piano Study in Mixed Accents*

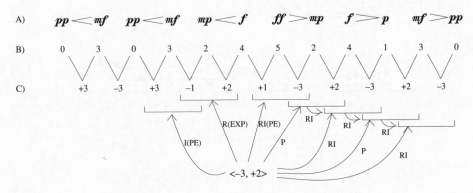

Example 2.113 Neumatic organization of rhythmic groupings with reference to <−3, +2> in *Piano Study in Mixed Accents*

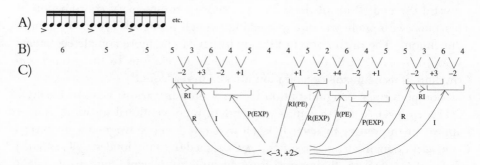

Example 2.114 Neumatic organization of registral high points with reference to <−3, +2> in *Piano Study in Mixed Accents*: A) first section with high points circled; B) analytical reduction

128

Example 2.115 Motive M1 projected in pitch, duration, and dynamics in *Diaphonic Suite No. 1* (for flute or oboe), fourth movement: A) mm. 33–end; B) rhythmic groupings; C) dynamics

A)

B)

C)

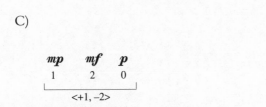

that make up the first section of the piece. As with the dynamics and rhythms, this registral pitch line can be understood in relation to <−3, +2>, its opening neume. These relations, based on projecting the same contour simultaneously in dynamics, rhythm, and pitch, are not systematic, but they are highly suggestive.

Example 2.115A shows the final phrase from the *Diaphonic Suite No. 1*, fourth movement, and identifies the two overlapping statements of Motive M1 with which it ends. The same motive is expressed both in the rhythms (Example 2.115B) and the dynamics (Example 2.115C).[136] As in the *Piano Study in Mixed Accents*, Crawford finds a way of projecting the same neume simultaneously in three dimensions: pitch, rhythm, and dynamics.

Crawford does not consistently structure her dynamics using this kind of neumatic organization. More commonly in her music, dynamics play a freely expressive role, not governed by readily apprehensible patterns and not coordinated in any systematic way with the rhythms and pitches. In heterophonic textures, for example, dynamics are used simply, along with many other factors, to distinguish clearly among the contrasting parts. Yet she does structure her dynamics often enough, and strikingly enough, to deserve acknowledgment for her pioneering work in this area. More specifically, she merits credit for two related achievements, for finding a way of organizing musical dynamics independently and, more significantly, for finding a way to project the same musical idea simultaneously in the domains of pitch, rhythm, and dynamics.[137] In both senses, she anticipates the concerns of the post-war serial composers from the following generation.

3

Six analyses

"Rat Riddles" from Three Sandburg Songs

Crawford's longstanding friendship with the poet Carl Sandburg resulted first in the Five Songs of 1929 and then, in the immediate aftermath of her studies with Seeger, in the Three Songs of 1930–32. The first of the Three Songs, all of which are among her most important compositions, sets a poem titled "Rat Riddles."

> There was a gray rat looked at me
> with green eyes out of a rathole.
>
> "Hello, rat," I said,
> "Is there any chance for me
> to get on to the language of the rats?"
>
> And the green eyes blinked at me,
> blinked from a gray rat's rathole.
>
> "Come again," I said,
> "Slip me a couple of riddles;
> there must be riddles among the rats."
>
> And the green eyes blinked at me
> and a whisper came from the gray rathole:
> "Who do you think you are and why is a rat?
> Where did you sleep last night and why do
>   you sneeze on Tuesdays? And why is the
>   grave of a rat no deeper than the grave
>   of a man?"
>
> And the tail of a green-eyed rat
> Whipped and was gone at a gray rathole.[1]

Crawford provides an elaborate and original setting of this brief lyric, one that captures both its ironic, mocking tone and the more disturbing connection it draws between the life of a human being and the life of a rat.

"Rat Riddles" is scored for two opposed groups of instruments. The principal group, which Crawford calls the "concertanti," consists of the singer, oboe, piano, and a mixed percussion group, including Chinese block, triangle, tambourine, cymbal, and bass drum. This group of instruments provides the essential musical substance and continuity of the song. The secondary instrumental group, called "ostinati," and consisting of strings, winds, and brass, punctuate the music with staccato chords.

Seeger offers an accurate and expressive general description of the work, which he considered one of Crawford's finest:

> The piano and the oboe chase each other around in the most surprising arabesques to a percussion accompaniment, the two instruments and the voice and percussion giving the impression – such is the independence of parts – of a whole small orchestra, busily engaged in a contrapuntal tutti. Upon the gay irregularity of the fabric of these instrumentas, as *concertanti*, has been superimposed a slow and solemn orchestral *ostinato* of a purely percussive character, whose regular tread makes a very unusual effect – a counterpoint between two groups, one in florid counterpoint, the other independently homophonic.[2]

The two instrumental groups are quite independent of each other, and were in fact written separately. The concertanti-only version of the song was written during the spring of 1930, before Crawford left for her year in Europe on a Guggenheim Fellowship. The ostinati, for this and all three of the songs, were written months later, after Crawford had returned to New York, and they may be omitted in performance, as Crawford suggests in her performance instructions:

> The concertanti section is complete in itself, and can be performed with or without the ostinati. The ostinati should be seated apart from the concertanti – if possible, at the rear of the stage. The concertanti and ostinati should, if possible, be rehearsed once or twice separately, in order that the independence of the two sections be understood by the players.[3]

Within this basic heterophony of concertanti vs. ostinati, the concertanti parts themselves comprise a disparate trio of voice, oboe, and piano, with irregular interjections from the percussion. The vocal line is probably the most integrated and motivically unified melody Crawford ever wrote. Its first six notes comprise a prototype, a basis for all that happens subsequently (see Example 3.1).

Example 3.1 Opening vocal melody, "Rat Riddles," mm. 18–21

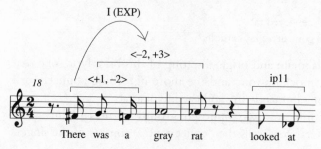

The prototype begins with Motive M1, <+1, –2>, which is overlapped with an inverted expansion of itself, <–2, +3>. The last two notes present a leap of eleven semitones. The obvious inversional symmetry of the prototype around its first two notes, F♯–G, will be taken up shortly. In each of these respects, the melodic fragment is entirely typical of Crawford.

Virtually the entire melody can be understood in relation either to M1 and its expansion, often overlapped, or to the leap of eleven semitones (see Example 3.2). The entire melody can be read from left to right moving down the page.[4] Musical material is vertically aligned with its prototype in the first six notes. Each horizontal staff, then, contains a variation of the prototype that begins with M1 and/or its expanded variant and concludes with a leap of eleven semitones. While notes are occasionally added or omitted, the entire melody can thus be understood as a six-note theme and twenty-one variations. At the end of each variation, the melody usually leaps by tritone to the beginning of the subsequent variation. Indeed, the tritone usually has a kind of carriage-return function in this melody, demarcating the end of one melodic unit and the beginning of another.[5]

This extraordinary motivic compression, with the constant repetition of a few elements, captures very nicely the restricted vocabulary of the poem, with its hypnotic repetition of a few words and phrases. The words "rat" and "rathole," or "gray" and "green," occur almost as often in the poem as M1 and ip11 do in the melody.

These twenty-two brief melodic units coalesce into larger groups that conform generally to the structure of Sandburg's poem. Nonetheless, the smaller units often cut across the syntactic boundaries of the poem. The prototype itself ends right in the middle of a grammatical unit in the poem, and grammatical units frequently end in the middle of variations. There is thus a kind of heterophony within the text setting. The text establishes one kind of periodicity, the melody establishes another, and the two need not coincide. Some of the repetitions in the music underscore significant repetitions or near-repetitions in the text. For example, the melodic figure of a descending ip11 followed by a tritone is used to link related figures of speech ("looked at me" and "blinked at me"), but the same figure is used many times with no apparent textual significance.

The melody is responsive to the text in many obvious ways, particularly in the correspondence between musical rhythm and poetic accentuation, but there is at the same time a tension between them, a sense of each pulling in its own direction. The musical structure is so strong, so well-formed, that it does not and cannot support the text at every point. Like the heterophony in this song between concertanti and ostinati, and among the concertanti parts, the music and text of the vocal line coexist in shifting, and not always mutually supportive, ways.

As with all of Crawford's melodies, distinctive musical fragments are transposed along musically significant paths. Example 3.3 shows the ten statements of the descending ip11 in the first sixty-two measures of the song, that is, up to the point where the rat itself begins to speak. Leaving out the first one, the ip11s

Example 3.2   Analysis of entire vocal melody in relation to the opening melody, in "Rat Riddles"

describe three binary twist neumes, of which the first is M1 (the first motive in the melody), the second is an exact doubling of it (MULT), and the third expands each of its intervals by a semitone (EXP). Each of these motives has a high point which, when taken together, describe an even larger form of M1. The ip11s thus follow a large–scale path that replicates the motivic shapes of the musical surface.

Example 3.3   Projection of ip11 along a motivic path, in "Rat Riddles"

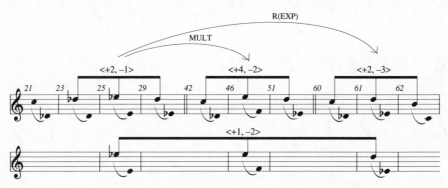

Example 3.4   Inversional balance around F♯/G in the opening melodic phrase of "Rat Riddles"

In the first four notes of the voice part, there is a sense of a musical wedge expanding outward from the initial F♯–G to F–A♭. Indeed, inversional balance around the initial F♯–G helps to organize the entire first phrase of the melody (see Example 3.4). The notes of the melody are slurred to their inversional partners, which are usually found in close proximity. Some of the notes of the melody do not participate, but most do, including the highest and lowest, giving the melody a palpable sense of balance around the inversional axis defined by its opening notes. Those notes thus act as a kind of pitch center for the melodic phrase, exerting on the remaining notes a gravitational pull.

Inversional balance, and the centricity it induces, shape the remainder of the vocal line as well. The centers are often ambiguous or rapidly shifting, but they come into particularly clear focus at the end of the vocal line, where the rat begins to speak (see Example 3.5). Of the last three phrases of the song, the first balances around B♭/B, the second around G/A♭, and the third around A♭/A. In the second phrase, the inversional balance is strongly reinforced by the piano accompaniment (to be discussed later), which states the inversional pairs as vertical dyads, and the third phrase is organized almost entirely as a literal

Example 3.5   Inversional balance and a progression of inversional axes in "Rat Riddles," vocal
melody, mm. 63–84

expanding wedge. The inversional centers trace a near-motivic path, moving
down three semitones and then up one semitone. This is a virtual imitation, at a
deep structural level, of <−2, +1> or <−3, +2>, which, along with their
"conversions," are so pervasive in this song.

The vocal line, then, has a compelling internal structure. It is highly charged
with motivic life, and finds ways of projecting its motivic concerns over large
musical spans. Some of its motivic concerns infiltrate the other instrumental
parts, which otherwise contrast with it.

The oboe's countermelody has a somewhat different character. It is less declamatory, often moving in rapid values, scampering from register to register in apparent imitation of the eponymous rat. Nonetheless its pitch organization is similar to that of the voice part, frequently embedding its motives, particularly M1 and its near variants, and the leap of ip11.

Amid its rapid movements, the oboe part does occasionally come to rest on certain pitches, particularly D4, E4, F5 and G5, and these notes are often further emphasized with trills. Furthermore, they often participate in larger-scale statements of the motives of the song (see Example 3.6). The trilled D4 and E4 lead to the sustained E♭4 in measure 17, which completes a statement of M1. The D in the following measure is prepared by two interlocked statements of the same motive. The voice enters in measure 18 with yet another statement of the motive, creating a clear imitative link between the parts.

Example 3.6   Motive M1 in the oboe countermelody in "Rat Riddles," mm. 13–19

Apart from their similar content and their mutual adherence to the large stanzaic plan of the poem, however, the oboe and voice parts are in a constantly changing vertical relationship. Compare, for example, the two passages shown in Example 3.7. In the second passage, the voice has been transposed up a semitone. Such an exact transposition is relatively rare in the voice part, but is obviously reflective of the nearly repeated text. The oboe part in the second passage, however, is transposed up initially at ip3, and then at ip2.[6] This sort of transposition is entirely characteristic of the oboe part. Indeed, after the first thirty-three measures, virtually all of the rest is either the transposition at T_2 or T_3, those prominent motivic intervals, or the exact repetition of music previously heard. As a result, these two passages have a virtually identical melodic content, but entirely different intervals formed between the parts. As we have seen, this is characteristic of Crawford's heterophonic practice. The melodies tend to go their separate ways, allowing for subtly shared intervallic concerns. The relationship between them is fluid and shifting, best understood as the by-product of the primary melodic activity.

The piano plays two kinds of music, relatively slow-moving chordal passages and rapidly scampering passages, occasionally in octaves. The scampering music is like the rapid passagework in the oboe part, both in character and content, although the oboe and the piano rarely scamper at the same time. The chordal passages make frequent use of vertical ip11s in the right hand. Usually the ip11

Example 3.7   Shifting contrapuntal relations between vocal melody and oboe countermelody, in "Rat Riddles," mm. 24–27 and 45–48

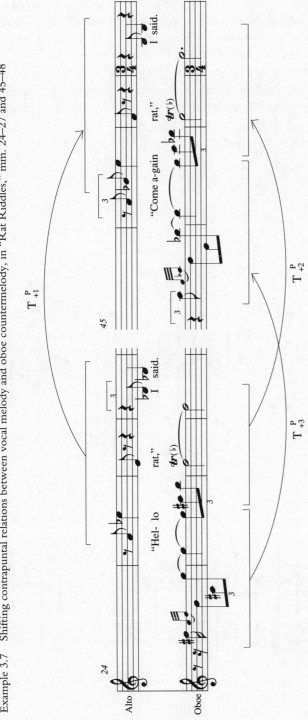

is harmonized with a bass note that creates a tight chromatic cluster, (012), as in the first chord of the piece (see Example 3.8). In this case, the chord is spaced to describe, in register, the familiar Motive M1, so prevalent on the melodic surface. The piano chords and the vocal melody are thus closely related: the principal piano chord represents a simple verticalization of the vocal motive.

Furthermore, like Motive M1 in the melody, this chord is developed in systematic ways, particularly through the use of inversional pivoting. Example 3.9 shows two characteristic passages in which this chord progresses to other chords

Example 3.8   First piano chord in "Rat Riddles," m. 4

Example 3.9   Two chord progressions in "Rat Riddles," piano: A) mm. 4–7; B) mm. 79–80

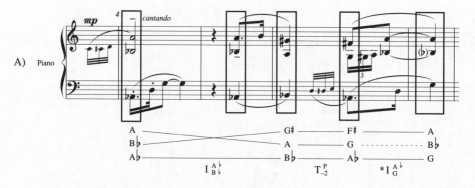

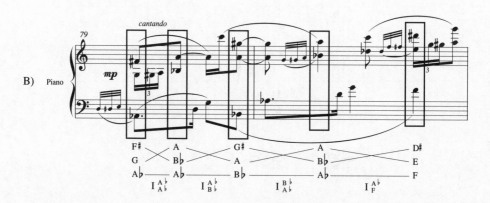

of the same type, or a near-variant. The progressions can be understood in various ways, but inversional pivoting appears to be the preferred means of getting from place to place, with the bass usually acting as a fulcrum around which the upper voices pivot. In Example 3.9A, the motion from the first chord to the second inverts the upper parts around the bass's A♭–B♭. After the second chord is transposed down two semitones onto the third, the upper parts again invert around the bass, this time A♭–G, although this is a "near," not a true inversion. The progression in Example 3.9B operates in similar, and even more consistent fashion, with the upper parts always inverting around the bass. As a result of all these pivotings, the last chord is spaced identically to the first, but twenty-one semitones higher. In its reliance on a continuous process of inversional pivoting amid a changing musical surface, the harmonic organization of the piano part is thus typical of Crawford's mature practice.

The percussion parts consist entirely of scattered occurrences of the rhythmic figure ♪ ♫ in the Chinese block interspersed with single attacks on the beat in the other instruments, occasionally sustained by a roll. There does not appear to be any larger pattern of recurrence or transformation. The Chinese-block figure occurs sometimes isolated and sometimes as many as four times in succession. It is sometimes followed by a single stroke in another instrument, but sometimes it is not. Crawford's only concern appears to be a persistent irregularity.

Even leaving aside the irregular percussion parts, it is difficult to generalize about the ensemble harmonies formed among the parts. Aside from the chorale-like passage where the rat poses the last of its riddles, there is no moment in the song where the voice, oboe, and piano sustain notes simultaneously even for as long as a quarter note. When one part has longer rhythmic values, one or both of the other parts are sure to be moving rapidly. As a result, the intervals formed between the parts, even insofar as they can be perceived amid the rapid figuration, are extremely varied.

The chorale-like setting of the rat's words deserves a closer look, if only as an instance of Crawford's handling of a rare homophonic texture (see Example 3.10). The passage as a whole is preoccupied with inversional balance around an axis of G/A♭, the first two notes in the voice and oboe melodies and the first vertical dyad in the oboe and piano. The melody moves among inversionally-balanced pairs of notes (see Example 3.5 above) and the same pairs are also heard vertically between the other instruments. The oboe and piano begin with a voice exchange involving G–A♭, then expand outward to F♯–A, and end the passage on C♯–D. That final pair is heard melodically in the oboe, just as the first one was.

The harmonies formed among all three parts are varied, but the accompanying notes frequently create a fulcrum around which the voice leaps. The voice moves from B♭ to F around the sustained A♭–G, and later leaps from C♯ to D around a sustained F♯–A. The passage as a whole is spanned by the inversion of the first chord into the last chord, a progression whose voice leading is reflected exactly in the instrumental assignments: B♭ to B in the voice, A♭ to C♯ in the oboe, and

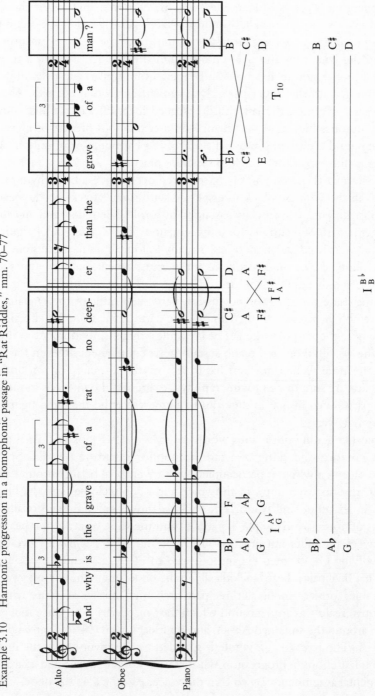

Example 3.10   Harmonic progression in a homophonic passage in "Rat Riddles," mm. 70–77

G to D in the piano. In this homophonic chorale setting, then, the harmonies progress by transposition and inversion, and the voice leading induced by those transformations is reinforced by the actual registral and instrumental lines.

The concertanti parts describe Crawford's heterophony as we have come to understand it. The individual parts maintain a high degree of internal coherence and independence from each other. At the same time, they share a motivic focus and, in those rare moments when they can be heard clearly in relation to each other, they progress together in consistent ways.

With all of the contrapuntal activity within the concertanti parts, the basic musical issue of the song involves the contrast between concertanti and ostinati. Where the concertanti parts are relatively free and flexible, the ostinati are rigid, mechanical, and uniform. One can hardly speak of individual lines there. Instead, the texture is one of unbroken homophony, a series of staccato chords separated by rests. The chords are organized into eleven statements of a single rhythmic pattern (see Example 3.11). The notated meter of the ostinati is $\frac{2}{4}$, but the actual rhythms describe an unambiguous $\frac{3}{4}$. The repeated pattern consists of three statements of ♪ ⅞ 𝄾 𝄾, marked x on the example, followed by a single statement of ⅞ ♪ ♪ ⅞ 𝄾, marked y on the example. Each pattern thus describes four measures of $\frac{3}{4}$.

Apart from slight variants in the fourth, tenth, and eleventh statements, and an elongation in the eighth statement, the rhythmic organization is invariant throughout the song, the kind of rigid patterning that, as we have seen, defines one extreme of Crawford's musical style. This repeated rhythmic pattern is what earns this group of instruments the title "ostinati." The concertanti parts, in contrast, are free of any explicit rhythmic schemes. Furthermore, the beginnings and endings of statements in the ostinati usually do not coincide with points of articulation in the concertanti parts. Rhythmically, then, the opposed instrumental groups are thus both distinct in character and entirely independent of each other.

The ostinati draw from a repertoire of twelve different chords (labeled one through twelve beneath the staves in Example 3.11). These chords, particularly the first one, are frequently repeated and irregularly distributed with relation to the recurring rhythmic pattern. Chords are frequently repeated across the boundary between the rhythmic statements, and change within the statements. The first, third, and ninth statements consist exclusively of iterations of the first chord, while the remaining statements contain at least two different chords. The eighth statement, which is rhythmically elongated, contains the most different chords, and the most rapid chord changes. Measures 51–52 are thus striking both harmonically and rhythmically, but, for the most part, the rhythm and harmony are organized independently. Just as there is a larger heterophony between the two instrumental groups, there is thus a dimensional heterophony within the ostinati.

Now, let us examine the chords themselves (see Example 3.12, where the chords are given in their order of occurrence in the song, with immediate repetitions omitted). Each of the five string parts (violin, viola, cello 1, cello 2,

Example 3.11   Rhythmic organization of the ostinato parts in "Rat Riddles"

and bass) is doubled at the unison (or, in the case of the bass, at the octave) by one of the five woodwind or brass parts (trumpet, clarinet, horn, trombone, and bassoon). The five lines cross in only one instance (in measure 28, cello 1 is above viola) and that crossing is rectified when the same chord returns in measure 82. There is no duplication or doubling between the parts and, as a result, each chord has five different notes.

Example 3.12   Harmonic organization of the ostinato parts in "Rat Riddles"

The intervallic make-up of the chords varies considerably. Chords 1, 2, and 5 are all five-note linear segments of the chromatic scale, but there is no other repetition or equivalence. The twelve different chords represent ten different chord types.[7] We thus find ourselves in a situation familiar in Crawford's music, amid a musical surface of strikingly varied content. The coherence of the progression cannot be based on repetition of chords or chord types, but must be sought elsewhere, in the transformations that take the music from chord to chord.

Each line moves conjunctly for the most part, using the smaller pitch intervals. In the bass part, for example, out of twenty-one linear intervals, thirteen are ascending or descending semitones, and the others are a tritone or less. There is nothing consistent or systematic about these linear intervals, but they do create a sense of smooth linkage from chord to chord.

A deeper linkage is created by the transpositions and near-transpositions that connect the chords. Chords 1, 2, and 5 are of the same type, so motion among them is by actual transposition. More commonly, the chords are connected by near-transposition (see Example 3.13, which looks more closely at the climactic passage between measures 40 and 53). With a few gaps, adjacent chords are connected by near-transpositions, which can be grouped into larger patterns. The overall path from Chord 1 back to Chord 1, shown as T_0, thus runs through a series of inexact transpositional moves. In this case, uncharacteristically for Crawford, the intervals of transposition do not bear any obvious relationship to the intervals of the chord being transposed.

Example 3.13   Harmonic progression in the ostinato parts in "Rat Riddles," mm. 40–53

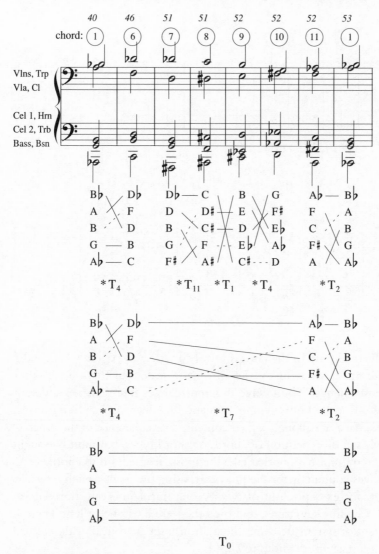

Because of the independence of its constituent parts, it is difficult to discuss the form of the song as a whole. Rather, one must discuss its *forms*, including the twenty-two segments and three large sections in the voice part and the eleven repetitions of the ostinato. The song resists any single interpretation. There is no single place from which to view the whole, no way, in fact, to perceive a whole at all in the face of the irresolvable contrasts among the parts.

As in other works by Crawford, the basic duality here pits one group that is flexible and free against another that is rigid and constrained. There is a temptation to see in this a metaphor for the unreconciled dualities of the poetic text, its mocking, colloquial tone and the gravity of its central section, its juxtaposition of rat and man. The concertanti parts seem to scamper about freely, but their freedom is only possible because they remain ignorant of the ineluctable heavy tread of the ostinati, which plod along indifferently. The ostinati suggest our inevitable destiny, one we share with rats and all living things. We may scamper about and feel ourselves free, but we must be always dimly aware of what awaits us.

"Prayers of Steel" from Three Sandburg Songs

The second of the Three Songs is "Prayers of Steel," a setting of Carl Sandburg's poem with that title:

> Lay me on an anvil, O God.
> Beat me and hammer me into a crowbar.
> Let me pry loose old walls.
> Let me lift and loosen old foundations.
>
> Lay me on an anvil, O God.
> Beat me and hammer me into a steel spike.
> Drive me into the girders that hold a skyscraper together.
> Take red-hot rivets and fasten me into the central girders.
> Let me be the great nail holding a skyscraper through
> blue nights into white stars.[8]

The two stanzas are roughly parallel in construction. In the first, the narrator wants to be transformed into a crowbar that demolishes an old building and, in the second, to be a steel spike holding together the new skyscraper that takes its place. As a celebration of violent change, and of new structures erected on the rubble of the old, the poem welcomes a setting in Crawford's dissonant, ultramodern style.

As in "Rat Riddles," the instrumental forces in "Prayers of Steel" are divided into two groups, the ostinati (strings, winds, and brass) and the concertanti (consisting of an alto voice in a heterophonic trio with piano and oboe, their melodies punctuated by percussion). Crawford's setting is in two virtually identical large sections, each of which sets the entire poem.

The vocal line is declamatory in style, and, while it is the only melodic line in the song that is free of precompositional schemes in both its pitch and its rhythm, it has less of the breadth and extended spinning-out of Crawford's other free melodies. Indeed, much of the vocal line is a kind of recitation, with many syllables of the text intoned on single notes. G$\sharp$4 in particular is used in this way (see Example 3.14). As Seeger describes the melody, "tonally, it is centered rigidly upon G sharp."[9]

The sense of fixity and focus created by the restricted range and frequent repetition of individual notes is reinforced by intensive motivic concentration.

Example 3.14   Vocal melody in "Prayers of Steel"

Example 3.15   Analytical reductions of the vocal melody in "Prayers of Steel": A) pitches listed in order; B) large gestures involving symmetrical expansions and contractions; C) large-scale projections of Motive M1

Occurrences of Motive M1 are indicated with brackets below the staves. Many of these are concatenated into RI–chains, and most of the notes of the melody participate in at least one form. Two additional RI–chains, involving motives other than M1, are indicated with brackets above the staves. As in other melodies by Crawford, a generative process remains the same even as the intervallic content changes. This permits Crawford a nice opportunity for expression of the text, particularly with the first of these non-M1 RI–chains, beginning at the end of measure 6. When the second stanza of the poem begins, the narrator still wants to be forged into a piece of steel, but now into a steel spike to be used in construction instead of a crowbar to be used in demolition. Crawford creates a musical analogue by picking up the G4 that completed the previous RI–chain and using it to initiate a new RI–chain, one with a different intervallic content.

The frequent M1s and RI–chains of the surface help to organize the melody into a series of large, interlocked gestures (see Example 3.15). The pitches of the melody, which gradually rises to its highest point just before its final return to the music of the opening, are listed in Example 3.15A. Example 3.15B groups them into four gestures, each of which involves expansion from a registrally central form of Motive M1 outward to the local registral boundaries, usually ip11 apart.

The first gesture, spanning the entire first stanza of text, begins with a form of Motive M1, G♯–A–G, expands symmetrically outward to the registral high and low points, C5 and E♭4, then contracts back to its starting point, as the section ends. The second gesture begins with a restatement of the same M1, expands symmetrically to Crawford's familiar boundary interval of ip11, D4–C♯5, then again contracts to M1, but with its pitches now reordered. This reordered M1 is followed by its transposed retrograde inversion, and the two motives together form the center for a third registral expansion to ip11, E4–D♯5. Finally, a new form of M1, beginning on D5, forms the center for a nearly symmetrical expansion to a final ip11, the last note of which is decorated by a last statement of M1, with the same pitches as the first, but reordered. The surface forms of M1 thus help shape the larger gestures, either by establishing a midpoint that lies symmetrically between registral boundaries, or by elaborating one of the boundaries.

The melody also projects large, contour-defined statements of Motive M1 (see Example 3.15C). The stemmed notes occur as either local or long-range contour turning points, either high points (stems up) or low points (stems down). These may be thought of as phrase-neumes, projecting the prevalent M1s of the surface over large melodic spans. While the vocal melody is more restricted in range, more chant-like than many of Crawford's melodies, then, it is nonetheless typical in many respects, particularly in its focus on Motive M1, its use of RI–chains and inversional pivoting, and its projection of its motives over large spans.

As in "Chinaman, Laundryman," the free declamatory vocal melody in "Prayers of Steel" is heard in heterophonic counterpoint against a strict, serial melody, and the radically contrasting character of the melodies conceals a subtle motivic correspondence between them. In "Chinaman, Laundryman," the duality had an obvious dramatic significance, contrasting the yearnings of the narrator with the oppressive world in which he is trapped. In "Prayers of Steel," the same duality has a similar dramatic meaning, again placing a human narrator within a mechanistic setting, in this case the skyscraper. What is different is the relationship between the narrator and the world in which he finds himself. In "Chinaman, Laundryman," the relationship was one of antagonism; in "Prayers of Steel" it is one of attraction and longing. This difference is reflected musically, as we shall see.

The serial melody in "Prayers of Steel" is in the oboe part, and is based on a seven-note series, designed to feature overlapping statements, a small RI-chain, of Motive M1 (see Example 3.16A). The remaining notes of the series can also be understood as an RI-chain, something that is seen most easily when the series is rotated to start on D♯ (see Example 3.16B).

Example 3.16   Seven-note series in the oboe part in "Prayers of Steel": A) an RI-chain involving Motive M1; B) two RI-chains

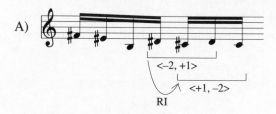

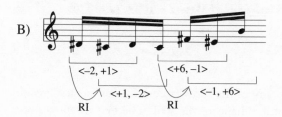

Example 3.17   First set of rotations in the oboe part in "Prayers of Steel," mm. 1–2

The oboe part as a whole consists entirely of Crawford's customary rotations and transpositions. In the first two measures of the piece, the series is stated, then systematically rotated to begin on its second, third, fourth, and fifth notes (see Example 3.17). The first note of each statement is emphasized with an accent,

151

and these accented notes are identified with stems beneath the staff to show the projection of the series at this higher level.

In other serial works by Crawford, the series is rotated exhaustively – there are as many rotations as there are notes in the series. Here, in "Prayers of Steel," there appear to be two reasons for truncating the rotations. The first has to do with the statement of Motive M1, C♯–D–C, that ends the series (marked with brackets). These notes present the same intervallic ordering, <+1, –2> as the opening vocal statement, G♯–A–G, and are thus marked for special attention. As the series is rotated, that final trichord gradually moves toward the beginning, and initiates the last rotation in the group. It is the only trichord that retains its original ordering throughout the rotations. Its progress from the last position to the first articulates the phrase and brings the rotations to an end.

A second reason involves the metrical organization of the passage, an organization that is retained in each of the sections of the work. In the two serial melodies discussed previously, *Diaphonic Suite No. 1*, third movement, and "Chinaman, Laundryman," the series fit exactly within the prevailing metrical unit. In the oboe melody of "Prayers of Steel," however, the seven-note series does not fit evenly among the regular groups of four sixteenth notes. As a result, the series moves immediately out of rhythmic alignment, and then slowly realigns itself (see Example 3.18).

Example 3.18   Metrical organization of the first set of rotations in the oboe part in "Prayers of Steel," mm. 1–2

The accented notes can fall on any of the four sixteenth notes in each group, and their actual placement is indicated beneath the staff. The first accented note falls on the first of a group of four sixteenth notes. The accented notes then jump ahead to the fourth of a group, falling back gradually until the last accented note is once again on a first beat. Once the alignment has been reestablished, the rotations cease. The durational intervals that separate the accented notes can also be calculated. The accented notes move ahead three places, then fall back one place at a time.

In other words, the serial rotation is matched by a metrical rotation. Just as the notes of the series change their position in the pitch-class ordering, moving back one place upon each statement, they also change their position in the metrical ordering, again moving back one place upon each statement. There is thus an interesting, if not particularly complex, coordination of pitch structure and rhythmic structure in this melody.

As we saw in our discussion of rhythmic neumes, Crawford was interested in finding correspondences between pitch and rhythm, of projecting the same musical idea simultaneously in both dimensions. In "Prayers of Steel," she has found a somewhat different way of acheiving this, one that involves not contours of rhythms but series of time points. She has understood that just as a note can be located in a modular pitch-class space (as, say, an F♯, or a C), it can similarly be located in a modular metrical space (as, say, on beat 1 or beat 3). This is an analogy she pursues with greater intensity in the String Quartet and the Suite for Wind Quintet, and, in so doing, she significantly anticipates the concerns and procedures of the post-war serialists.[10]

Over the course of the song, the series is heard at six levels of transposition reflecting, in order, the first six notes of the series itself. Each transposed series is heard in five rotations, except for the last, which displays the full set of seven rotations.[11] As a result, the series is projected at three levels of structure: from sixteenth note to sixteenth note, from accented note to accented note, and from section to section.

While the pitch-class succession is highly constrained by the transpositional-rotational scheme and by the invariant metrical layout of each rotational unit, the melody's motions in pitch space, its actual registers, are considerably freer. In the first statement of the series, the notes occur as close together as possible, within the span of seven semitones, and lie virtually at the bottom of the oboe's range. Over the course of the piece, the melody expands registrally. Later series statements tend to occupy larger registral spans, and to include pitches from all parts of the oboe's range. Occasionally, Crawford takes advantage of these widely-ranging motions to project additional forms of the crucial Motive M1 in register, but more often, she seems interested simply in gradually increasing the level of activity without concern for the intervallic consequences.

The relationship between the free vocal melody and the serialized oboe melody is unusually close, despite their obvious differences of character. Indeed, for much of its length, the vocal melody can be understood entirely in terms of motives drawn from the series (see Example 3.19). The series can be thought of as in Example 3.19A, as an RI–chain of M1, preceded by its MULT, <+4, –2>. The characteristic section of the vocal melody in Example 3.19B can be understood in virtually the same way, as an RI–chain of M1, flanked by two isolated occurrences of M1, and preceded by its MULT, <+4, –2>. The narrator's vocal melody is thus embedded within the series just as the narrator seeks to be embedded within the skyscraper.

The character of the piano melody, played in four octaves at once, is similar to that of the oboe. It rattles along in uniform rhythmic values, and has the constrained, mechanistic quality of the oboe part. In its clattering and banging, it is clearly designed to evoke the sounds of a construction site. Although it is not serialized in any consistent way, it does show some of the same deliberate precompositional planning of Crawford's serial melodies.

Example 3.19   Affinities between the oboe series and the vocal melody: A) motivic organization of the series; B) same motives embedded in the vocal melody, mm. 3–4

A)

B)

Example 3.20   Piano melody in "Prayers of Steel," mm. 1–4

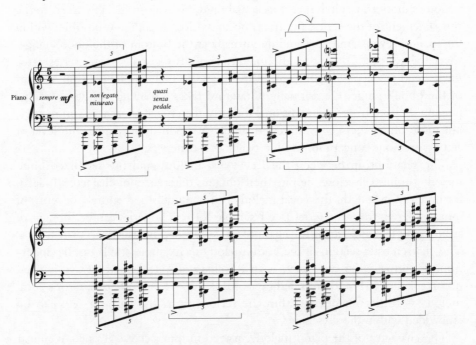

The first four measures of the piano melody are given in Example 3.20, and the rhythmic organization of these measures remains consistent throughout the entire song. Within each measure, the piano plays ten notes, in two groups of eighth-note quintuplets. Two measures in which the quintuplets are separated by a rest alternate with two more in which they are preceded by a rest.

The notes in measures 3–4, and others in the song with the same rhythm, give a hint of the rotational schemes that occupy Crawford's serial melodies. Measures 4 and 8 rotate measures 3 and 7, respectively, while measure 12 rotates measure 11 in a somewhat freer way. These three small rotational schemes, however, are independent of each other – no single series is involved in all of them – and the remaining notes of the melody show no similar plan.

There are internal repetitions and redundancies, however, that give the piano melody some of the same constrained, repetitive intervallic profile of Crawford's serial melodies. Brackets above the staves identify the numerous occurrences of Motive M1 in the melody, many of which are organized into the familiar overlapping RI-chains.

Larger groups of notes also recur. If we imagine the first five notes of the melody as a kind of basic melodic unit, a five-note neume, the melody as a whole contains numerous statements of it, occurring within almost every measure. It occurs five times in the first four measures, identified with brackets below the staves, and the last two are rotated retrogrades of the first one. The others in these measures and elsewhere in the piece are the unordered transpositions or inversions of the first, and of each other.[12] Other pentachords also recur throughout the melody, particularly those containing three or four semitones, again imparting a sense of tight intervallic focus. The piano melody is not strictly serialized but, in Crawford's dichotomy of mechanized and free, it certainly belongs, at least in spirit, in the first camp.

The accompaniment as a whole is organized into inflexible four-measure groups. Each instrumental part has its own individual rhythmic pattern, which shifts in relation to the others. Only at the beginning of each four-measure group are all the parts in alignment (see Example 3.21).[13] The bass drum and cymbal divide the twenty beats into five groups of four, in contrast to the notated meter, which divides them into four groups of five. Among the smaller rhythmic values, the piano and oboe create a similar conflict of quintuple and quadruple divisions.

The pattern shown in Example 3.21 is heard in its entirety three times in the first half of the song and three times in the second half. Both halves end with a statement of the first measure of the pattern and a full measure of rest. After its initial four-measure phrase, the vocal part ceases to observe the groupings in the other parts. Instead, it breaks free, spiralling off both registrally and rhythmically, cutting across the rigid groupings in the accompaniment.

Indeed, the vocal part, as we have seen, does not participate in any rigidly predetermined scheme, of either pitch or rhythm. Compared to the other parts, it is relatively free. Nonetheless, there are important points of contact between the vocal part and the accompaniment. First, there is an affinity of character. Despite the relatively free organization of the vocal line, it has a controlled, constrained feeling, due in large measure to the frequent returns to, and extended intonations of, G♯4. The accompanying parts are rigid, mechanical, unyielding, and the vocal part seems to aspire to the same condition. Second, the voice part, as we

Example 3.21   Rhythmic organization of the concertanti parts in "Prayers of Steel" have seen, is constructed almost entirely from statements of M1 and other shapes embedded in the serialized oboe part and the partly mechanized piano part. Finally, the vocal part joins the others in creating twelve-note aggregates, which function as basic harmonic units in this song. Consider, for example, the first two measures of the song (see Example 3.22). The seven-note series in the oboe excludes five notes. Four of those excluded notes, G–G♯–A–B♭, are the entire pitch-class content of the vocal part. The remaining note, E, is the first note in the piano part. The piano part, in turn, contains eleven pitch classes, excluding only G♯, which is, of course, the featured note in the vocal part. These relationships, of exclusion and completion, link the disparate lines of the texture.

Example 3.22   Concertanti parts in "Prayers of Steel," mm. 1–2

There is unquestionably a narrative significance to these links between the vocal and the other melodies. Just as the narrator of the poem seeks to be embedded within the skyscraper, the steel spike that sustains the structure, the vocal line is embedded within the accompaniment that swirls around it, drawing its essential structural material, particularly Motive M1, from the other parts.

The concertanti parts (voice, piano, oboe, percussion) simply repeat in the second half of the song the music, and the text, from the first half. The ostinati, however, are through-composed. As in the ostinati from "Rat Riddles," the strings punctuate the texture with sharp chords, consisting in this case of single notes doubled at the unison and octave. The chords are widely separated by rests. The winds are more active, doubling each of the string notes, then going on to interpolate additional notes of their own, in the manner of melismas elaborating single tones of a chant.

The strings describe a much slower, and vastly augmented, version of the oboe part, beginning with the seven-note series transposed at T_8, then continuing with an incomplete set of rotations.[14] The ostinato strings thus require the entire song to do once what the oboe does every two measures.

Example 3.23   Rhythms and pitches of the ostinato parts in "Prayers of Steel," mm. 1–8

The first eight measures of music in the ostinati are shown in Example 3.23.[15] In this passage, the strings, doubled by the winds, state the seven-note series, and begin the first rotation of it. The winds interpolate additional notes, and create melodic fragments of 1–2–2–3–3–4–5–6 notes in length. As the music continues beyond the example, that grouping pattern is repeated once more, and then stated twice in retrograde. In its interest in large-scale retrograde symmetry, this melody thus belongs to a family of similar melodies, including the *Piano Study in Mixed Accents, Diaphonic Suite No. 4* (first movement), and the String Quartet (fourth movement). The four statements of this rigid grouping pattern in the winds are not aligned, however, with the serial rotations in the strings. In the song as a whole, there are five series statements in the strings, but only four rhythmic grouping patterns in the winds, replicating at this highest level the four-versus-five rhythmic conflicts within the concertanti parts. As a result, string and wind patterns begin together, but are not aligned thereafter. Furthermore, neither pattern is fully aligned with patterns and periodicities in the concertanti parts. Thus, as we have seen, it becomes impossible to describe *the* form of the piece. Instead, we must describe the patterning within each part, suggest some ways in which the patterns interact, and leave it at that.

The piece is thus heterophonic in many ways, both within the ostinati and concertanti and, more dramatically, between them. Nonetheless, there are significant similarities among the heterogenous parts, more in this song, perhaps, than in most of Crawford's works. Like a family gathering where everyone is talking at the same time, no single, unified discourse emerges, but one is nonetheless aware of the resemblances among the speakers.

String Quartet, third movement

The String Quartet is Crawford's greatest and most important work, her most frequently performed, recorded, anthologized, and analyzed.[16] Each of the movements is distinctively and compellingly constructed. The third movement in particular is remarkable in evoking masses of sound moving through space, colliding, expanding, breaking apart. In their slow ascent to their high point, and the much more rapid descent that follows, the instruments play continuous sustained notes, and the harmony changes one note at a time. The harmonies generally occur in a register common to all four instruments and often form dense chromatic clusters within small registral spans, as the instruments intertwine. The sustained chords are animated by independent patterns of crescendo and diminuendo in each of the instruments, lending them a surface shimmer.

In the representative passage in Example 3.24, the instruments intertwine in close proximity, frequently crossing over each other. The sound mass the instruments jointly describe gets higher and louder until measure 43, then begins to get lower and softer. Amid this larger motion, the sustained notes in each instrument are animated by alternations of crescendo and decrescendo, with each instrument reaching its dynamic high point on a different beat from the others. The overall effect is similar to that of music by Varèse, and anticipates in striking ways Ligeti's sound-mass pieces from thirty years later, in which a densely packed sonority expands, contracts, and moves through the musical space.

Example 3.24   String Quartet, third movement, mm. 37–48

The harmony changes one note at a time, and that series of new notes comprises what Crawford imagined as the basic melodic line of the movement: "As for melodic line – as in the second movement, it travels from instrument to instrument; there is only one line."[17] In her own copy of the score, Crawford circled all of the new notes and connected them with lines to emphasize their integral linearity. In the published score, each new note enters with a distinctive *tenuto* marking that distinguishes it from the prevailing chorale texture. The four instruments take turns, although not in any systematic way, introducing new notes.

The melody is thus a kind of *Klangfarbenmelodie*, its instrumental coloring constantly changing. Once a note is introduced, it is sustained until it is that instrument's turn to state another one. The harmonies are thus produced as the lingering after-effects of the sustained melodic tones.[18] The harmonies are not merely verticalized segments of the melody, however, since the instruments do not enter or exit in any regular order. In the passage in Example 3.24, for example, the viola contributes only one new note, the E in measure 39, while the others provide two or three. The harmony sustained at the end of such a passage will combine notes that are not adjacent within the melody. The harmony is thus derived from the melody, but not in a predictable or systematic way.

It is ironic that the main melody, which gives rise in this movement to such striking harmonic effects, should be so entirely characteristic of Crawford's customary melodic practice (see Example 3.25).[19] The melody is in two large sections, the first (measures 1–76) generally ascending in slow arches, and the second (measures 77–99) rapidly descending to its starting point.

The melody begins with a gradual ascent to a plateau around D4 in measures 19–25, the point where the first violin enters and where all four instruments play together for the first time. A second ascent leads to D♯5 in measure 43, and is followed by an increasingly fragmented approach to the climax in measures 72–74, which contain both the highest (E6) and lowest notes heard so far. The melody ceases in measures 75–76, which are truly harmonic in conception, then resumes in measure 77, rapidly descending to its starting point (C♯3), and beyond, to its conclusion on C2. In its winding motions, the melody thus establishes nodal or boundary points that are separated from each other by thirteen semitones: C2–C♯3–D4–D♯5–E6–F7. This division of the musical space is familiar from other works by Crawford, and its significance in this movement will be explored later.

The intervallic structure of the melody is also typical of Crawford in its general avoidance of pitch or pitch-class repetition, its creation of chromatic zones in both pitch and pitch-class space, and its varied surface. As usual, there is some degree of internal motivic repetition, particularly with reference to the ubiquitous Motive M1, indicated with brackets in Example 3.25.

Like Crawford's other melodies, its movements can be described as gaps created and filled, inversional centers asserted, and pivotings where the fulcrum is constantly changing. The opening section of the melody, for example, twists and turns in familiar ways (see Example 3.26). It begins by ASSERTing C♯2, one of the registral nodes, then ADJOINing notes a semitone above and below it to create Motive M1, <+1, –2>.[20] An ascent follows in which notes leap-frog over each other, creating small chromatic zones as they do so. At the top of the ascent, two additional forms of M1 are created via RICH. Virtually the entire melody,

Example 3.25   Main melody shared among the four instruments in String Quartet, third movement

Example 3.26   Melodic transformations and pivotings in the opening section of the main
melody in String Quartet, third movement, mm. 1–20

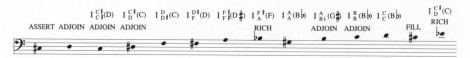

Example 3.27   Neumatic transformations in the concluding section of the main melody in
String Quartet, third movement, mm. 77–end

including those places near its high point where it leaps widely, can be described
in similar fashion.

As in Crawford's other melodies, this one also coheres through a process of
neumatic transformation, often involving intervallic expansions or multiplica-
tions, and even more often involving simple preservation of contour. The rapid
melodic descent from measure 77, for example, begins by using only the smallest
intervals, but concludes with wide leaps. A single contour-neume, however,
persists throughout (see Example 3.27). The first four notes form what Seeger
would call a ternary line-twist neume, or <–, –, +>. This basic shape, and its
inversion <+, +, –>, retrograde <–, +, +>, and retrograde inversion <+, –, –>,
permeate the melody, and are identified with brackets on the example. All of the
bracketed segments belong to either of two CSEG classes, the one that contains
the first four notes, <3201>, or the one that contains the second four notes,
<1320>. Some of the contour relations are reinforced by intervallic relations, but
this becomes less and less true as the melody progresses and the intervals get far
larger. The contour relations do persist, however, and create a sense of coherence
even as the intervals change.[21] Through familiar melodic and neumatic transformations, then, the melody is made coherent, although it is far from uniform.

The rhythmic organization of the melody is not systematic, although there are
hints of intriguing structural possibilities. Crawford makes frequent use, for
example, of a certain pattern of durations and its inversion or retrograde inversion (see Example 3.28). The four-note segment in measures 1–8, for example,
begins with its second shortest duration, then continues with its longest, its
second longest, and finally its shortest. A durational pattern of that kind can be
expressed as <1320>, where 0 represents the shortest duration, 1 the second
shortest, 2 the second longest, and 3 the longest. That durational CSEG, its
inversion, <2013>, and its retrograde inversion, <3102>, occur frequently in the
melody and take in both the first four notes of the melody and the last four.

Example 3.28   Seven statements of the duration–neume <1320> or its TTOs in the main
melody of String Quartet, third movement

Example 3.29   Coincidence of duration and pitch contours in the main melody of String
Quartet, third movement, mm. 39–46

Those duration-contours have an independent motivic life in the piece, uncoordinated with the pitch structure. There are, however, isolated points in the piece where the duration contours and the pitch contours are precisely the same (see Example 3.29). In the brief melodic fragment at measure 39, the pitches and durations track each other precisely. This is not a consistent procedure in this movement, however, and suggests the tentative and experimental nature of Crawford's efforts to integrate pitch and rhythmic structure.

The melody, as we have observed, is shared among the four instruments. In the first half of the melody, leading to the climax in measures 72–76, there is no consistent pattern in the instrumentation. After the opening measures, adjacent tones in the melody are virtually never played by a single instrument. Conversely, a single instrument may sustain its note while as many as seven new melody notes are played by the other three instruments. Within those limits, the instruments seem to enter and sustain virtually at random.

In the concluding section of the melody (m. 77 to the end), however, the instrumentation is almost entirely systematic (see Example 3.30). For the first thirty notes of the section, only the upper three instruments participate, and the melody moves down ten times in a row from first violin to second violin to viola. When the cello joins in, there is a momentary suspension of the pattern, which then returns for the last four notes of the melody, played in order by the first violin, second violin, viola, and cello. The instrumental patterning tends to group the melody into segments that are three notes long, with the beginning of each segment marked by the return of the first violin. This generally cuts against the intervallic structure of the melody with the four-note segments described above. This is another example of Crawford's dimensional heterophony: both the melody and the instrumentation are structured, but independently.

Example 3.30   Patterns of instrumentation in the concluding section of the main melody of String Quartet, third movement, mm. 77–end

3 = 1st violin   2 = 2nd violin   1 = viola   0 = cello

The main melody creates, and moves within, several different kinds of musical spaces. It moves among the four instruments and leaves in its wake four timbrally distinct instrumental lines. It moves among the four registral positions – soprano, alto, tenor, and bass – and leaves in its wake four distinct registral lines. Finally, it moves amid patterns of rising and falling dynamics, and leaves in its wake a new melody, consisting of notes at dynamic high points. Let us examine each of these musical spaces in turn.

In both the instrumentally free first section and the highly patterned second section, each instrument plays some of the main melody notes, and thus projects a timbrally distinct melodic line. These melodic lines, unfolding within each instrument, are structured to some degree independently of the principal melody, which is their source. Consider, for example, the notes played by the cello in the first half of the movement (see Example 3.31). Each of the beamed segments, comprising virtually the entire cello melody, describes a form of set class (025),

164

Example 3.31   Motivic organization of the cello melody in String Quartet, third movement, mm. 1–74

Example 3.32   Motivic organization of the highest registral line in String Quartet, third movement, mm. 1–32

one that is virtually absent from the main melody. The last four (025)s are organized into two RI-pairs, the first overlapping <+3, +2> with <+2, +3>, and the second overlapping <–2, –7> with <–7, –2>. Both of these RI-pairs begin on G♯. The cello part thus has some degree of internal coherence, and of autonomy from the main melody. The same is true of the other instrumental parts.

The instruments intertwine with each other, and each spends some time at the bottom, middle, and top of the texture.[22] Together, they project a reasonably consistent four-part texture, from which one can extract distinct registral lines: a soprano, alto, tenor, and bass. These registral lines, like the instrumental lines, show a surprising degree of internal coherence and independence. Example 3.32 shows the registral soprano, the highest sounding notes, in measures 1–32 (the main melody itself is also given for the sake of comparison). The two lines coincide to some extent, but they diverge whenever the main melody descends, leaving some previously stated note sounding at the top of the texture. In the opening measures, for example, when the main melody dips down to C3, C♯3 is left sounding above it as the registral soprano. As a result, a form of Motive M1 is created in the soprano that did not exist in the main melody. This is followed, in both the main melody and the soprano, by an RI-chain, overlapping <+1, +3> with <+3, +1>. The same RI-chain is then heard again, but only in the soprano, not in the main melody. The soprano thus shows, at least in these measures, a high degree of internal structure. The same is true, in varying degrees, of the rest of the soprano, and of the other registral lines as well. The main melody thus

Example 3.33   Patterns of dynamic high points in relation to the four instruments (0=cello, 1=viola, 2=violin 2, 3=violin 1) in String Quartet, third movement, mm. 19–52

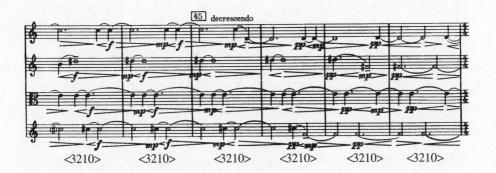

creates, and moves through, two four-part counterpoints, one defined by the four instruments, and one defined by the four registral parts.

The main melody also moves through another musical space, defined by the dynamics. Indeed, a "heterophony of dynamics" is, for Crawford, the central defining idea of the movement:

> The underlying plan is heterophony of dynamics – a sort of counterpoint of crescendi and diminuendi. The crescendo and diminuendo in each instrument occurs in definite rhythmic patterns, which change from time to time as the movement proceeds. The crescendos are intended to be precisely timed; the high point is indicated to occur at some specific beat of the measure . . . No high point in the crescendo in any one instrument coincides with the high point in any other instrument.[23]

The pattern of crescendi from measure 19, where all four instruments begin to play together, through measure 52, where the instruments begin their final ascent to the climax of the movement, is shown in Example 3.33. In measures 19–23, the viola reaches its loudest point on the first beat, violin 2 on the second beat, cello on the third beat and violin 1 on the fourth beat. We can describe that particular "firing order" as <1203>, where 0=cello, 1=viola, 2=violin 2, and 3=violin 1. To describe it in that way will permit us to track changes in the firing order, and to compare patterns in this dimension with patterns in other dimensions, including pitch and duration contours.

After a brief transitional passage, measures 24–27, where, despite Crawford's claims to the contrary, cello and violin 2 crescendo on the same beat, a new pattern, <0123>, establishes itself in measure 28, and requires two measures to complete.[24] That in turn inverts in measure 35 to <3210>, which expands temporally in measure 39 to fill a 5/4 measure. That pattern is metrically displaced in measure 43, to begin on the last beat of each measure, and then gives way in measure 49 to <0312>, the retrograde inversion of the opening pattern. These patterns, their transformation through the familiar TTOs, and their rhythmic contractions and expansions, create an independent dimension of musical structure that interacts in interesting ways with other musical dimensions.

The dynamics act, above all, to create a new melody, formed by the notes found at each successive dynamic high point (see Example 3.34).[25] This melody of dynamic high points is shown for measures 34–43 in relation to the main melody. Since each new note in the main melody occurs at the top of a crescendo in some instrument, it is thus represented at precisely that moment in the dynamic melody. The dynamic melody has many more notes, however, and is constantly recalling notes that the main melody has previously presented. In measures 37–38, it takes the straight chromatic descent B–A♯–A–G♯ from the main melody and reorders it in a motivic way, presenting three statements of Motive M1. In measures 40–43, the dynamic melody links tones that were not adjacent in the main melody, again with occasional motivic effects. By recalling the main melody's B from back in measure 33, the dynamic melody is able to present three RI-pairs involving Motive M1 (the low E, which does not participate in these motivic statements, is given in parentheses).

Occasionally, the dynamic melody creates shapes that are present also in other melodies or in the durations (see Example 3.35). The pitch contours of

Example 3.34   Melody formed by successive dynamic high points in String Quartet, third movement, mm. 34–43

Example 3.35   A single contour, <1320>, projected simultaneously in the pitches and durations of the main melody and the melody formed by the dynamic high points, in String Quartet, third movement, mm. 19–31

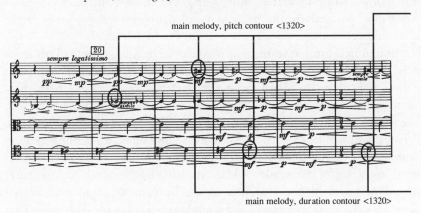

the main melody, beginning in measure 20, give two statements of <1320>. In the same passage, the durations of the same melody describe the same shape, as does the melody comprised of dynamic high points.

Musical structures can thus be shared among the many melodies: the main melody, the instrumental lines (violin 1, violin 2, viola, cello), the registral lines (soprano, alto, tenor, and bass), and the melody defined by dynamic high points. The same structures can also be projected in the durations of any of these melodies. The relevant musical spaces are so numerous, and the connections within them and between them are so complex, that no larger synthesis is possible. The complexities do not resolve to an underlying simplicity nor the diversity to unity. The music is multivalent, rewarding attentive listening from many directions.

Despite Crawford's emphasis on melody, reflected in the preceding discussion, the movement can also be understood, can perhaps be most easily understood, as a series of sustained harmonies, a kind of chorale, where the chords change one note at a time. The harmonies are enormously varied. The consistency and coherence of the progression depends not upon recurrence of the actual harmonies (or their transposed or inverted equivalents), but upon consistently applied transformations, particularly the by now familiar inversional pivotings at the local level, and coherent transpositional plans at the higher levels.[26]

Each chord differs from its immediate predecessor by a single note. That series of new notes is what I have been calling the main melody, so rather than focus on the immediate chord-to-chord succession, and thus largely duplicate the previous discussion, let us focus on the larger moves and the higher structural levels.

At the level of the single pitch, the dyad, the trichord, and the tetrachord, the music gradually moves from place to place, expanding outward, turning in upon itself, shifting and changing shape as it moves. Certain large gestures emerge as the music moves (see Example 3.36). At the highest level of structure, represented in Level A, the first half of the movement projects an initial C3–C♯3–D3–D♯3 up three octaves and a semitone to C♯6–D6–D♯6–E6. That greatly compounded semitone can be understood as a composing-out of the first melodic interval of the movement. In the second half, a slightly different type of tetrachord, [C♯, D♯, E, F], is transposed downward by T_8, although the transposition is not a literal pitch transposition as in the first half. Notice that the lowest notes of these two harmonies, C♯6 and C2, are related by compound semitone, just like the lowest notes of the two principal harmonies in the first half.

In Level B, these motions are partially filled in. In the first half, the principal harmony is transposed up an octave, then twice by T_4 and finally, breaking the pattern, by T_5. Following the initial octave, the larger T_1 is thus partitioned almost equally. In the second half, the larger descent of T_8 is divided into an octave descent, a pitch transposition down four semitones, and then another octave descent. In Level C, the initial move up T_4 is divided into two T_8s. A simultaneous move up four semitones each time is indicated in an upper voice. In the second half, the initial octave descent is equally divided into two descending tritones, the second of which is itself equally divided into two descending minor thirds.

The principal harmonic motions involve asserting a basic harmony, set class (0123) in the first half and set class (0124) in the second half, and projecting it through a series of transpositions, often involving the symmetrical division of the octave. It is worth emphasizing that there is no single motion that spans the movement as a whole. The basic harmonies and the paths they follow are different in the two halves. There is surely a sense of departure toward a climax and return to the starting point – the music concludes in the same register in which it began, and the viola's sustained C♯3 is heard at both points. Nonetheless, the movement resists any attempt to capture it in a single analytical gesture.

Let us dwell for a moment on the musical space within which these small motions and these larger gestures unfold – the principal nodal points that

Example 3.36   Large-scale harmonic organization of String Quartet, third movement articulate that space are shown at the beginning and end of each of the structural levels in Example 3.36. The first note of the piece is C♯3. In measure 19, the first violin enters on D4. This is the first, and virtually the only, doubled note in the movement. It concludes the reduced instrumentation of the opening section – from this point forward to the climax in measure 75, four voices will be the norm. After a brief plateau, the music begins to ascend. At the apex of a musical arch, D♯5 is attained in measure 43. The arch is one of dynamics as well as pitch – measure 43 is the climax of a long crescendo and is followed immediately by a decrescendo. The high point D♯5 is harmonized by set class (0123), as shown on the example. Notice that the harmony is bounded by D4 on the bottom and D♯5 on the top.

The music then recoils into the 4-octave, preparatory to a long and relatively uninterrupted ascent to the climax of the piece. In the climactic passage, measures 73–76, E6 is attained as the high point. In measure 76, it is harmonized as part of the chromatic tetrachord C♯6–D6–D♯6–E6. At this climactic moment, the tones are closely compressed; in the overall musical space, the same tones are spread out evenly, separated by pitch interval 13 instead of 1. In the climactic and loudest chord, on the downbeat of measure 75, the low point of the piece, C2, is stated together with the high point E6.

The descending final section of the piece moves through the same musical space, most obviously in the concluding measures of the movement. The movement ends, of course, with the dyad C2–C♯3. That dyad recalls the first note of the movement, and combines it with a note thirteen semitones lower. That low C2 was heard only once before, at the climax of the piece. Locally, the C2 may be understood as the result of the pitch inversion of D4 around C♯3. In that way, the boundary tones become an explicit part of the small-scale process of musical unfolding.

String Quartet, fourth movement

The fourth movement of the String Quartet pits two contrasting musical lines (one in the first violin, the other played in octaves by the other three instruments) against each other. The relationship between them is not the traditional hierarchical one of melody and accompaniment. They are not even coordinated with each other, as they might be in a traditional polyphonic setting. Instead, the two lines are designed to contrast maximally with each other, each responding to its own musical and dramatic imperatives. The result is like a vigorous dialogue in which the participants are somewhat better at expressing their own views than at listening to each other.

Both lines consist of distinct musical statements separated by rests (see Example 3.37). Voice 2 (second violin, viola, and cello) moves in steady streams of eighth notes, and its first statement contains twenty pitch attacks.[27] Its second statement is one pitch attack shorter, as is each successive statement until its

Example 3.37   Basic heterophony of two voices in String Quartet, fourth movement, mm. 1–18

twentieth, which consists of a single pitch attack. At that point, which Crawford calls the "turning point," the process reverses, adding a note with each statement until the original twenty are reattained. Indeed, the second half of the piece, in both voices and in virtually every musical dimension, is the precise retrograde of the first, further evidence of Crawford's longstanding interest in large-scale retrograde symmetry.

In pitch attacks per statement, Voice 1 (first violin) is the exact complement of Voice 2. The first statement in Voice 1 contains a single pitch attack, and (with a single slight anomaly) each successive statement contains one more than the previous, expanding to twenty-one notes in its twenty-first statement. At that turning point, the same place in both voices, the process reverses – each statement is one note shorter than the previous until the movement ends, as it began, with a single note.

The movement begins with two statements in Voice 1, and then the two voices alternate. As the statements in Voice 1 get longer, those in Voice 2 get shorter; one line waxes as the other wanes. This durational plan is reinforced by dynamics – as the statements in each voice get longer, they get softer, and as they get shorter, they get louder. Thus Voice 1 begins loud, gets progressively softer approaching the midpoint of the piece, then progressively louder during the second half, while Voice 2 does just the opposite. In Crawford's words:

> The two voices are written to be independent of each other dynamically. Voice 1 begins with its single tone fortissimo and, with the increase in number of tones in each entry, it decreases in dynamics to pianissimo at measure 55. Oppositely, Voice 2 begins its greatest number of tones at measure 3 with pianissimo, and increases in tone to fortissimo as the number of tones in each entry decrease. There is therefore a sort of dissonance within each voice between volume in dynamics and number of tones, and also a sort of dissonance between the two voices, in volume and number.[28]

This basic complementarity of durations and dynamics in Voices 1 and 2 is reinforced by the rhythmic distinctions between them. Where Voice 2 moves exclusively in regular streams of eighth notes (although grouped irregularly by slurs), Voice 1 uses eighth- and quarter-note triplets, quintuplets, sextuplets, dots, and ties, to produce an enormous range of rhythmic values and a resulting sense of "rhythmic fluidity."[29] Where Voice 2 is regimented and restricted, Voice 1 is florid and free. As we will see, this basic distinction in character applies in many musical domains.

The pitch classes of Voice 2 are derived from a single ten-note series (see Example 3.38). The series is a typical, if brief, Crawford melody. It turns in and jumps out, winding around and pivoting on itself as it creates and fills gaps. By the end, it creates a chromatic decachord – only B♭ and B are excluded. It is intervallically less varied than many of her melodies: it excludes 4s and 5s and contains only a single 6. It embeds Motive M1 once and the chromatic tetrachord (0123) three times.[30]

Example 3.38   Ten-note series in Voice 2 of String Quartet, fourth movement, mm. 3–4

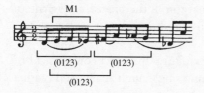

After its initial statement, the series is systematically rotated in what we have come to understand as Crawford's customary fashion. The second statement begins with the second note and ends with the first; the third statement begins with the third note and ends with the second; and so on. When the entire set of ten rotations is completed, the series is transposed up two semitones (starting on the second beat of measure 21), and a new set of rotations begins. When that new set of rotations is completed, the original untransposed series is stated once (beginning in measure 47). The sustained E♮ that follows is the second note of the series and thus initially suggests that a new set of rotations has begun. Instead, it simply marks the turning point of the movement.

Example 3.39   Identity of intervallic structure in A) large-scale transformations of the series and B) the first four notes of the series in String Quartet, fourth movement

$$\text{A)} \quad +2 \quad +1 \quad -2$$
$$< T_0, \quad T_2, \quad R(T_3), \quad R(T_1), >$$

$$\text{B)} \quad < D, \quad E, \quad F, \quad E\flat, >$$
$$+2 \quad +1 \quad -2$$

In the second half of the piece, the music of the first half is repeated, but in retrograde and transposed up one semitone, creating the overall plan shown in Example 3.39A.[31] As in all of Crawford's serial works, the transformations applied to the series reflect its internal structure. The big transpositional move in the first half is an ascending whole tone (from T_0 to T_2). That is answered in the second half, one semitone higher, by a descending whole tone (from $R(T_3)$ to $R(T_1)$). That overall transpositional progression, 0–2–3–1, recapitulates the first four notes of the series, D–E–F–E♭ (see Example 3.39B). The large-scale transpositional plan thus reflects the initial intervallic ordering of the series. Furthermore, the set of transpositional levels – 0, 1, 2, and 3 – creates the chromatic tetrachord-type found three times in the series (refer back to Example 3.38).

There are three levels of rhythmic patterning at work in Voice 2: the series statements (always ten notes in length); the phrases separated by rests (ranging in length from twenty-one eighth notes down to a single eighth note and back again); and the irregular slurs (articulating the constant eighth notes into groups of one, two, three, or four notes). Both the durational and rotational plans are quite regular, but they intersect with each other, and with the irregular slurs, in constantly shifting patterns (see Example 3.40). The periodicities are occasionally aligned, as at the beginning and end of the excerpt, but more commonly cut against each other. There is thus a kind of rhythmic heterophony within Voice 2.

Example 3.40   Rhythmic patterning in Voice 2 of String Quartet, fourth movement, mm. 20–41

That rhythmic heterophony creates additional pitch-class voices. Consider, for example, the melody that consists of the first note in each slurred group (see Example 3.41). It has the characteristics of a typical Crawford melody, including an RI-chain with three members. Furthermore, it embeds two segments, identified by the first two brackets, that are related by transposition to segments of the series. The first of these is the familiar chromatic tetrachord. It thus reveals a high degree of internal structure.

A second additional pitch-class voice is created by the first note of each series rotation. This melody is extracted in Example 3.42A, and some information

Example 3.41   Motivic organization of the melody formed by the first note in each slurred group, in String Quartet, fourth movement, mm. 20–24

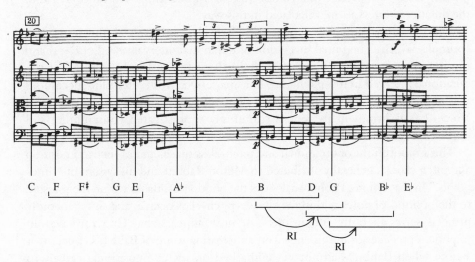

Example 3.42   Metrical organization of melody formed by the first note in each series rotation, in String Quartet, fourth movement, mm. 20–41

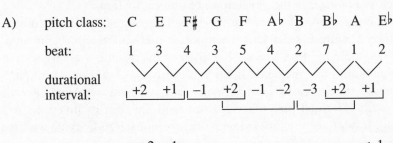

A)   pitch class: C   E   F♯   G   F   A♭   B   B♭   A   E♭

beat: 1   3   4   3   5   4   2   7   1   2

durational interval: +2   +1   −1   +2   −1   −2   −3   +2   +1

B)   series (T_0)   <+2, +1>   D   E   F   E♭   F♯   A   A♭   G   <−1, +2>   D♭   C   (D)

series R(T_0)   C   D♭   G   A♭   A   <−3, +2>   F♯   E♭   F   E   D   <+2, −1, −2>

177

about its metrical organization is also provided. After the initial C, the first note of the tenth rotation of the series at T_0, the pitch classes simply describe the series at T_2. This is an inevitable result of Crawford's rotational plan: the first notes of each successive rotation will spell out, over a large span, the series being rotated. What is not inevitable is the metrical placement of each of the pitch classes, or the remarkable metrical organization that results.

Each note of the line occurs on one of the eight beats of the measure. The C occurs on the first beat, the E on the third beat, the F♯ on the fourth beat, and so on. One can calculate the intervals between two beats, counted in eighth notes, just as one might calculate the interval between two notes, counted in semitones. From C to E we advance two eighth notes, from beat one to beat three, and from E to F♯ we advance one eighth note, from beat three to beat four. All of the durational intervals are calculated in this way.

The durational intervals reflect the pitch-class intervals of the series (see Example 3.42B). The initial succession of durational intervals, <+2, +1>, is also the initial succession of pitch-class intervals of the series. Indeed, all of the durational intervals in this pitch-class line are derived from intervallic successions within the series, as the example shows. The seemingly simple rotational plan of Voice 2 thus brings in its train a stunningly sophisticated contrapuntal and rhythmic organization.

This isomorphism of durational and pitch-class space, and of metrical position and pitch class, is generally attributed to Milton Babbitt and his system of "time-points." In that system, Babbitt analogizes the position of attacks within the measure to the position of notes within the twelve-pitch-class octave, and simultaneously projects series in both dimensions.[32] It now appears that Crawford was an important predecessor in this endeavor, anticipating some of Babbitt's concerns at a time when Babbitt had not yet embarked on his compositional career. In taking steps to ensure that the rhythmic/metric organization and the pitch-class organization of her music were shaped by similar musical concerns, Crawford may be seen as a pioneer in the serialization of musical rhythm.

The pitch organization of Voice 1 stands in radical contrast to that of Voice 2. Where Voice 2, with its strict serial rotations, is mechanical and regimented, Voice 1 is rhapsodic and free. Voice 1 has many of the qualities we have seen in others of Crawford's free melodies. It has a relatively equal distribution of pitch classes (although the aggregate is not pursued in any systematic way) and intervals (although with the usual preference for the semitone and its inversion and compounds). It twists its way forward with the inversional leap-frogging we have seen in other melodies and frequently employs RI-chains.

The overall shape of Voice 1 involves two large ascending waves, leading to a high point in the middle of the movement, and generally moving through larger and larger registral spaces as it rises. In the second half of the movement, the melody is heard in retrograde, transposed a semitone higher, and thus descends in two large waves, until it reattains its starting point.

While Voices 1 and 2 have distinct and, in some respects, complementary characters, they do share common intervallic concerns. Although Voice 1 contains many intervals not found in the series of Voice 2, particularly members of interval classes 4 and 5, there are long stretches of Voice 1 that can be understood in terms of segmental subsets of the series or its transformations. In the passage in Example 3.43, all of the bracketed segments, comprising virtually every note in Voice 1, represents a segment of the series (allowing for transposition, inversion, retrograde, and retrograde inversion). Needless to say, the same segments are heard again and again as the series is rotated in Voice 2, and they thus comprise a significant affinity between the voices.

Example 3.43   Segmental subsets of the series from Voice 2 (or their TT0s) embedded in Voice 1, in String Quartet, fourth movement, mm. 30–40

Aspects of the large-scale design of Voice 1 also show an affinity with the series. Example 3.44A shows its first six notes, its turning point, and its last six notes. The first three notes describe Crawford's ubiquitous Motive M1, which also occurs as a segmental subset of the series. The next three notes transpose the first three at T_2. At the end of the movement, these T_2-related M1s are heard in retrograde a semitone higher. The transpositional plan for the motive – T_0–T_2–$R(T_3)$–$R(T_1)$ – is thus identical to the transpositional plan of the series (see Example 3.39 above). A related design is formed by the first note, the turning point, and the last note. These three notes, A♭–G–A, recapitulate over a very large span the first three notes of the movement. The large progression in Voice 2 is virtually identical – its first note, turning point, and last note also compose-out Motive M1, creating a deep bond between the voices (see Example 3.44B).

Example 3.44   Large-scale organization in String Quartet, fourth movement: A) Voice 1; B) Voice 2

A)

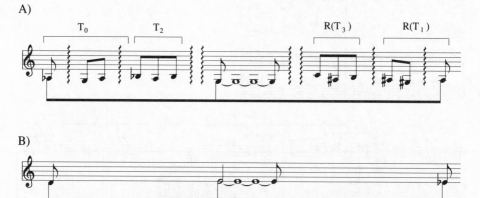

B)

Example 3.45   Projections of Motive M1 in Voice 1 of String Quartet, fourth movement, mm. 16–17 and 24–27

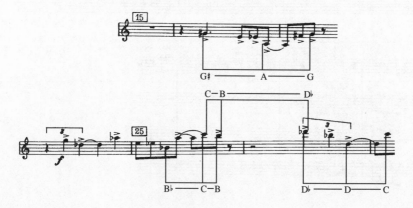

This same structural unit – first note, turning point, last note – also helps to shape some of the phrases and sub-phrases of Voice 1. Example 3.45 shows the sixth, ninth, and the beginning of the tenth phrases. In four cases, an initial tone, a contour turning point, and a terminal tone (also a contour turning point) are identified, and in all four cases a form of Motive M1 is spelled out. The first of these involves the same pitch classes as the large-scale statement discussed above (refer back to Example 3.44A) and the last three form an RI-chain. Motive M1, and others that occur frequently on the surface of both Voices 1 and 2, thus shape Voice 1 at the deeper levels as well.

Because of the high degree of melodic integrity of both Voices 1 and 2, typical of Crawford's heterophony, the contrapuntal relationship between the voices is difficult to specify. Two general principles can be adduced, although neither is pursued systematically or consistently. First, when the two voices are sounding together, they tend to form harmony types that occur also as segmental subsets of the series in Voice 2. In measures 19–21, where the voices begin for the first time to overlap by more than a single tone, the harmonies created, (012), (013), and (0135), are all found as segmental subsets of the series (see Example 3.46). At the turning point of the movement, the sustained E in Voice 2 similarly combines with the moving line in Voice 1 to create harmonies each of which is found three times in the series (see Example 3.47). The form of (012) spells out, in attack order, F–E– F♯, a form of Motive M1.

A second type of relationship between the two voices involves a sustained note in one voice acting as an inversional fulcrum for the notes in the other. This principle operates at the turning point, where the last two notes in Voice 1, C♯

Example 3.46 Similarity of harmonies formed between the voices and those found in the series in String Quartet, fourth movement: A) mm. 19–22; B) segmental subsets of the series

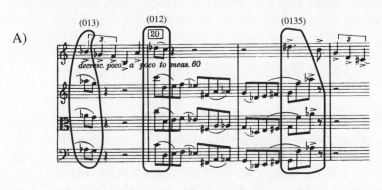

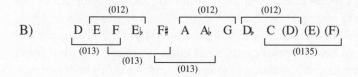

Example 3.47   Similarity of harmonies formed between the voices and those found in the series in String Quartet, fourth movement: A) mm. 54–59; B) segmental subsets of the series

A)

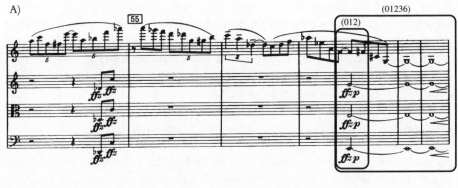

B)

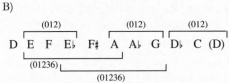

and G, are symmetrical around the sustained E in Voice 2, but only sporadically elsewhere in the movement.

Despite the inconsistent nature of the intervals formed harmonically between the voices, the two voices share enough common motivic content to cause us to reevaluate our original impression of the movement as a dialogue between mutually indifferent and irreconcilable musical characters. Like the partners in many relationships, these melodies conflict with each other, but nonetheless belong together. In this sense, the duality of the opposing melodies is created only to be subverted. The movement thus suggests, to an attentive listener, that even the most apparently irreconcilable conflict can in fact be mediated, indeed, can be heard to dissolve amid the subtle connections between the parties.

Suite for Wind Quintet, first movement

The Suite for Wind Quintet marked Crawford's return to composition after twenty years of silence. Following an extraordinarily fertile period in the early 1930s, when she wrote the String Quartet, the Three Songs, the two Ricercare ("Sacco, Vanzetti" and "Chinaman, Laundryman"), and several other works, Crawford turned her professional attention to collecting and arranging American folk music, first as an assistant to Charles Seeger, whom she married in 1933, and later on her own. I will speculate in Chapter Four about the reasons for her long abandonment of her own music and her decision to return to it. For now, it suffices to observe that when she did return, she picked up right where she had left off. Because of her premature death from cancer in 1953, she produced only one work during her compositional renaissance, the Suite for Wind Quintet, and this work is stylistically indistinguishable from her earlier music, apparently unmarked by her long years of immersion in folk music.

Example 3.48   Suite for Wind Quintet, first movement, mm. 10–15

A seven-note ostinato runs, without any break, through the first movement of the Suite for Wind Quintet, and forms the basis of the entire structure. In the representative passage in Example 3.48, it occurs in the bassoon, once per measure. The ostinato is remarkably similar to that of the second movement of the Violin Sonata, written in 1926 (see Example 2.57). The rhythmic similarities are obvious, as are the shared initial leap of ip11 from G to F♯, followed by a rough wedge inward toward the center of that interval. As Judith Tick observes, the resemblance between the ostinati involves "resurrecting [the Sonata] . . . and by implication resurrecting herself as a composer."[33]

The resurrection was not exact, however, because the ostinato is used in the Wind Quintet in a manner Crawford could not have envisioned at the time of the Violin Sonata. The work to which it bears the closest resemblance structurally is the third movement of the String Quartet. In that work, a single melody, by sustaining some notes while others entered, left a progression of shifting harmonies in its wake. In the Wind Quintet, the ostinato functions in a similar way, spawning the melodies in the other instruments and the harmonies formed between them.

In Example 3.48, the sustained lines in the non–ostinato parts at first appear to be independent of the ostinato, but turn out to be slavishly dependent upon it. Each attack in the sustaining parts occurs in unison or octave with whatever note the ostinato happens to be attacking at that moment. On the first eighth note of the measure, no note other than G may be attacked in the upper parts; on the third eighth note, no note other than F♯, and so on. The melodic lines and harmonies that result from this severe constraint are interesting and will be discussed in due course.

As for the ostinato itself, it begins with a melodic leap of eleven semitones, so characteristic of Crawford's melodies, then moves in an inexact wedge inward to a place slightly off of the center of the initial leap. This produces a sense of melodic imbalance to match the rhythmic instability, caused by the asymmetrical division of measure: Crawford gives the time signature as 10 ♪ (2 ♩. + 2 ♩). There is no duplication of pitch or pitch class and, apart from the two concluding semitones, no duplication of interval either. Its five segmental trichords represent five different types. In all of these respects, it is a typical, although brief, Crawford melody. As with the serial melodies, however, any initial sense of variety and freedom is immediately quashed as the melody begins a series of seemingly endless repetitions.

Although it is subject to mutations and transformations, the ostinato melody generally fits within a single measure and retains its distinctive rhythmic profile and contour. It has three principal forms in the movement, first in the bassoon, then, in strict pitch inversion, in the oboe, and finally back in the bassoon in a strict pitch transposition (see Example 3.49). The relationship between the first

Example 3.49   Three principal forms of the ostinato, in Suite for Wind Quintet, first movement

184

two forms can be thought of as $I_G^{E\flat}$, that is, the inversion that causes the E♭ and G to change places. This particular inversion causes the first note of the first statement to become the last note of the second statement, and vice versa. It also leaves B and F as the third and fourth notes in both figures. The common tones are thus disposed for maximum effect and provide a link between the forms (beyond their obvious shared rhythm and mirrored contour). The second and third forms, related by $I_B^{E\flat}$, share five common tones, again disposed for maximum effect. Four notes, the majority, are held in common among all three forms, and these include the first and last notes in each.

The first ostinato form is heard by itself, accompanied by sustained melodies to be discussed later, but the second and third forms are played in alternation with additional forms related by inversion (see Example 3.50A). The second form is associated with its inversion around D/D♯, and the third with its truncated and slightly scrambled inversion around B/C.

The ostinato itself can be understood in a very similar way, as three principal notes, related by $I_G^{E\flat}/I_B^{E\flat}$, and T_4, the latter two of which are conjoined with inversional associates (see Example 3.50B). I have suggested two alternative readings, both of which imagine G, B, and E♭ as the principal tones in the ostinato, a decision easily justified on the grounds of rhythm, contour, and position within the figure. From G to B is T_4, the same as the distance from the first ostinato (which begins on G) to the third ostinato (which begins on B). The ostinato gets from B to E♭ just as the second form gets to the third, and it gets

Example 3.50   Structural relations among the forms of the ostinato compared with its internal structure, in Suite for Wind Quintet, first movement

A)

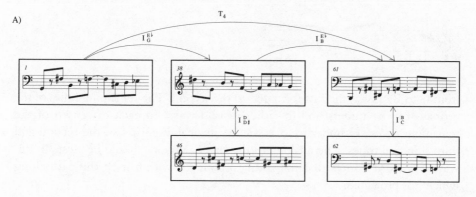

B)

Example 3.51   Note-by-note transformation of the ostinato into its inversion, in Suite for
Wind Quintet, first movement, mm. 1–38

from G to E♭ just as the first form gets to the second. The remaining notes of the
ostinato can be understood in either of two ways. In each case, two of the
remaining notes are understood as the inversional associates of the second and
third principal tones. The analogy to the larger network should be clear. In this
way, Crawford assures that the ostinato contains within itself the path along
which it is projected.

In the first section of the piece, the ostinato persists unchanged for seventeen
measures, then is gradually altered to lead the music from the initial figure to its
inversion in measure 38 (see Example 3.51). The rhythm becomes more rapid
and the figure more compressed as it changes, one note at a time. It also is
compressed in pitch-class space, and by measure 29 has become a seven-note
chromatic cluster, thus losing its distinctive intervallic profile. From that point
on, the figure is purposefully reassembled, still one note at a time.[34] The contents

of measure 32 are just one note off from being related at I_G^{Eb}, as an unordered collection, to the original figure. My hypothetical measure 38, given in parentheses, changes that single note (A♭ replaces F♯). In actual measure 38, the notes of hypothetical measure 38 are arranged as the ordered inversion of the original figure. Interestingly, the contents of measures 30 and 32 are also related by I_G^{Eb} – a smaller statement nested inside the larger. As in the chord progression in "Sacco, Vanzetti" the gradual alteration of a figure one note at a time carries us from some starting point to its transposition or inversion. The harmonies that intervene are not necessarily related either to the beginning and end points, or to each other. Rather, they are the by-products of the ongoing transformation.[35]

A similar piecemeal process of transformation leads in the second section of the movement from the principal form of the ostinato to its inversional associate, at $I_{D\sharp}^{D}$, (see Example 3.52). An alternation of the two persists throughout the remainder of the second section of the movement and well into the third.

The remaining instrumental parts simply double the tones of the ostinati. Some of the time, many or all of the instruments simply play in unisons or octaves, as in measures 20–37. More commonly, however, the non-ostinato parts attack a note in unison or octave with the ostinato, but then sustain for varying amounts of time, even as the ostinato continues to chug along. When it comes time to reattack, they do so again in unison or octave with the ostinato. The non-ostinato instruments thus play melodic lines that consist of notes attacked with the ostinato, and then sustained until their next attack. A wide variety of melodic lines, and a dense counterpoint, result from this practice.

In the first nine measures of the movement, the ostinato is heard in the bassoon, once in each measure and without variation (see Example 3.53). In the first measure of the example, each of its seven notes is assigned an ordinal number. The other parts play more sustained lines, the tones of which are also indicated with the appropriate ordinal number. At the beginning of the excerpt, for example, the clarinet attacks the second note of the ostinato in measure 2, then sustains it until it is time to play the fourth note of the ostinato in measure 3. Generally, one of the non-ostinato instruments is playing a principal melodic line, marked by Crawford with brackets. The oboe has the principal melody in measures 1–9, while the horn begins another principal line in measure 8, which continues beyond the end of the example.

The ostinato, and the melodic lines that are thus derived from it, share certain musical and intervallic characteristics with each other, and with Crawford's usual melodic practice. Like Crawford's typical melodic lines, the ostinato is intervallically quite varied. When the ostinato is changed one note at a time during the first section of the movement, an even greater variety prevails. Every ordered pitch-class interval except 7 and every trichord-type except (036) and (048) occurs in the passage. Returning to the original ostinato, however, there is some repetition in its segmental trichords, and in fact it can be understood in terms of two forms of (014) and two of (015) (see Example 3.54). Because the

Example 3.52   Transformation of the inverted form of the ostinato into its own inversion, in
Suite for Wind *Quintet*, first movement, mm. 38–46

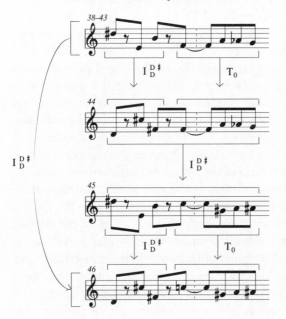

ostinato figure is repeated, its first notes are written again at the end, and two of
the trichords in the example result from this "wrap-around."

The melodic lines derived from the ostinato tend to have the same intervallic
concerns. To some extent, of course, this is an inevitable result of their derivation. The melodic lines are restricted to the seven notes of the ostinato, and
often simply reproduce its segmental subsets. In measures 5 and 6, for example,
the first three notes in the oboe simply state, in order, the first three notes of the
ostinato. In a slightly less direct way, the clarinet in measures 4–5 plays the first
two notes of the ostinato, but in reverse order. In cases like these, the relationship between the melodic lines and the ostinato is simple and direct.

More commonly, however, the melodic lines are constructed from non-
adjacent tones of the ostinato. The first three notes in the oboe (measure 3), for
example, are the second, fourth, and sixth notes of the ostinato. Those notes,
taken as a unit, constitute another member of (014), related by transposition or
inversion to the two (014)s directly present in the ostinato. The same principle
of construction is at work throughout this movement – the melodic lines
project the same musical structures as the ostinato itself.

In Example 3.55, the oboe's melodic line in measures 3–9 is analyzed in terms
of the same motivic trichords. The numbers above the oboe melody indicate
which ostinato note is being doubled. Some of these trichords are created when
the oboe melody doubles a segmental subset of the ostinato, but many more are
formed from tones that are not adjacent in the ostinato. The procedure is not

Example 3.53   Relation of the non-ostinato melodies to the ostinato, in Suite for Wind
Quintet, first movement, mm. 1–9

entirely systematic – in this example and throughout the movement there are
notes that do not conform. But Crawford clearly prefers to have the melodic lines
reflect the musical concerns of the ostinato from which they are derived.

Example 3.54   Segmental subsets of the ostinato, in Suite for Wind Quintet, first movement

Example 3.55   Segmental subsets of the ostinato represented in the oboe melody, in Suite for Wind Quintet, first movement, mm. 3–9

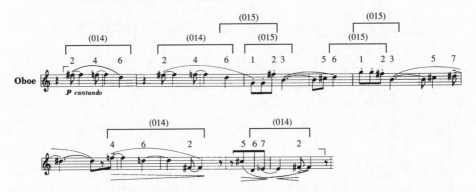

Example 3.56   Inversional pivoting in a melody from Suite for Wind Quintet, first movement, horn, mm. 8–10

At the same time, the melodies have a surprising degree of apparent independence. Despite their obvious constraints, they have something of the sound of typical free melodies from Crawford's other works. Consider the first six notes of the horn melody in measures 8–10 (see Example 3.56). The process of inversional pivoting moves the melody along. Certain of the melodic fragments, F♯–F–D and D–E♭–F♯, occur frequently in the melodies, although they are absent from the ostinato. The melodies are thus simultaneously derived from the ostinato, yet achieve a real degree of independence from it.

The melodic lines and the ostinato combine to form constantly shifting simultaneities. Consider, for example, the vertical harmonies in measures 10–11 (see Example 3.57). Some of these harmonies are formed simply by the piling up

190

Example 3.57   Harmonies formed between the parts in Suite for Wind Quintet, first
movement, mm. 10–11

of adjacent tones of the ostinato. The (015) formed above the third ostinato note in measure 10, for example, is simply a verticalization of the first three notes of the ostinato: G (sustained in the horn), F♯ (sustained in the flute and clarinet), and B (in the bassoon ostinato). The remaining verticals in measure 10, and the last three in measure 11 also, however, are formed by non–adjacent tones of the ostinato. In measure 10, for example, the notes sounding with the ostinato C♯ are F♯ (flute and clarinet) and F (horn) – a verticalization of the second, fourth, and fifth notes of the ostinato. Those three notes comprise a member of set class (015), a trichord-type that is found directly within the ostinato (e.g. its first three notes). The principle here is similar to the one that governs the melodic lines: notes are combined (as simultaneities) to create set classes that are also found as segmental subsets of the ostinato. And as with the melodic lines, this is more of a general preference than an absolute or systematic rule. Like the melody that winds through the third movement of the String Quartet, then, the simple, single-line ostinato brings a remarkable structural richness in its wake, with subsidiary melodies and harmonies that are derived from the ostinato, and share some of its concerns, but nonetheless achieve a significant degree of independence from it.

There is thus a profound paradox at the core of this movement. In one sense, this movement is nothing but an ostinato and its pale emanations. The upper parts are entirely dependent on the ostinato. They are not only restricted to the notes of the ostinato, but can only state a note when the ostinato is doing so also. Their only freedom is the freedom to sustain a note once it has been attacked. Remarkably, from that small freedom, structures of surprising integrity and independence are able to grow. The upper parts refer to the intervals and segments of the ostinato, as indeed they must, but like plants growing from an inhospitable rocky mountainside, they also push outward, to create their own distinctive shapes.

Suite for Wind Quintet, third movement

The third movement of the Suite for Wind Quintet is roughly in the form of a rondo: A1–B–A2–C1–A3–C2–A4. In each of the formal sections, a free melody or pair of melodies is combined with a serial melody based on the series shown in Example 3.58B, as it appears in the bassoon in the first measure. The series is remarkably similar to the series for the fourth movement of the String Quartet, which is shown for comparison in Example 3.58A. They begin with the same four notes in the same order. The next four notes are also the same but with the order scrambled. The last two notes in the String Quartet series are also the last two notes of the Suite for Wind Quintet series. In this very explicit sense, Crawford picked up in 1953 right where she had left off twenty years earlier. If, in this work, she is "resurrecting herself as a composer," as Tick suggests, then the resurrection is not merely one of abstract spirit, but in the flesh, right down to the fingernails. Her musical concerns, to the level of actual pitches and intervals, had not substantially changed in the intervening years.[36]

Example 3.58   Comparison of two series: A) String Quartet, fourth movement; B) Suite for
                Wind Quintet, third movement

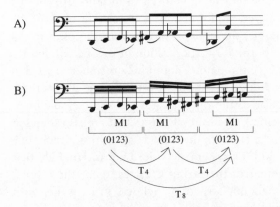

The series contains all twelve tones and, in this respect, is different from all of Crawford's other series. In other respects, it is typical not only of her series, but of her melodies generally. It embeds Motive M1 three times (shown with brackets)[37] and is explicitly concerned with filling the chromatic space. Each of its discrete tetrachords is a chromatic cluster, with the second and third related to the first at either T_4 or T_8.[38] The series as a whole, like all twelve-tone series, fills the entire available pitch–class space, and each of its tetrachords fills a small chromatic zone. The tendency toward chromatic completion, which we have observed in many of Crawford's melodies, is clearly at work here. The transpositions convey a sense of cyclicity: the first tetrachord is projected through an interval cycle which, if continued, would lead right back to itself. That sense of circling around, of an ending that leads right back to a beginning, is vital to the structure of the movement, and is felt in the rondo-like arrangement at the highest formal level.

The tetrachords are related not only as unordered collections but as ordered lines: the second is the ordered retrograde of the first and the third is the transposed rotation of the second (the third is thus the transposed, rotated retrograde of the first). In this sense, the first tetrachord propagates itself, through transposition, retrograde, and rotation, to generate the entire series. Transposition, retrograde, and rotation, applied within the series, will later be applied to the series itself as a whole. In this way, and in keeping with Crawford's usual practice, the same operations will shape the structure at all levels.

The series is structured in an even more intimate way, at the level of its dyads. Each of its tetrachords can be thought of as two whole tones a semitone apart (see Example 3.59). For the purposes of this discussion, the third tetrachord is unrotated to reveal its two whole tones. If the whole tones are understood as unordered collections, they describe the transpositional relationships shown on the example. These relationships are also crucial in shaping the structure of the movement as a whole.

The series can thus be understood as dyads combining to form tetrachords, and tetrachords combining to form a series. Within each dyad, the notes are related at T_2; within each tetrachord, the dyads are related at T_1; and within the series as a whole, the tetrachords are related at T_4. This multi-leveled structure is

Example 3.59   Series analyzed in terms of its whole-tone dyads, in Suite for Wind Quintet, third movement

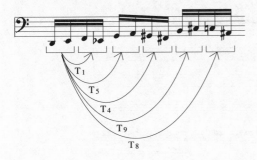

Example 3.60   Intervallic structure of the series, in Suite for Wind Quintet, third movement

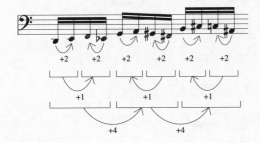

Example 3.61   A complete set of rotations of the series, in Suite for Wind Quintet, third
movement, A section, mm. 1–18

194

shown in Example 3.60, and, as before, the third tetrachord is unrotated for the purposes of the example.[39] These transpositional relationships influence the structure of the movement at various levels including, most obviously, Crawford's manipulation of the series as a whole. As in her other serial pieces, its treatment reflects its internal structure.

In each of the A sections of the movement (measures 1–17, 31–57, 85–100, and 128–145), the series is systematically rotated in Crawford's usual manner (see Example 3.61). The familiar rotations are played by the bassoon and flute together (three octaves apart) through the middle of the ninth rotation, and then by the bassoon alone until the end. Roughly at the point the flute drops out, a contrasting free melody enters. All of the A sections are laid out in just this way.

With two slight exceptions, each of the rotations is compressed within the minimum possible pitch space. That is, in each statement, only eleven semitones separate the lowest and highest pitch, and each pitch in between is heard once, testifying once again to Crawford's interest in chromatic saturation. Furthermore, we see again her propensity for organizing her melodies within a moving registral frame whose boundaries are eleven semitones apart, and which follows a motivic path. Example 3.62 shows the registral span of each of the twelve rotations, ignoring two notes in the eighth rotation and one in the twelfth that are out of register. Only the bassoon part is considered, but the flute, when it is present,

Example 3.62 Registral disposition of twelve rotated series-statements in Suite for Wind
Quintet, third movement, mm. 1–18: A) registral span of each series-form;
B) larger gestures reflect relations among the tetrachords of the series;
C) smaller gestures reflect relations among the dyads of the series

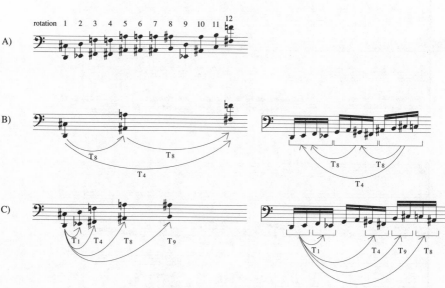

simply doubles each bassoon pitch three octaves higher. The general shape of the bassoon melody is evident here, as it rises slowly to a resting point in the fifth through eighth rotations, then begins rising again, farther and more rapidly, to the end of the section. The first ascent comes to rest eight semitones above the origin and the section ends sixteen semitones above. The pitch space is thus divided symmetrically. What is more, these particular intervals of transposition recall the relations among the tetrachords of the series, also T_4 and T_8 (see Example 3.62B). The partitioning of the pitch space can also be heard largely in relation to the dyads of the series, as a series of transpositions by 1, 4, 8, and 9 (see Example 3.62C).[40] The series thus shapes not only the pitch-class succession of the bassoon melody, but its precise registration as well.

As striking as this pitch organization is, the rhythmic organization is even more remarkable, projecting as it does in rhythmic space the basic pitch motives of the movement. In each of the A sections, the serial melody flows along in the continuous, almost uniform, manner we have come to expect from melodies of this type. The meter of the passage is three quarter notes, or twelve sixteenth notes, per measure. Given the rhythmic patterns in use, a note may occur on any of twelve different locations in a measure. This creates the potential for an analogy between pitch and rhythm, namely, that just as a note can occupy any of twelve different locations in pitch-class space, or any of the twelve order positions within the series, it can similarly occupy any of twelve different locations in any of the measures of the passage.

196

Consider, for example, the placement of pitch class D in the fourth through eighth rotations (see Example 3.63). Pitch class D is the first note of the series, and the first and last note of the movement, and thus seems worthy of special attention. Within these rotations, the D is moving backwards, occupying successively the tenth, ninth, eighth, seventh, and sixth order position in the series. In metrical terms, however, it is moving forward, occupying successively the eleventh, twelfth, first, second, and third sixteenth-note position within the measure. The principle of rotation, so central to the pitch organization, is thus also applied to the metrical organization. The analogy is not pursued systematically, but is an unmistakable part of the rhythmic design.

Example 3.63   Metrical position of pitch class D within the rotations of the series, in Suite for Wind Quintet, third movement, mm. 4–12

Example 3.64   Metrical position of pitch–class D within the rotations of the series, in Suite for Wind Quintet, third movement, mm. 31–46

The same pitch/rhythm analogy is pursued in a slightly different sense in the second A section (see Example 3.64).[41] The passage presents the usual rotations of the series, indicated with numbers above the staves. The rhythm moves in uniform eighth notes, six per measure. To make a comparison to the first section clearer, let us imagine joining the written measures into pairs, each of which will contain twelve eighth notes. Within these hypermeasures, pitch class D occupies successively metrical positions, or time points 1, 2, 12, 12, 2, 4, and 3.

Example 3.65   Durational intervals in relation to pitch intervals, in Suite for Wind Quintet, third movement, mm. 31–46

series-rotation: 1   2   3   4   5   6   7

metrical position
of pitch class D: 1   2   12 12 2   4   3

durational intervals: < +1, –2 >   < +2, –1 >

pitch intervals in series:

< +1, –2>   <+2, –1>   <+2, –1>

As with pitch classes, one can meaningfully calculate the intervals between successive points (see Example 3.65). The D begins on the first eighth note, advances one position for its second occurrence, then retreats two positions for its third occurrence. In other words, it describes in metrical terms the pattern <+1, –2>. The retrograde of the same pattern, <+2, –1>, is created immediately after. These, of course, are forms of Crawford's familiar Motive M1, which is also embedded within the series for this movement. The same motive is thus projected simultaneously in pitch and rhythm. In that profound sense, Crawford has "serialized the rhythm" of this passage and this movement, just as she did in the fourth movement of the String Quartet.

Toward the end of each of the A sections, another melody, which I will refer to as Countermelody 1, is heard in a heterophonic duet with the serial melody. This countermelody is slightly varied in its four appearances, but its shape in the first of the A sections can stand for the rest (see Example 3.66). Countermelody 1 is a nicely shaped, integral and self-contained melody that conforms to Crawford's usual style, including her preference for the filling of chromatic pitch and pitch–class space and her desire for intervallic variety, with an emphasis on intervals 1 and 2. The melody unfolds via the usual inversional pivots, and is impelled for much of its length by RICH.

The two melodies are arranged to contrast with each other rhythmically. In general, when one line has eighth notes, the other has sixteenth notes, and

Example 3.66   Serial rotations and non-serial countermelody, in Suite for Wind Quintet, third movement, mm. 13–17

contrary or oblique motion is preferred. There is one striking exception to both of these preferences, on the last beat of measure 16. There, the two lines move in parallel unisons for four notes. That suggests the possibility of deeper links between the serial line and the countermelody.

The two lines are intervallically distinct and are not direct transformations of each other. Nonetheless, as is characteristic of Crawford, there are subtle affinities between these contrasting melodies. They both count among their segmental subsets a number of shared trichord and tetrachord types. Furthermore, many of the actual pitch-class collections within the series find their way into the countermelody, usually with their order rearranged. The notes of the second tetrachord of the series, for example, F♯–A–A♭–G, can be found together toward the beginning of the countermelody, although not in that order. The most conspicuous shared collection is C–D–E–F, which does occur in the same order in both melodies, an identity that is emphasized in the music by the surprising parallel unisons in measure 16, and in each of the analogous spots when the A section repeats. The other intervals formed between the parts tend to be the dissonant ones, although there is nothing systematic involved. The countermelody is not derived from the series in any systematic or straightforward way; rather, it is constructed to embody some of the same pitch-class and intervallic concerns. Beneath the apparent contrast between the serial melody and the countermelody, then, lurks a deeper unity. This is characteristic, as we have seen, of virtually all of Crawford's heterophonic duets.

The A sections present and rotate the series at T_0. The B, C1, and C2 sections retrograde and rotate the series at T_2, T_{10}, and T_5.[42] As in all of Crawford's serial compositions, this larger transpositional plan reflects the structure of the series itself (see Example 3.67). The transpositions of the series take it up two semitones, then down four semitones, then up seven semitones. The series itself can be described in roughly the same way, in terms of its constituent whole tones. Beginning with the dyad C–D formed between the last and first notes of the series, the dyads A$\sharp$–C, D–E, and G–A are produced by applying successively T_{-2}, T_{+4}, and T_{-7}, the mirror image of the transpositions applied to the series over the course of the entire movement.[43] The remainder of the series is produced by conjoining the three generated dyads with another whole tone that lies a semitone higher or lower. There is no analogy for this final stage of generation in the larger transpositional plan.

Example 3.67   Using the same operations to generate the series from its whole tones and the larger transformations of the series itself

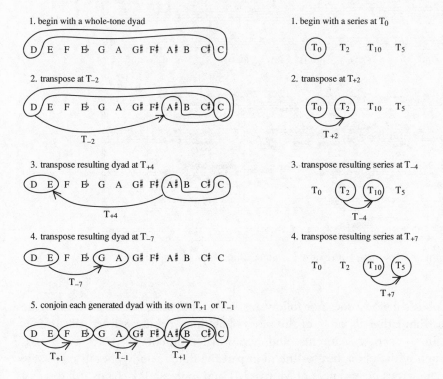

In Section B, the serial rotations in the bassoon and clarinet are heard in counterpoint with two other melodies, in the flute and oboe (see Example 3.68).

Example 3.68   Three-voice heterophony in *Suite for Wind Quintet*, third movement,
mm. 21–30

The oboe's melody does not follow any strict serial plan, but all of its notes are taken from either P_0 or I_8 of the series. The flute melody is freer still. It does contain some row segments, and occasional moments of exact pitch-class imitation of the oboe, but for the most part the flute melody goes its own way, with numerous occurrences of Motive M1 and multiple RI-chains. All three of the melodies in the B section have integrity and make sense on their own terms, allowing for the usual commonalities of intervallic and motivic structure.

Example 3.69   A serial melody and a free duet in Suite for Wind Quintet, third movement, mm. 58–72

It is impossible, however, to account in any systematic way for the harmonies formed between the lines. The harmony types formed on each of the quarter-note beats from the entrance of the flute in measure 21 to the end of Section B may be found beneath the staves of Example 3.68. There is a bewildering variety, with four of the six dyad types and nine of the twelve trichord types represented. No pattern is apparent.

This lack of consistency is one likely consequence of Crawford's heterophonic ideal. The more highly structured and numerous the melodies, the less likely it will be that the verticals will fall under similar compositional control. Instead, they will tend to be by-products of the complex melodic designs.[44]

The same may be said of the contrapuntal organization of the two C sections, which are similarly heterophonic in design (see Example 3.69, the opening part of the first C section.)[45] The bassoon and horn share a slow, expressive melody that begins and ends freely, but is largely devoted to the serial rotations of $R(T_{10})$. The serial line's heterophonic counterpart is a free duet, in slow rhythmic values and largely note-against-note. The duet occurs primarily in the remaining three instruments, although the horn and bassoon both participate in the second half of the section, when they are not occupied with the serial rotations.

The duet itself consists of two distinct bits of material. The first is a kind of refrain, usually heard in the oboe and clarinet. The refrain normally consists of three intervals, the third of which is an octave, usually octave Cs. The second constituent of the free duet, usually heard in the flute and clarinet, is longer and conforms much more closely to Seeger's principles of dissonant counterpoint (see Example 3.70, which extracts the free duet). Beneath the music, a hypothetical species-counterpoint reduction is offered. Apart from the arrivals on octave Cs in each of the refrains, consonance and dissonance are treated as in Seeger's model, with the consonances relegated to the weaker beats, within a prevailing dissonant framework.

Neither the melodies of the duet nor the intervals formed between the parts have any explicit relationship to the series and its rotations. Even more than in the B section, the principle of heterophony prevails. At the same time, the heterophony is moderated, and its oppositions mediated, by subtle associations among the parts. The central characteristic of Crawford's music, both structurally and dramatically, is a tension between the highly structured and the rhapsodically free. In that way, Crawford recreates musically one of the familiar binary oppositions of Western thought. The immediate effect of her music is a sense of utter and irreconcilable conflict between the two kinds of melodies, a mere inscription of duality. The melodies seem to go their own way, each hardly acknowledging the other's presence. Gradually, however, one becomes aware of the subtle ties that bind the disparate parts, their underlying affinities, their shared concerns. In this sense, Crawford's music offers a healing vision, one in which the seemingly rigid dualities and oppositions of our lives can be heard to melt, thaw, and resolve themselves, if not into a transcendent synthesis, then at least into a sense

Example 3.70   The free duet and a species–counterpoint reduction of it in Suite for Wind
Quintet, third movement, mm. 58–72

of respectful coexistence. Each kind of melody, that is, without compromising
its own integrity and individual character, nonetheless gives signs of having
listened to, and heard, the other.

4

Crawford's music in its contexts

In the context of her biography

Ruth Crawford was born on July 3, 1901, in East Liverpool, Ohio.[1] Her father was a Methodist minister and the family, which included her parents and an older brother, moved frequently following his assignment to a succession of ministerial positions. The family lived briefly in several towns and cities in Ohio and Indiana before arriving in Jacksonville, Florida, in 1911. That is where Crawford's father died in 1914, and that is where Crawford spent the remainder of her childhood and youth, while her mother supported the family by renting out rooms to boarders.

Her early musical experiences were those of middle-class, small-town America. She studied piano, first with her mother, then with local teachers. For two years after graduating from high school, she taught piano to help support the family, and piano teaching would remain her primary source of income until much later in her adult life. At the age of nineteen, with the encouragement of her mother and her music teachers, she left Jacksonville for Chicago, to pursue advanced study in music.

In the fall of 1920, she entered the American Conservatory in Chicago and she stayed there until 1929. During these student years, she supported herself by ushering and checking coats at theaters and concert halls, and later by teaching piano and theory. Initially, she had ambitions to become a professional pianist, but muscular problems caused her to turn away from the piano toward theory and composition.

Her principal teacher of theory and composition at the Conservatory was Adolf Weidig, a German-American violinist and composer, and a former student of Hugo Riemann. Weidig's approach to traditional tonal harmony was based on the theories of Riemann.[2] He had no particular affection for modern music – he described atonality as a form of "musical communism" which obliterated all musical "standards, values and traditions"[3] – but he apparently did not discourage Crawford's early compositional experiments: "Sprinkling sevenths and ninths plentifully and insistently, and observing or breaking the solemn rules of harmony with equal regularity, I was guided with great understanding during the next years by Adolf Weidig of the American Conservatory in Chicago, who seems to me to have had an unusual balance between necessary discipline and necessary allowance for individuality."[4] Crawford's experience with Weidig and the Conservatory provided her with a solid, standard musical training, oriented toward the masterworks of the past. For a sense of new compositional possibilities in a rapidly changing musical world, however, she had to turn elsewhere.

The musical climate in Chicago of the 1920s was conservative, with its large, mainstream institutions devoted almost exclusively to the standard repertoire of the dominant European tradition. Interest in new music by American composers was confined to small, informal groups, including a circle of composers, performers, and other interested parties centered on the pianist Djane Lavoie Herz.[5] Herz had been a student of Artur Schnabel in Berlin, and was for two years a pupil and disciple of Scriabin, in Brussels. In Chicago, she and her husband, Siegfried Herz, a concert manager and impresario, created a musical salon, where regular guests included central figures in the emerging avant-garde, including Henry Cowell, Dane Rudhyar, and Edgard Varèse.

By studying piano with Djane Herz, Crawford entered an iconoclastic musical and intellectual circle, with profound effects on her musical outlook: "Contact in 1925 with Djane Lavoie Herz, with whom I studied piano, and with Dane Rudhyar, and later with Henry Cowell, established a definite turning-point in my work, and enabled me to see far along the way toward which in my numerous student compositions I had been groping. I discovered Scriabine [*sic*] at this time; the music of Schoenberg and Hindemith I did not hear until later; Stravinsky's "Sacre" and "l'Oiseau de Feu" came to me too about this time."[6]

In the long run, Crawford's friendship with Henry Cowell would prove decisive, both in shaping the content of her music and in guiding her career, but during her remaining years in Chicago, Rudhyar was the more important influence.

Rudhyar is not well known today, but in ultra-modern circles in the 1920s and 1930s, he was considered a major figure. He was born and educated in Paris, but moved to America in 1916, where he pursued varied interests, not only in music but in film and mysticism, including astrology – the latter preoccupied him from around 1930 until his death in 1985. He was a founder of the International Composers' Guild, and is consistently identifed in contemporary press accounts as a leader of America's musical avant-garde. Crawford was deeply impressed by him, not only by his music, but by his charismatic personality:

> Tonight at Djane [Herz's] . . . Rudhyar reads some very beautiful poems. I begin to feel his beauty as never before. Previously when he was here I have admired and stood afar worshipping vaguely, you might say, intellectually, because I was dazzled by his erudition. Now I begin to "feel" his greatness. Some part of the film has been lifted from my eyes, there is a rift in the clouds which before were so dense.[7]

Rudyhar influenced Crawford in three areas. First, he along with Herz was a principal conduit for Scriabin's music and ideas. Crawford's interest in "almost-whole-tone" harmonies, including but not limited to Scriabin's "mystic chord," her reliance on sequential transposition (which I have called transpositional projection) as a means for organizing large musical spans, and her preference for relatively static harmonies animated by linear motives can all be traced to Scriabin, by way of Rudhyar and Herz.

A second area of influence was Rudyhar's interest, again shared by Herz, in Eastern mysticism and Theosophy.[8] While these ideas evidently intrigued Crawford, their impact on her music is only occasionally evident, in isolated moments or brief works identified with character designations such as "mystico."[9] The only larger works to bear their full imprint are the Three Chants, particularly the third, with its evocation of massed prayer in a Buddhist monastery.

The third area of influence, having to do with Rudhyar's specifically musical ideas and compositions, is more pervasive. Through Rudhyar, Crawford became committed at this relatively early stage in her career to dissonance as a structural principle, long before she knew about Seeger's version of dissonant counterpoint. For Rudhyar, consonance was isolating because it tended to gather music into discrete areas, each organized around a tonal center. Dissonance, in contrast, could liberate music by shattering traditional schemes of tonal organization. As Tick summarizes: "Consonance was 'tribal' because it represented exclusiveness or the primitive expression of sectarian conditioning. Dissonance was 'universal' because it symbolized the inclusiveness of the theosophical 'Universal Brotherhood.'"[10]

Rudhyar's ideas helped to justify for Crawford the dissonant and atonal underpinnings of her own music, which nonetheless differs from Rudhyar's music in basic and substantial ways. Rudhyar's music, such as the piano works *Paeans* (1927) and *Granites* (1929), is characterized by massive, static harmonies, in contrast to the restrained polyphony of Crawford's. His music is full of exact repetitions, designed to create an atmosphere of incantation, while hers rarely contains exact repetition, preferring instead a sense of continual evolution. His music is relentlessly harmonic in conception, while hers contains lines or strands that are relatively independent. In a letter to Seeger, Crawford later claimed that she had "scorned counterpoint for two years" because of Rudhyar,[11] but her music was always more contrapuntal, more embryonically heterophonic than his.

During Crawford's years in Chicago, as her mature style began to take shape, she also began to receive performances of her works, in both Chicago and New York.[12] By 1929, with her reputation rising and, with it, her sense of her own abilities, she decided to move to New York, then as now the center of new musical activity in the United States.

It was at this point that Henry Cowell, a tireless promoter and publisher of other people's work, began to exert himself decisively on Crawford's behalf. He arranged for her to live in the New York apartment of Blanche Walton, an important supporter of new music. That not only provided for Crawford's most pressing material needs, a crucial consideration for a young composer with no sources of income beyond piano teaching, but placed her right at the lively center of new music activity in New York. Walton's salon in New York thus played the same role for Crawford that Herz's had in Chicago: it brought her into close contact with major figures in the world of ultra-modern composition.

For Crawford, the most important of these figures was unquestionably Charles Seeger. Through his teaching, writing, and, to a lesser extent, his own compositions, Seeger was well established by this time as a central figure in the ultra-modern movement, particularly by virtue of his association with Henry Cowell. He had been Cowell's first, and only, composition teacher, and Cowell regarded him as "the greatest musical explorer in intellectual fields which America has produced."[13] Cowell arranged for Crawford to study with Seeger, overcoming Seeger's initial objection to teaching a woman, and the lessons took place at Blanche Walton's apartment, beginning in the fall of 1929 and continuing through the spring of the following year.

In the summer of 1930, Crawford and Seeger continued to work together outside the city, first at Seeger's parents' home in upstate New York, then at Walton's summer cottage in Connecticut. During this period, the lessons became more and more frequent, and eventually they worked together every day, with their efforts directed toward both Crawford's compositions and Seeger's theoretical treatise. A romance between them also began at this time, but both the romance and the musical studies were interrupted in August when Crawford departed for a year in Europe on her Guggenheim fellowship, the first ever awarded in music to a woman.

Crawford described studies with Seeger as "the second great turning point of her life" as a composer, the first having been her contact with Herz, Rudhyar, and Cowell.[14] Seeger persuaded Crawford of the inadequacy of her earlier music, and advised her to adopt his own approach: "The first lesson with Ruth was spent mostly on my critique of European and American composition up to the year 1930 and my criticism of her work as being too diffuse, having too much reliance on Scriabinian harmony, and advising that she should start off first in making single melodic lines that would be dissonated in accord with my theory that the sooner you could dissonate a melodic line the better."[15]

For Crawford, Seeger's discipline of dissonant counterpoint provided a means of purging her music of romantic excess, of paring it down to its essentials: "[Seeger] shared with me his conception of the aspects and as yet untried possibilities, both in form and content, of a new music, and his views as to various means of bringing some organic coordination out of the too often superabundance of materials in use at present. As a result of this study, my work began at last to take a 'handleable' shape, to present itself in some sort of intelligible continuity."[16] Crawford's music in this period does take the dissonant melodic line as its basis, and thus breaks clearly with her earlier music. Nonetheless, and despite the self-effacing quality of Crawford's remark, the "shape" and "continuity" of her music were ultimately the products of her own compositional imagination, however much she may have been stimulated by Seeger's ideas.

209

Crawford's year spent in Europe represented a continuation of the compositional path she had begun to travel in her studies with Seeger. Although she met with many important composers, including Béla Bartók, Alban Berg, Josef Hauer, Arthur Honegger, and Maurice Ravel, she studied with none of them. Instead, she spent most of her time completing pieces she had begun in New York, perfecting the original compositional language she had forged the previous year. The year in Europe was the most productive of her career and saw the composition or completion of what are probably her best works. She wrote the Three Chants, the first two movements of the String Quartet, and two of the Three Songs ("Rat Riddles" and "In Tall Grass"), while completing the last two movements of the String Quartet and the four *Diaphonic Suites*. All of these works are in her distinctive idiom and none bears any evident trace of her European experiences. In her words: "I am sure that the work I did during this time [the period of study in Europe] was by far the best I had done – a fact which I attribute not so much to Europe itself (though the experience abroad was invaluable to me in a general sort of way) as to the financial freedom to work, and to the natural course of my growth."[17] Europe, then, was simply a place for her to work, not a significant source of influence.

Even before her trip to Europe, Crawford had some knowledge of contemporary musical developments there. Her knowledge tended to be superficial, however, and her music bears little trace of it. Like her mentors, Cowell and Seeger, she condemned neoclassicism.[18] One might imagine that Schoenberg's twelve-tone idea would have appealed to her more. She studied some of Schoenberg's early twelve-tone music, including the Piano Suite, Op. 25, and Wind Quintet, Op. 26, during the early period of her work with Seeger,[19] and she met with Berg, Josef Rufer and Egon Wellesz (all students of Schoenberg) during her Guggenheim year. Furthermore, she was close friends with Adolph Weiss, who had been Schoenberg's first American student.[20] Nonetheless, Crawford's few comments on the subject are not particularly well informed (the same is true also of her mentors, Cowell and Seeger.)[21] Schoenberg's twelve-tone idea may have attracted her mild intellectual interest, but it had little impact on her music. Certainly Crawford's conception of serialism as a rigid system of rotations and transpositions is profoundly at variance with Schoenberg's conception of it as a process of "developing variation," wherein a series is a basic shape to be endlessly reshaped.[22]

At an even more basic level, Crawford was largely immune to the kinds of nostalgia, or anxiety, toward the music of the past that so preoccupied her European contemporaries. European music of the period, including twelve-tone music, is haunted by the past, by the forms of older music, by its sonorities, by its rhythmic and melodic gestures.[23] The ghosts of Beethoven, Wagner, and Brahms can be heard speaking, from a distance but distinctly, in the music of Schoenberg and his followers. The neoclassical music of Stravinsky and his followers is also haunted by ghosts of music past, but in a somewhat different way. European modern music can be understood, to a surprising extent, as an elaborate attempt to neutralize and incorporate an overwhelming and oppressive musical tradition.

Crawford apparently felt little of this burden. She and her fellow ultra-moderns were certainly interested in establishing an American countertradition, but that apparently did not require them to grapple in each piece with an all-too-present past. As a result, the musical gestures of European classical music are consistently absent from Crawford's music. As we will see in a subsequent section, her characteristic anxiety was an anxiety of authorship, a concern about her own worth and competence, not an anxiety of influence.

Upon her return to New York in November 1931, Crawford began living with Seeger – they were not married until the following year, after Seeger's divorce from his first wife had become final. She completed her Three Sandburg Songs, and got somewhat involved in the Composers' Collective of New York. This was a group of professional musicians eager to enlist their art in the service of their politics, and willing to do so under the overall control of the American Communist party.[24] At its height in 1933–35, it included twenty-four composers, including Crawford, Seeger, and Cowell.

Crawford was not closely involved with the Collective and wrote only two pieces for it: "Sacco, Vanzetti" and "Chinaman, Laundryman," first performed in 1933 at a concert called "Workers' Music Olympiad." The texts of these works obviously reflect her new political commitments, and her use of *Sprechstimme*, a technical novelty for her, reflects her concern that the biting, politically radical words be clearly understood. The accompaniments, however, while strikingly individual, do not depart significantly from her mature, ultra-modern idiom as it has been described in these pages. In this sense, Crawford's politics did not impinge in any deep way on her music.

When her politics really took hold, rather than altering the style of her compositions, they impelled her to abandon them entirely. Following the composition of those two "Ricercari," Crawford essentially stopped composing for almost twenty years. Instead, she devoted her professional energies to collecting, editing, transcribing, and anthologizing American folk music. Crawford had some prior knowledge of American folk music, having contributed several piano arrangements to Carl Sandburg's *American Songbag* in 1927, when she and Sandburg were friends and neighbors in Chicago.[25] During the 1930s and 40s, however, Crawford dedicated herself to this subject, transcribing recordings in the Library of Congress, editing collections, writing song accompaniments, and publishing her own songbooks for children.[26]

Crawford's decision to stop composing – what she referred to as "a decision born of indecision" – had many apparent causes.[27] The first was the same that had drawn her to the Composers' Collective, namely a sense that her ultra-modern art music served only a narrow elite and ignored the large mass of Americans then suffering under the effects of the Great Depression:

We discovered the Anglo-American folk music at the same time in the early thirties and were both carried away with it. It was partly the reaction to the depression in which we were very much embroiled, and it might be partly a sense of the increasing pointlessness of the composition of those days. I think she felt as I did that the fine art of composition, the great tradition of Bach, Beethoven, Brahms, and so forth down to Bartók, had practically exploded into many pieces sometime around the first World War, and her turn to folk music I think was probably in a single line from a certain amount of disappointment in the trend of the compositions of the twenties.[28]

Ruth and I were completely flabbergasted by the situation – that here we were – people who called ourselves American composers and we didn't know anything about America or American music, so we simply decided that we would lay aside for a while our interest in dissonant counterpoint and try to find out something about America.[29]

A second reason for abandoning her own music involved the press of family obligations, first to a husband with somewhat traditional ideas of marital responsibility, and then to children, eventually four in number. Seeger traces the beginning of her compositional silence, and its roots in her relationship to him, back to the end of her year in Europe. Crawford had applied to the Guggenheim Foundation for an additional year of fellowship support, but when she was turned down "the tears ran down and she said 'What's going to happen to me?' So I put my arm around her . . . and I told her what was going to happen to her was that we were going to get married and that we would have some lovely children."[30] Those who celebrate a woman's traditional family role may find this anecdote comforting; others may find it chilling. In either case, it suggests strongly the kinds of domestic pressures to which Crawford was subjected.

A further reason was certainly Crawford's habitual sense of her own inadequacy as a composer, what I have referred to earlier as her "anxiety of authorship."[31] In all of her creative endeavors, she was shadowed by the sense that she was not up to the task, that she had little to offer, nothing of value to say, that, indeed, she had no business composing music at all. Her comments on her Five Songs, written just before she began to study with Seeger, are typical, if somewhat more pointed than usual:

A wild, mournful day. Work on my songs all morning with no zest, finally crying hard; no inspiration. No will to write, no desire, no vision, no facility. I ask myself why under God's heaven, I am a composer. I say damn, I ask what I am good for. I am not brilliant along any line, I do nothing easily. Have I anything to say? Why write when I have nothing to say? I am sterile, dry. The song I am trying to write is called "Joy."[32]

Crawford's persistent uncertainty about the value of her compositions may have contributed to her decision to stop composing altogether.[33]

Whatever Crawford's ultimate motivation, her decision to stop composing brutally truncated a highly promising compositional career. She had created a stable musical style, one that satisfied her desire for compositional coherence and permitted her to say what she wanted to say. She had already written a number of significant works in that style, and could have gone on doing so, had she chosen to. Without questioning the value, to her and others, of the way she spent her time during the two decades from 1933 to 1952, I find it hard not to regret the loss of the music that might otherwise have been created.

During that period, she wrote only one original composition, a slight orchestral work titled *Rissolty, Rossolty*. This work is entirely and traditionally tonal throughout, incorporating actual folk tunes, and thus is radically at variance with her usual compositional practice. Toward the end of that period, she began to consider returning to her own music, imagining that she might try to incorporate the folk idioms she had so thoroughly assimilated:

> I am still not sure whether the road I have been following the last dozen years is a main road or a detour. I have begun to feel, the past year or two, that it is the latter – a detour, but a very important one to me, during which I have descended from stratosphere onto a solid well-travelled highway, folded my wings and breathed good friendly dust as I travelled along in and out of the thousands of fine traditional folktunes which I have been hearing and singing and transcribing from field-recordings, for books and for pleasure . . . Whether I ever unfold the wings and make a start toward the stratosphere again, and how much of the dust of the road will still cling to me, is an interesting question, at least to me. If I do, I will probably pull the road up with me.[34]

When Crawford did resume composing, however, she returned uncompromisingly to her former ultra-modern idiom. Her Suite for Wind Quintet, completed in 1952, bears no discernible trace of folk influence. Instead, it makes explicit reference to her earlier music, particularly the Violin Sonata and the String Quartet, and in its construction is a virtual companion piece to the String Quartet. Indeed, a scholar trying to establish a date for the Wind Quintet on internal evidence alone would certainly place it back in the early 1930s, in the heyday of ultra-modern composition and dissonant counterpoint.

Ironically, by the time Crawford actually did complete the work, the musical world had changed dramatically. Her brand of ultra-modern composition was ultra-modern no longer, having been supplanted by the still more radical music of the post-Webern generation in both Europe and America. It is impossible to know how Crawford would have responded to these new developments, because her renaissance as a composer was cut sadly short by her premature death in 1953.

In the context of the ultra-modern movement

The period between the end of World War I and the beginning of the Great Depression, the period when Crawford came to maturity and wrote her most important works, was one of unprecedented ferment and experimentation in American music, marked by an upsurge of groups dedicated to performing modern music. By the late 1920s, when she was writing her principal works, the new music scene was divided roughly into two competing circles. The first was centered around the League of Composers, and included composers oriented toward Europe and European models, such as Copland, Piston, Sessions, and Thomson. The second was centered around the Pan American Association of Composers, and included "Americans who have developed indigenous materials or are specially interested in expressing some phase of the American spirit in their works," and "Foreign-born composers who have made America their home, and who have developed indigenous tendencies in their works."[35] This latter group, which included, among others, Ives, Varèse, Cowell, Ruggles, Rudhyar, Seeger, and Crawford herself, adopted the designation "ultra-modern" to describe their idiom which, of course, varied from composer to composer.[36]

The ultra-modern composers were bound together as a group by a complex network of personal and professional connections. Seeger taught Cowell and Crawford. He also exerted a strong influence on Ruggles, whom he met through Cowell. Ruggles acknowledged that "my style began with Seeger"[37] and dedicated *Angels* to him. Seeger expressed his esteem for Ruggles by dedicating *Psalm 137* to him, and by writing a celebratory essay about him.[38] The Pan American Association of Composers was founded by Varèse and Cowell, and was partly funded by Ives.[39] Several of the composers in the circle, including Cowell, Rudhyar, and Crawford, shared an interest in Theosophy.[40] The composers participated in the same salons, such as that of Djane Lavoie Herz in Chicago, where Crawford met Rudhyar and Cowell, and were supported by the same patrons, including Blanche Walton, at whose apartment Crawford took her first lessons with Seeger. Later, after the Great Depression had taken hold, several of the composers, including Cowell, Seeger, and Crawford, were active in the Composers' Collective.

By far the most important focal point for the ultra-moderns, however, was the series of enterprises organized by Henry Cowell under the name New Music, which included not only the periodical by that name, but also performances and recordings.[41] Cowell's stated intention in creating The New Music Society, the first of his enterprises, was to introduce audiences in Los Angeles, far outside the new music center of New York, to "the works of the most discussed composers of so called ultra-modern tendencies, such as Stravinsky, Schoenberg, Ruggles, Rudhyar, etc."[42] In addition to The New Music Society, which gave concerts in Los Angeles in 1925–26 and in San Francisco in 1927–36, Cowell also created two publication series – *New Music Quarterly* (begun in 1927) and the *Orchestra Series* (begun in 1932) – and a recording series, the *New Music Quarterly Recordings* (begun in 1934). Crawford was on the advisory board of the New Music Society as early as 1926, and participated actively in the other enterprises as well. The money for all of these efforts came largely, and anonymously, from Ives. The composers in this circle depended heavily on Cowell and his New Music conglomerate for the performance, publication, and recording of their works.[43]

Cowell supported Crawford in a particularly generous fashion. He promoted her music in public lectures as early as 1926. Her music was included in many of the concerts in the New Music Society Concert Series. Four of her Piano Preludes, the *Piano Study in Mixed Accents*, the String Quartet, and one of the *Diaphonic Suites*, were all published in the *New Music Quarterly*.[44] Her Three Songs were published in *New Music Orchestra Series*, with a cover designed by Ruggles.[45] The third movement of her String Quartet was the first work recorded as part of the *New Music Quarterly Recordings*.[46] In a letter to Ives to persuade him to finance the recording, Cowell wrote: "As to the value of the Crawford quartet, I think it is without question the best movement for quartet that any American has written, and I would rather hear it than almost anything I can think of . . . a genuine experience, and rises far above Crawford's earlier works. I would like to make the record, if only to have you hear it."[47] Cowell's patronage was crucial to Crawford, for she had no works published or recorded during her lifetime except under his auspices.

Cowell's admiration for her music, and his ceaseless patronage of it, placed Crawford at the center of the ultra-modern circle. Her music can be understood, to some extent, in relation to the musical and aesthetic concerns shared by the composers in that circle. It is difficult to generalize about a group of composers as diverse and highly individualistic as this, a group that includes such powerfully idiosyncratic figures as Varèse and Ives, but certain affinities can be identified.

The first involves a declaration of independence from Europe.[48] American composers had traditionally gone to Europe, particularly Germany and, more recently, France, to study, and had generally emulated European musical models. The ultra-moderns became the first group to turn away from Europe, both physically and mentally. They generally shunned studying abroad or, in the cases of Varèse and Rudhyar, expatriated to America. They avoided the forms, gestures, and sonorities of traditional European music, and the revival of those forms in modern neoclassicism.

Instead, the ultra-moderns tried in various ways to create an authentically American mode of musical expression. For Cowell and the others, nationalism was not so much an end in itself but, for Americans so long under the sway of European models, a necessary condition for originality and independence, which are the truly desirable ends.

> Certain music may be called essentially American because it expresses some phase of American life or feeling. Other music may be named American if it contains new materials which are created by an American composer or the American folk.
>
> Nationalism in music has no purpose as an aim in itself. Music happily transcends political and racial boundaries and is good or bad irrespective of the nation in which it was composed. Independence, however, is stronger than

imitation. In the hands of great men independence may result in products of permanent value. Imitation cannot be expected to produce such significant achievements.

American composition up to now has been tied to the apron-strings of European tradition. To attain musical independence, more national consciousness is a present necessity for American composers. The result of such an awakening should be the creation of works capable of being accorded international standing. When this has been accomplished, self-conscious nationalism will no longer be necessary.[49]

Unlike Ives, Crawford never incorporated any vernacular elements, such as hymn tunes or folk songs, directly into her music. Nonetheless, in its almost austere rejection of the forms and shapes of European music, her music achieves the musical independence of which Cowell speaks.

The independence is made possible, in part, through disciplined strategies of avoidance, ways of assuring that no traditional formations emerge unbidden. For the most part, ultra-modern music is characterized by its avoidance of traditional triadic harmony, and of the traditional melodies and rhythms associated with it, in favor of new harmonic combinations, new melodies, and new rhythms.

One strategy, which we have seen in Crawford's music and Seeger's writing, involved avoiding emphasizing any single note through repetition. This principle of non-repetition also shapes the melodies of Ruggles, as Cowell describes:

> Carl Ruggles has developed a process for himself in writing melodies for polyphonic purposes which embodies a new principle and is more purely contrapuntal than a consideration of harmonic intervals. He finds that if the same note is repeated in a melody before enough notes have intervened to remove the impression of the original note, there is a sense of tautology, because the melody should have proceeded to a fresh note instead of to a note already in the consciousness of the listener. Therefore Ruggles writes at least seven or eight different notes in a melody before allowing himself to repeat the same note, even in the octave.[50]

The avoidance of repetition is one aspect of a deeper commitment to dissonance as a structural basis, a commitment that entails, above all, the suppression of triads and tonal implications. When Seeger speaks of "dissonation," or of "dissonant counterpoint," this is what he has in mind. The systematic avoidance of traditional intervallic combinations and sonorities is one of the defining characteristics of ultra-modern composition, one of which all of the ultra-moderns spoke in strikingly similar language. Varèse, for example, was not known as a teacher as Seeger was, but their approaches were virtually identical on this basic point. In the words of André Jolivet, one of Varèse's few students: "The atonal discipline to which Varèse constrained me was much more severe than that of the dodecaphonists . . . It avoided all tonal connections and even hints of tonality, not only in the simultaneous harmonies, but also in the melodic successions."[51]

Beyond their commitment to avoiding "tonal connections and even hints of tonality," the ultra-moderns shared a vision of a new musical language based on dissonance, of melodies and harmonies structured upon the non-triadic intervals.

> Let us, however, meet the question of what would result if we were frankly to shift the center of musical gravity from consonance, on the edge of which it has long been poised, to seeming dissonance, on the edge of which it now rests. The difference might not be, any more than in Bach's practice, a matter of numerical proportion between consonant and dissonant effects, but rather an essential dissonant basis, the consonance being felt to rely on dissonance for resolution. An examination in fact would reveal that all the rules of Bach would seem to have been reversed, not with the result of substituting chaos, but with that of substituting a new order. The first and last chords would be now not consonant, but dissonant; and although consonant chords were admitted, it would be found that conditions were in turn applied to them, on the basis of the essential legitimacy of dissonances as independent intervals. In this system major sevenths and minor seconds and ninths would be the foundation intervals; major seconds and ninths, diminished fifths, and minor sevenths might be used as alternatives; all thirds, fourths, fifths, and sixths would only be permitted as passing or auxiliary notes. Octaves would be so far removed from the fundamental intervals in such a system that they would probably sound inconsistent and might not be used except in the rarest circumstances.[52]

Cowell envisions a world of harmonies built not from stacks of thirds, but from fourths/diminished fifths/fifths and from seconds, the latter possibility comprising what he calls a "tone-cluster."[53] Ultimately, he imagines harmonies in which "all the notes in any chord [are to be considered] as equal and independent."[54] He thus imagines the sound-world of ultra-modern music generally, in which the normative triads of traditional music are supplanted by a wide range of sonorities with varied intervallic profiles, a sound-world in which tritones, major sevenths, and minor ninths come to play preeminent structural roles.

This, of course, is the sound-world not only of Crawford and the American ultra-moderns, but of their European contemporaries as well, including particularly Schoenberg and his followers. Cowell's harmonies of equal and independent notes and Seeger's dissonant counterpoint describe what Schoenberg would have recognized as inevitable consequences of the emancipation of dissonance.[55] Crawford's commitment to atonal harmony places her right in the European–American modernist mainstream.

In some cases, an interest in new, nontraditional sounds led ultra-modern composers to expand radically their timbral palette. They did so either by using traditional instruments in unusual ways, as in Cowell's works that require striking the piano keys with fist or forearm, or by incorporating sounds made by non-traditional instruments, as in the sirens and *ondes martenot* of Varèse's *Ionisation* and

Ecuatorial, part of his life-long interest in "the liberation of sound and my right to make music with any sound and all sounds."[56]

Crawford, however, showed little interest in new instruments, instruments of indefinite pitch, or even in new instrumental techniques. Her instrumental combinations are not always traditional, aside from the Suite for Wind Quintet and String Quartet, but she always uses traditional instruments. Furthermore, the traditional instruments usually play in their traditional way. Her affiliation with the ultra-modern program comes in other areas.

As a general matter, the ultra-moderns turned their backs on the rich, lush harmonies of late romanticism in favor of a taut polyphony of independent lines. Seeger's comment about Ruggles could be applied also to Crawford and others in the circle: "The sustained melodic line is of prime importance . . . Counterpoint has challenged the chordal origins of [his] technique."[57] In its mildest form, this rejection of the "chordal" led simply to a shift in the prevailing texture from homophonic or melody-with-accompaniment to a counterpoint of relatively equal melodies. In a somewhat more intense form, it led to the heterophony of music like Crawford's, in which the component melodies have a very high degree of independence, and little attention is paid to the intervals or sonorities formed between them. Such music cultivates sounding-apart as opposed to sounding-together, in Seeger's phrase, a description that applies to Ruggles as well as it does to Crawford.[58]

In its most extreme form, the rejection of chordal homophony led to a radical heterogeneity of elements within a piece, with distinct musical materials, each with an independent structural basis, clashing and competing. Ives's music is probably an extreme in this regard, with its characteristic amalgam of tonal tunes embedded in an atonal environment. Ives uses quotation and collage as ways of opening up the work, shattering its boundaries, and drawing the outside world in. Crawford's music, in contrast, is hermetically sealed and, compared to Ives at least, stylistically uniform. Furthermore, while many of the ultra-modern composers changed style dramatically from piece to piece – Cowell is particularly noteworthy in this regard – Crawford's style, once she achieved her musical maturity, is remarkably stable. She avoids the extremes of heterogeneity both within and between her works.

At the same time, it is in the heterophony of her music that she, like her fellow ultra-moderns, offers her most profound challenge to the Western tradition. Her music presents elements that are distinct in basic ways, and offers no ready synthesis. It offers multiple perspectives, and privileges none of them. In her music, and in ultra-modern music generally, there can be no overarching unity, no *Grundgestalt* or *Ursatz* from which all the details of the musical surface can be derived. Instead, such works offer an irreducible multiplicity.

This is also the aspect of Crawford's music that proved most decisively influential for later generations of American composers. In its moderate form, the heterophony of ultra-modern music led directly to the music of Elliott

Carter, particularly the string quartets, so often characterized by vigorous independence of the parts, both melodically and rhythmically.[59] In its more extreme form, the heterogeneity of much ultra-modern music points ahead to the music of Cage and other composers who celebrate the independence of musical events from any subsuming context.

The ultra-modern composers shaped the concerns of later generations also by their interest, shared with their European contemporaries, in various kinds of precompositional planning. Like the twelve-tone serialism of Schoenberg, the canons and retrogrades in Ruggles's *Sun Treader* and Crawford's rotational plans offer a way of bringing order to the potential chaos of atonality.

Occasionally, different musical parameters are planned independently of each other, creating a situation that Nicholls calls "total polyphony," which he defines as the "deliberate independence of musical ideas or parts, or their component parameters."[60] This "kaleidoscopic" effect caused by the shifting relationship among the components of a single musical idea can be heard in music by Ives and Cowell, and by Crawford as well, in the first movement of the String Quartet, for example, where the pitches and rhythms of the opening melodies are treated independently when the melodies return at the end of the movement.[61]

More commonly, however, the ultra-moderns used precompositional plans as a way of integrating, not disassociating, the musical parameters, particularly pitch and rhythm. Crawford, as we have seen, brought about this integration in two ways, first by projecting the same shape or neume simultaneously in different musical dimensions and second through the proto-time-point system of her String Quartet and Suite for Wind Quintet. Cowell described an even more sweeping integration of musical parameters in his treatise *New Musical Resources*, and realized his ideas in two works, the *Quartet Romantic* and the *Quartet Euphometric*. What Cowell called his "theory of musical relativity" involved generating all the components of a work, including pitch, rhythm, dynamics, and timbre, from the ratios of the overtone series.[62] A concern with deep, precompositional, systematic links between particularly pitch and rhythm is thus a defining feature of ultra-modern music, and links it strongly to post-war serialism. When critics discuss the music of Babbitt and other American integral serialists, they generally do so in relationship to Schoenberg, Webern, and other European serialists. It now appears, however, that the impulse toward precompositional planning in which all musical parameters are integrated also had indigenous roots, in the music and writing of Cowell, Seeger, Crawford, and others.[63]

At the same time, there is a paradox in the precompositional planning of the ultra-moderns, in that it is used to create either maximum integration of the musical parameters or its opposite, maximum disassociation. Perhaps it would be most accurate to say that the ultra-moderns were interested in exploring the extremes of control and freedom, and that they often used precompositional plans to assist in that exploration. Ultra-modern music, then, is characterized by two deep, and deeply contradictory, impulses: one toward heterogeneity and multiplicity, the other toward integration and unification. It pushes both terms of the dichotomy to their outermost limits.

I do not wish to exaggerate the cohesion or uniformity of the ultra-modern composers. Any group that purports to encompass composers of such striking originality and individuality as Ives, Cowell, Crawford, and Varèse must define its identity in a loose, flexible way. Nonetheless, beyond their ties of friendship and patronage, the ultra-modern composers did share a common core of musical concerns, including a self-conscious Americanism, a desire to assert independence of traditional, European forms and structures, an interest in combining disparate musics into a single piece without the possibility of a higher unifying synthesis, and a desire to explore a variety of precompositional systems. In all of these respects, and despite her own powerful originality and independence, Crawford's music defines her as an essential member of the group.

In the context of the history of women in music

In the early nineteenth century, in America as in Europe, women in music were either middle- or upper-class amateurs who made music at home, or professionals, usually from a musical or theatrical family.[64] An unbridgeable divide separated these two groups, as professional musicians were not respectable members of middle-class society and respectable, middle-class women were not permitted to enter the public sphere. By the end of the century, however, with increased educational opportunities for women (including musical education) and the impetus provided by the women's movement, women began to emerge, in small numbers, as professional performers and composers of vernacular and parlor music and later of art music. Women began to attend music conservatories and to enter the profession of music teaching in significant numbers. By the turn of the century, America had produced its first generation of women composers of art music, including Amy Beach (1867–1944), who remains probably the best known.

As a conservatory student, a piano teacher, and a composer, Crawford took full advantage of these new opportunities for women. It would be an exaggeration, however, to imagine her as participating in a vital subculture of women composers of art music, because they remained, during Crawford's lifetime, few in number and geographically isolated. It seems unlikely that Crawford would have known art music by women composers of earlier generations. No tradition existed to sustain her; there were no viable models for her to emulate. Women writers of her generation could look back to a long, rich, and continuous tradition of women as novelists and poets, but women composers were not so fortunate. Effectively cut off from their forebears, they were forced not only to confront the musical challenges shared by their male colleagues, but simultaneously to engage the more difficult task of even imagining themselves as composers. This is what I have referred to earlier, following Gilbert and Gubar, as the "anxiety of authorship."

If she was unfamiliar with art music by her female precursors, Crawford would certainly have been aware of the nineteenth-century tradition of domestic music making. Indeed, as the daughter of a piano teacher, and as one who supported herself by teaching piano, she was an active participant in that tradition. Her professional career also benefitted from the tradition of domestic music making in the form of the musical salons of Djane Herz and Blanche Walton.[65] Both women transformed their homes into important centers of musical activity. It was in these domestic settings that Crawford not only heard the music and met the composers who became most important to her, but also enjoyed first performances of many of her own works.

Crawford's attitude toward the domestic tradition would have been complicated, however, by what Gilbert and Gubar, in another useful coinage, refer to as the "female affiliation complex," a network of ambivalent attitudes women authors have toward their female precursors. One strand in that complex may involve the reluctance of a woman author to identify herself with a tradition that, because it is female, has been widely devalued. She may turn in "renunciation of her desire for a literary mother to the tradition of the father."[66]

This renunciation is central to the stance of modernist women composers like Crawford, as Catherine Parsons Smith has argued:

> In music, numerous middle-class white women of the generation of romantic Americanism, the most famous being Amy Beach, were able, like their male contemporaries, to build constructively on the nineteenth-century American tradition of domestic music that preceded them. But the modernist generation firmly turned away from the domestic tradition, identifying it with "feminization." The younger women thus rejected their romantic Americanist foremothers, alienating themselves from female role models along with their "feminized" heritage. Simultaneously, they themselves were rejected and isolated as composers by the male modernists who were their contemporaries.[67]

Crawford maintained close and sustaining ties with her female music teachers, including her mother, with female patrons, including Herz and Walton, and with an important female contemporary composer, Marion Bauer.[68] By adopting a dissonant, ultra-modern idiom in her music, however, Crawford effectively cut herself off from the consolation and continuity of a distinctly female tradition in music. Her abandonment of her compositions and her turn to American folk music in the mid 1930s may have been motivated, in part, by a desire to reestablish links to the tradition she had renounced.

Ignorant of previous women composers of art music, and cut off musically from the women's tradition of domestic music, Crawford chose to make her way in a male-dominated world of musical modernism, one that was hostile to women in a deep and pervasive way. Recent feminist scholarship has shown the surprising extent to which modernism is shaped not only by an interest in breaking free of traditional forms and structures, but by a deep and misogynistic anti-feminist reaction:

The literary phenomenon ordinarily called "modernism" is itself – though no doubt overdetermined – for men as much as for women a product of the sexual battle that we are describing here, as are the linguistic experiments usually attributed to the revolutionary poetics of the so-called avant-garde.[69]

In music, the "sexual battle" was waged by modernist men using an intensely misogynist rhetoric, one which defined their own work as variously hard, powerful, abstract, learned, and above all, virile, as they sought to reassure themselves of the masculine nature of their career and their music. The most conspicuous example of this kind of rhetoric in music is Charles Ives.[70] For him, both the tradition of domestic music, dominated by women, and most of the European art-music tradition, was "sissy," "emasculated," "ladylike," etc. As Frank Rossiter observes, Ives had

> a vision of music as divided into two great opposing camps. On the one side lay music of the cultivated tradition – effeminate, aristocratic, pretentious, easy on the ears, commercial and lacking in ideals in spite of its pretensions, only rarely breaking its bondage to women. On the other side lay music of the vernacular tradition – masculine, democratic, down to earth, fervent, speaking to men of the substance of their daily lives.[71]

For Ives then, the battle between two kinds of music was explicitly also a battle between the sexes. For Ives, and for others, musical dissonance was a primary weapon in the battle, a means of differentiating the manly from the sissified.[72] Crawford's decision to compose under the banner of dissonant counterpoint, then, placed her in the extraordinarily awkward position of subscribing to a program that, for some at least, was designed explicitly to demean and exclude her.

A fainter echo of the same gendered language may be found in Cowell's claim that "American composition up to now has been tied to the apron-strings of European tradition."[73] For Cowell, American modernism is a young man asserting his independence of his overbearing mother. Cowell, of course, was Crawford's greatest supporter, and defended her music when Ives wondered whether it was sufficiently "mansized."[74] Nonetheless, he too seems to have been unable to resist imagining his modernism as a male response to an overly feminized past, as part of an ongoing battle of the sexes.

Seeger initially resisted initiating Crawford into his brand of musical modernism precisely because she was a woman.

> Cowell was much impressed with [Crawford's] writing and spoke to me about her several times, and of course I saw some of her first compositions published in *New Music*. I was very snooty in those days about women composers and had come more or less to the conclusion that the great tradition of European music, say from 1200 to about 1930, had been created mostly by men and that it was a bit absurd to expect women to fit themselves into a groove which was so definitely flavored with machismo (and, of course, the early music of the

twentieth century and the late music of the nineteenth century was machismo with a capital M).[75]

Crawford thus faced barriers beyond those that hampered any woman attempting a career in the public sphere. In allying herself with the ultra-modern movement, she placed herself in a camp that was hostile to her, that was committed, in a deep philosophical and aesthetic sense, to her exclusion. If all of the ultra-moderns were outsiders in relation to prevailing musical tastes, then Crawford was an outsider among outsiders.

While her resulting isolation may well have contributed to her later abandonment of her music, it is difficult to assess what impact it may have had on the music she composed in her ultra-modern heyday. Does Crawford's music speak "in a different voice?" Can it be positioned within the network of dualities that permeate Western thought, dualities that analogize male/female with good/evil, reason/emotion, culture/nature, self/other, content/process, stable/unstable, hierarchy/network, and so on? I have previously described Crawford's music in terms that might arouse optimism. I have emphasized its reliance on process rather than content as a means of establishing coherence, its resistance to hierarchical explanations that derive the musical surface from single generating ideas, and its tendency constantly to turn back in upon itself rather than striving toward well-established goals.

I am reluctant, however, to insist on the gendered nature of these musical attributes for several reasons. First, these qualities of Crawford's music are perhaps more accurately described as qualities of my analytical model. It is my model that is transformational, non-hierarchical, and anti-teleological, not necessarily Crawford's music, which might also be profitably modeled in other ways. Second, even imagining that I have succeeded in capturing essential features of Crawford's music, it is beyond question that the other, male ultra-moderns compose in a similar way and I would be uncomfortable arguing that, therefore, all ultra-modern music speaks with a different, and distinctly female, voice. Finally, the dualities themselves are too vague, and too inherently unstable to work as viable analytical categories.

The duality of consonance and dissonance, so central to Crawford's music and the ultra-modern program generally, is a case in point. In traditional tonal music, that duality can be mapped onto the duality of male and female in precisely contradictory ways. Either consonance is the stable, privileged term with dissonance its dark, chaotic Other, or dissonance is the active, striving term and consonance merely the passive place upon which dissonance discharges its energies.[76] Musical modernism, which takes dissonance as its structural basis, might seem to favor the latter interpretation – certainly Ives imagined the dissonance of his music as a barrier against softness and effeminacy – but Crawford herself seems to have identified dissonance with the natural and the feminine.[77] The dualities are thus too unstable and too easily reversed to provide a reliable basis for evaluating Crawford's musical voice.

Rather than asking about Crawford's voice in the abstract, it might be more profitable to ask whether gender, including the network of dualities discussed above, is at issue within individual compositions. Certainly a basic duality, between melodies that are strictly patterned and melodies that are free, is an explicit feature of many of Crawford's works.

The problem comes in mapping that duality of melodic types onto more abstract, philosophical dualities, particularly in the absence of a verbal text. In the fourth movement of the String Quartet, for example, a free melody in the first violin is poised against a strictly serialized melody played in octaves by the other three instruments. One might argue that the serial voice, with its rational, orderly patterning, lines up with the first term in each of the familiar male/female, reason/emotion, stable/unstable oppositions.[78] One might argue equally plausibly, I think, that the free melody in the first violin asserts a striving, autonomous individuality against the cyclical melody shared communally by the other instruments, and thus that the free melody should be lined up with the first terms in the dualities. It is unprofitable, then, to imagine Crawford's music as lining up in any straightforward way with a network of philosophical dualities.

It might be more useful to imagine her music, particularly those works that juxtapose strict and free melodies, as reveling in the instability of oppositional categories and playfully breaking down the barriers between them. Crawford always takes care in such works to emphasize the connections between the opposing terms, not merely their distinctions. The strict melodies (be they serialized, confined to ostinati, or regimented in some other way) and the free melodies always betray a subtle kinship, a shared motivic life. Similarly, the free melodies are often constrained by some kind of systematic control, such as verse form, while the strict melodies often engage in a free registral play that is independent of any serial plan. In that way, Crawford's music can be understood to create and invoke a system of dualities, including possibly the binarism of gender, only to question and undermine it.

As difficult as it is to situate Crawford's music persuasively in relation to a trans-historical network of dualities, it is no less so to find her proper place in relation to actual music written by actual women under certain social and historical conditions. Our first problem is how little we know at present about the music women did write. In music, we are still at an early stage of recuperative history, discovering previously unknown or obscure music by women. Given the almost complete absence of systematic description of music by any woman composer, it is virtually impossible, at this time, to generalize about its style and structure, or even to assert that there may be something distinctive about music written by women. Real progress in this area must await the kind of close study of music by women that its quality and interest merit.

One can hope that when we do have a critical mass of satisfying accounts of music by women composers, these might begin to cohere to create a musical equivalent to the "distinctively female literary tradition" that feminist literary critics have persuasively described.[79] Optimism in this area, however, has to be tempered by the sobering realization of the extent to which women composers, much more than women writers, were isolated from each other even when they were permitted to speak at all. Would Clara Schumann have been aware of her female predecessors? Would Amy Beach have known Clara Schumann's music? Would Ruth Crawford have known music by either Beach or Schumann? I think the answer has to be a depressing no in each case. The chains of knowledge and influence needed to bind a community together have largely been absent for women composers. As a result, I think we will always face fairly severe limits in any attempt to describe a coherent, stable countertradition of women composers of art music in the West.

Nonetheless, it is possible to make a few, tentative, generalizations about music by women since about 1750, although these have much more to do with style than structure, and there are striking exceptions in each case. First, women have tended to write music for voice accompanied by piano; what instrumental music they wrote was usually for the smallest groups of instruments, including particularly solo piano. There have been, until relatively recently, very few symphonies or operas by women. Second, women have tended to favor pro-grammatic or character pieces over the large, abstract forms like sonata or fugue. These preferences of instrumentation and genre reflect a more general stylistic orientation toward music with explicit links to the domestic or salon traditions. These choices were all highly constrained by social and economic forces: women were rarely permitted to emerge into the public sphere, and when they were, they were not permitted to emerge very far. Finally, women have rarely, until recently, been structural innovators or musical revolutionaries and, again, one does not have to look far for the social forces constraining them in this area.

Like most of her female precursors, Crawford also usually wrote for small groups of instruments, although the ostinati in the Three Songs and the *Music for Small Orchestra* might challenge that limitation somewhat. As for the other style characteristics generally shared by women composers, Crawford sets herself radically apart in each case. Although she did write songs, most of her music is textless and abstractly structured, often over the largest musical spans. While she participated in the tradition of domestic music making by virtue of her studying and teaching piano and her involvement in the salons of Djane Herz and Blanche Walton, her music itself is utterly severed from the traditions of domestic music, not only by virtue of its uncompromising dissonance but also because of its technical difficulty – the String Quartet, for example, can be played only by a highly skilled professional quartet. Finally, her music is extraordinarily innovative structurally, as it has been the principal task of this book to show. For all of these reasons, it is difficult to see Crawford as the inheritor of a distinctive counter-tradition, to write a narrative called "the history of women in music" that would lead to her in some compelling way.

During her lifetime and since, however, many of the profound discontinuities in that narrative have begun to be repaired. The isolation of women composers from their precursors and from each other, the pressure on them to remain within or close to the domestic sphere, the hostility toward them of prevailing musical movements, have all considerably abated. One may hope that, in this century, a distinctive countertradition, a community of women composers, has indeed begun to form. If that is the case, then Crawford's music, although significantly cut off from music by women before it, may come to be seen as a nourishing source for music by women, and for all music, that has come after.

Notes

1 Introduction

1 A note about names: The composer who is the subject of this book was born as, and wrote virtually all of her music as, Ruth Crawford. When she married Charles Seeger, she took his name, and is identified as Ruth Crawford Seeger in most works about her and in the catalogue of the Library of Congress. The title of this book conforms to that prevailing usage. Late in her life, when she resumed her compositional career after a long silence, she identified herself as Ruth Crawford-Seeger. Among these alternatives, I will refer to her throughout this book as Ruth Crawford, or simply Crawford.

2 The ultra-modern movement is described in standard histories of the period, including Gilbert Chase, *America's Music: From the Pilgrims to the Present*, rev. 3rd edn (Urbana: University of Illinois Press, 1987); Charles Hamm, *Music in the New World* (New York: W. W. Norton, 1983); H. Wiley Hitchcock, *Music in the United States: A Historical Introduction*, 3rd edn (Englewood Cliffs, NJ: Prentice-Hall, 1988); and Wilfrid Mellers, *Music in a New Found Land: Themes and Developments in the History of American Music* (New York: Alfred A. Knopf, 1965). See also more specialized studies, including Henry Cowell, ed., *American Composers on American Music: A Symposium* (Palo Alto: Stanford University Press, 1933; repr. edn New York: Frederick Ungar Publishing, 1962); Steven Gilbert, "'The Ultra-Modern Idiom': A Survey of *New Music*," *Perspectives of New Music* 12/1–2 (1973–74), 282–314; Rita Mead, *Henry Cowell's New Music 1925–1936: The Society, the Music Editions, and the Recordings* (Ann Arbor: UMI Research Press, 1981); and David Nicholls, *American Experimental Music, 1890–1940* (Cambridge: Cambridge University Press, 1990).

3 For a history of efforts to create an independent American music, and the place of the ultra-modern movement in that history, see Barbara Zuck, *A History of Musical Americanism* (Ann Arbor: UMI Research Press, 1980).

4 There is a growing secondary literature on Crawford, including Matilda Gaume, "Ruth Crawford Seeger: Her Life and Works" (Ph.D. dissertation: Indiana University, 1973), and *Ruth Crawford Seeger: Memoirs, Memories, Music* (Metuchen, NJ: Scarecrow Press, 1987); Felix Meyer, "'Thoughtful Bricklaying': Zu einigen Werker der americanischen 'Ultramodernistin' Ruth Crawford," in *Festschrift Ernst Lichtenhahn*, ed. Christoph Ballmes and Thomas Gastmann (Winterthur: Amadeus, 1994), 167–92; Mark Nelson, "In Pursuit of Charles Seeger's Heterophonic Ideal: Three Palindromic

Works by Ruth Crawford," *The Musical Quarterly* 72/4 (1986), 458–75; Charles Seeger, "Ruth Crawford," in Cowell, *American Composers on American Music*, 110–18; Judith Tick, "Dissonant Counterpoint Revisited: The First Movement of Ruth Crawford's *String Quartet 1931*," in *A Celebration of American Music: Words and Music in Honor of H. Wiley Hitchcock*, ed. Richard Crawford, R. Allen Lott, and Carol Oja (Ann Arbor: The University of Michigan Press, 1990), 405–22; also Tick, "Ruth Crawford's 'Spiritual Concept': The Sound-Ideals of an Early American Modernist," *Journal of the American Musicological Society* 44/2 (1991), 221–61, and her biography, *Ruth Crawford Seeger: An American Woman's Life in Music* (Oxford: Oxford University Press, 1995), which I was unable to consult before its publication. Valuable context is also provided in David Nicholls, *American Experimental Music, 1890–1940*, and Ann Pescatello, *Charles Seeger: A Life in American Music* (Pittsburgh: University of Pittsburgh Press, 1992).

5 This distinction between theoretical and cultural contexts is taken from Arnold Whittall, "Experience, Thought and Musicology," *Musical Times* 134 (1993), No. 1804, 318–20: "A composition can never be plausibly interpreted as self-contained, and can never be understood (experienced, enjoyed) 'in its own terms', as the glib phrase has it. The impulse behind the glibness is commendable: we all want to do justice to what is special, original and particular about a composition. But we are unlikely to get very far with this project if we make a determined effort to isolate the work, seal it away in a vacuum so that it remains unsullied by contact with the very circumstances within which it first saw the light of day. Music analysis, today, tends to see these circumstances as extending in two different directions from the work itself. In one direction, there is the theoretical context: this is, those various ideas about the structural substance of musical form and language that have been devised as interpretative tools – ideas which may themselves have evolved during different periods of musical history. Then there is the cultural context, and in approaching this the analyst extends the hand of friendship to musicologists who (with varying degrees of enthusiasm) wear the labels of 'historian' or 'critic'" (319).

6 The standard works in this area are Allen Forte, *The Structure of Atonal Music* (New Haven: Yale University Press, 1973); David Lewin, *Generalized Musical Intervals and Transformations* (New Haven: Yale University Press, 1987); Robert Morris, *Composition with Pitch-Classes* (New Haven: Yale University Press, 1987); George Perle, *Serial Composition and Atonality* (Berkeley: University of California Press, 1977); and John Rahn, *Basic Atonal Theory* (New York: Longman, 1980).

7 This treatise exists in four versions, two at the Library of Congress, dated December 1930 and September 1931, and two at the Library of the University of California at Berkeley, dated November and December 1931. More than sixty years after it was written, it has finally been published in *Studies in Musicology II*, ed. Ann Pescatello (Berkeley: University of California Press, 1995).

8 Henry Cowell, *New Musical Resources* (New York: Alfred A. Knopf, 1930; repr. edn New York: Something Else Press, 1969).

9 Ruth Crawford, letter to Charles Seeger, September 20, 1930; cited in Gaume, *Memoirs, Memories, Music*, 152.

10 Seeger, *Tradition and Experiment in the New Music*.

11 In Seeger's words: "In all the weeks that she handed in those weekly assignments, there wasn't a single exercise; there was simply a steady flow of real compositions and most of them have been published, in the *Diaphonic Suites* and eventually in the last two movements of the String Quartet, which were both assignments but with which she made the indefinable extra that really makes the composition." Quoted in Ray Wilding-White, "Remembering Ruth Crawford Seeger: An Interview with Charles and Peggy Seeger," *American Music* 6/4 (1988), 447.

2 Elements of a style

1 Charles Seeger, *Tradition and Experiment*. Seeger refers to "progression," that is, the motion from one note to another, rather than to the notes themselves. This emphasis on process rather than content, on transformation rather than object, permeates Seeger's treatise, and will strongly influence my own analytical approach to Crawford's music.

2 Crawford's role in the preparation of Seeger's treatise may have extended to writing, or helping to write, some of the music examples. The melodic fragments cited in my Example 2.1, and others throughout the treatise, resemble Crawford's in many ways. In this example, each fragment begins with an ascending semitone followed by a descending whole tone, a favorite motive of Crawford's from before her first contact with Seeger, and all are structured as loose inversional wedges around the first note, another familiar practice of hers.

3 Ibid. Seeger's concept of dissonance, which refers to the avoidance of triadic implications, will be discussed in detail later in this chapter.

4 In this and all of Crawford's music other than the four *Diaphonic Suites*, accidentals affect only the notes before which they occur; they are not effective throughout the measure.

5 This observation is drawn from a statistical survey undertaken by Larry Polansky in "Envisioning Ruth Crawford Seeger's *Piano Study in Mixed Accents*," a paper presented at the joint meeting of the American Musicological Society and the Society for Music Theory, November 1993, Montreal.

6 A *pitch* represents a point on the continuum of musically useful frequencies. Each of the eighty-eight keys of the piano keyboard represents a single pitch. When I speak of *pitch space*, I am locating a note along the continuum of pitches. A *pitch class* is the class of all pitches that are one or more octaves apart. Every pitch is a member of one of only twelve pitch classes. All the B♭s in the world, for example, whatever their pitch, are members of the same pitch class. When I speak of *pitch-class space*, I am locating a note within the modular, circular space defined by the twelve pitch classes. In this book, I will use the term "note" when I do not wish or need to distinguish between pitch and pitch class. For more formal definitions of pitch and pitch class, and of pitch and pitch-class space, see Morris, *Composition with Pitch Classes*.

7 Pitches are identified in this book according to the notation suggested by the Acoustical Society of America: pitch class is identified by an uppercase letter and specific octave placement by a number following the letter. An octave number refers to pitches from a given C through the B above. Middle C is C4.

8 A similarly equal distribution is maintained throughout the piece, as Polansky has shown. See "Envisioning Ruth Crawford Seeger's *Piano Study in Mixed Accents.*"

9 The numbering of the four *Suites* does not correspond to their order of composition. No. 2 (for bassoon and cello) was written in February 1930; No. 3 (for two clarinets in B♭) in March 1930; No. 1 (for flute or oboe) in April 1930; and No. 4 (for oboe and cello) in December 1930. Nos. 1, 2, and 3 were written during the period of Crawford's study with Seeger, while No. 4 was written when she was living in Europe.

10 Charles Seeger, "On Dissonant Counterpoint," *Modern Music* 7 (1930), 28.

11 The term is Charles Rosen's, coined with reference to Schoenberg: "The saturation of musical space is Schoenberg's substitute for the tonic chord of the traditional musical language. The absolute consonance is a state of chromatic plenitude." Charles Rosen, *Arnold Schoenberg* (New York: Viking, 1975), 57–58.

12 This preference could be phrased as a general rule, as follows: By the end of a melodic phrase, for every note X in the line, there must be a note Y a semitone away. This rule freely adapts David Lewin's rule for the diatonic melodies of species counterpoint, namely that, "for every note X of the counterpoint line lying above (below) the cadence tone, some note lying one step lower (higher) than X must appear in the line at some point subsequent to X." "An Interesting Global Rule for Species Counterpoint," *In Theory Only* 6/8 (1983), pp. 19–44.

13 In pitch space, we might speak of filling in all the semitones between, say, C♯4 and F5. In modular pitch-class space, we might refer to the chromatic zone between C♯ and F, that is, C♯–D–D♯–E–F in any register.

14 The serial organization of this and other melodies will be discussed extensively below.

15 Seeger wrote music criticism for the *Daily Worker* during 1934–35 under the pseudonym Carl Sands. For an account of the Composers' Collective, and Seeger's role in it, see David K. Dunaway, "Charles Seeger and Carl Sands: The Composers' Collective Years," *Ethnomusicology* 24/2 (May 1980), 159–68, and Barbara Zuck, *A History of Musical Americanism*, 103–38. Crawford was not an active member of the collective: "Chinaman, Laundryman" and "Sacco, Vanzetti" were her only contributions to the group's efforts.

16 Ray Wilding-White, "Remembering Ruth Crawford Seeger," 451.

17 The *Sprechstimme* notes in the published score were originally given as actual pitches in Crawford's handwritten manuscript. Crawford offers the following note for performers: "The singer must *modulate* from the sung to the spoken words – there must be no sudden break. The pitches given are only approximate."

18 Angle brackets <> denote ordered successions (of pitches, pitch classes, or intervals). Intervals are counted in semitones, with the signs + and – denoting ascending and descending motion.

19 The motive occurs in four versions: <−2, +1>, <+2, −1>, <+1, −2>, and <−1, +2>.

20 Note that retrograde refers to the relations among the pitches, not the intervals. When two motives are related by retrograde, they will have complementary intervals in reverse order.

21 Crawford, letter to Gerald Reynolds (conductor of the Women's University Chorus, which commissioned the works), October 13, 1930; cited in Judith Tick,

"'Spiritual Concept,'" 247. My account of the genesis of the Chants is based on Tick's.

22 Crawford, letter to Carl Sandburg, January 26, 1931; cited in Tick, "'Spiritual Concept,'" 247.

23 In motives related by inversion, each interval will be replaced, in order, by its complement.

24 Crawford originally wrote this piece for either two cellos or cello and bassoon, but the published version suggests only the latter instrumentation.

25 If two motives are related by retrograde inversion, they will have the same intervals in reverse order. An RI-pair involves the last interval of the first motive becoming the first interval of its retrograde inversion. RI-pairs are a persistent feature of Crawford's melodies, and will be discussed in detail below. David Lewin provides a general model for discussing RI-pairs and longer RI-chains in *Generalized Musical Intervals and Transformations*, 180–89.

26 Crawford's Nine Preludes were written in two groups, the first five in 1924–25 (these remain unpublished) and the last four in 1927–28.

27 Seeger, letter to Crawford, October 7, 1930; cited in Tick, "'Spiritual Concept,'" 251.

28 Crawford, letter to Gerald Reynolds, November 10, 1930; cited in Gaume, *Memoirs, Memories, Music*, 162. In describing the Chant to Reynolds, Crawford adopted Seeger's terminology, even quoting him verbatim. See Tick, "'Spiritual Concept,'" 252.

29 The notes are not introduced in strict ascending order: G♯ comes before G. As a result, a small RI-pair is produced from forms of Crawford's favorite motive: F♯–G♯–G overlapped with G♯–G–A.

30 I will be talking regularly about four different kinds of intervals in this book. 1) An *ordered pitch interval* is the interval between two pitches, counted in semitones, either ascending (indicated with +) or descending (indicated with −). 2) An *unordered pitch interval* is the space between two pitches, counted in semitones, without consideration for its direction. 3) An *ordered pitch-class interval* is an interval between two pitch classes calculated by moving upward from one pitch class to the nearest available member of the other pitch class. There are eleven different ordered pitch-class intervals. 4) An *unordered pitch-class interval* is the smallest distance between two pitch classes. There are six unordered pitch-class intervals, which are also called *interval classes*. Interval class 1, for example, contains pitch intervals 1, 11, and their compounds; interval class 2 contains 2, 10, and their compounds, and so on. I will commonly abbreviate pitch interval as ip and interval class as ic. In all of this, I follow standard formulations, like those of John Rahn in *Basic Atonal Theory* (New York: Longman, 1980).

31 Seeger, *Tradition and Experiment*. Seeger's use of the term "degree" is not entirely clear, but I take it to mean both size and type, as in "minor thirds" or "perfect fourths."

32 Any group of three notes will describe one of only twelve possible combinations of interval classes. A chromatic cluster like D–D♯–E, for example, contains two 1s and a 2, whereas a major triad contains a 3, a 4, and a 5. These twelve distinct intervallic combinations correspond to the twelve trichord-types, defined by equivalence under transposition and inversion.

33 The same intervallic preferences characterize the work as a whole, as Polansky has shown. See "Envisioning Ruth Crawford Seeger's *Piano Study in Mixed Accents*."

34 A trichord is an unordered collection of three pitch classes. The trichords can be grouped into twelve distinct equivalence classes, also known as set classes or set types. Within each set class, each set will be related by transposition or inversion to all of the others. I will generally identify set classes by their prime form, the most compressed possible representation, which I will present in parentheses. For example, all of the major and minor triads are members of set class (037), all the diminished triads are members of (036), and all the augmented triads are members of (048). The twelve trichord-types or trichord-classes are as follows: (012), (013), (014), (015), (016), (024), (025), (026), (027), (036), (037), and (048). Any group of three notes is a representative of one of these types.

35 Seeger, *Tradition and Experiment*.

36 "Even if a composer does treat all the intervals as though they were all of one class, it is to be doubted whether he is entirely honest with himself in stating that he is actually so free of the old tonality. For ourselves, and for many we know, there is still a lot of life in the old tonality and it will be read into or 'heard in' such music whether the composer expects it or not. Such a powerful element will not die for many years – perhaps centuries. Composers do not entirely make themselves and their work . . . So – admitting the general force of the argument as regards the gradual consonant-becoming of the intervals of the duodecuple scale, we would propose for the present as a working hypothesis: until more tones, making additional dissonances, can be added to the present twelve, the list of consonances and dissonances shall stand as is conventional for chordal sounding." Ibid.

37 Ibid.

38 Ibid.

39 Recall that accidentals affect only the notes before which they occur; they are not effective throughout the measure.

40 Seeger, *Tradition and Experiment*.

41 In Milton Babbitt's words, "The trichord is the minimal structure which can reflect the transformations of twelve-tone thinking." *Milton Babbit: Words About Music*, ed. Stephen Dembski and Joseph N. Straus (Madison, Wis.: University of Wisconsin Press, 1987).

42 Seeger, *Tradition and Experiment*.

43 Ibid.

44 Seeger did speculate on the possibility of analyzing timbre, and relating it to pitch, via the overtone series: "From a physical viewpoint, timbre is not a fundamental or simple phenomenon but a complex of pitches and dynamics. What musicians call the pitch of a tone is simply the loudest of this complex. It is the order among and relative loudness of the various pitches that constitutes the tone-quality or timbre. Thus, a valve-horn has a great many strong, low partial-tones or over-tones, giving it its rich, full sound; a tuning-fork, on the other hand has only very high and very faint ones (as can be noted from the "ring" it gives when struck) thus giving it its characteristic cold, pure sound. A clarinet is distinguished from a flute in that it tends to sound its uneven partials louder than its even, whereas the flute is the reverse – it sounds even louder." Timbres might thus be systematically distinguished and compared based on the partials that define them, but Seeger concludes: "Such a thing as a

scale of tone quality, however, much as it is needed, is still to be worked out." Ibid. Cowell's discussion of timbre takes a strikingly similar form in *New Musical Resources*, 32–35. Systematic study of timbre continues to engage music theorists. See Robert Cogan, *New Images of Musical Sound* (Cambridge, Mass.: Harvard University Press, 1984) and Wayne Slawson, *Sound Color* (Berkeley: University of California Press, 1985).

45 Seeger, *Tradition and Experiment*.

46 The most important recent work on contour may be found in the following studies: Michael Friedmann, "A Methodology for the Discussion of Contour: Its Application to Schoenberg's Music," *Journal of Music Theory* 29/2 (1985), 223–48; Elizabeth West Marvin, "The Perception of Rhythm in Non-Tonal Music: Rhythmic Contours in the Music of Edgard Varèse," *Music Theory Spectrum* 13/1 (1991), 61–78; Elizabeth West Marvin and Paul Laprade, "Relating Musical Contours: Extensions of a Theory for Contour," *Journal of Music Theory* 31/2 (1987), 225–67 (see also in same issue, Michael Friedmann, "A Response: My Contour, Their Contour," 268–74); and Robert Morris, *Composition with Pitch-Classes*.

47 Seeger, *Tradition and Experiment*.

48 There are a couple of small glitches in the chart, but these need not concern us here. In the first group of neumes, D–D♯–E♯ does not belong, since the E♯ is not related by semitone to either D or D♯. The second group of neumes is missing a member: D–E–C♯ has been inadvertently excluded.

49 Seeger, *Tradition and Experiment*.

50 I have adopted the notation and terminology of Friedmann's Contour Adjacency Series (CAS), which "describes a series of directional moves up and down in the melody . . . [thus producing] a rather blunt, general description of a series of moves between temporally adjacent pitches." Friedmann, "A Methodology for the Discussion of Contour," 226.

51 This concept and notation are adopted from Marvin and Laprade, "Relating Musical Contours," where they define a contour-segment (CSEG) as "an ordered set of c-pitches in c-space," where c-pitches (contour pitches) are "elements in c-space, numbered in order from low to high, beginning with 0 up to (n–1), where n equals the number of elements," and c-space (contour space) is "a type of musical space consisting of elements arranged from low to high disregarding the exact intervals between elements" (255). I will have frequent occasion to describe contours as CSEGs.

52 "The inversion of a CSEG comprised of n distinct contour pitches . . . may be found by subtracting each contour pitch from (n-1)." Ibid.

53 The four contours that Seeger describes as "constituting one basic form" comprise a CSEG class, which is defined as "an equivalence class made up of all csegs related by identity, translation [=transposition], retrograde, inversion, and retrograde-inversion." Ibid. All the CSEGs identified in Example 2.20 are members of the same CSEG class.

54 Seeger, *Tradition and Experiment*.

55 I am starting on D4 because Crawford's melodies so frequently use that pitch as a starting point and grant it special, centric status, and I have arbitrarily designated <+2, –1> as the prime ordering. Inverting the notes replaces each interval, in order, by the same interval in the opposite direction, or <–2, +1>. Retrograding the notes

reverses the order of the intervals and replaces each with its opposite, <+1, –2>. Retrograde inverting the notes keeps the intervals the same, but presents them in reverse order, <–1, +2>.

56 The dotted double bar is one of several symbols that Crawford uses to designate phrase or section boundaries. This topic will be discussed more fully below.

57 Most commonly a motive is overlapped with its own retrograde inversion to create what I previously called an RI-pair, and what David Lewin calls an RI-chain, or RICH. See *Generalized Musical Intervals and Transformations*, 180–89. I will have more to say about RICH applied to M1 and other motives later on.

58 In choral part III, Crawford appends this comment to the concluding F: "The F has much harmonic value, and must be clearly marked," adding at the bottom of the page, "Wherever there is a minor or major chord dissonated by one tone, the dissonating tone must be strongly marked." The F in question is dissonant against an E♭-minor chord in the other voices, which accounts for Crawford's interest in it. It also reveals much about her conception of harmony, which, like melody, must suppress traditional triadic implications. We will return to this subject at a later point.

59 Seeger, *Tradition and Experiment*. Seeger's list of neume transformations is remarkably similar to a list provided by Adolph Weiss, Schoenberg's first American student and a friend of both Crawford and Seeger, of Schoenberg's "methods of varying a motive." See "The Lyceum of Schoenberg," *Modern Music* 9/3 (1932), 101. The resemblance suggests not so much direct influence as the independently shared concerns of Schoenberg and Seeger. Taylor Greer also observes this resemblance in his commentary on Seeger's *Tradition and Influence in the New Music* in *Studies in Musicology II*.

60 Seeger, *Tradition and Experiment*. Seeger's own music, what little of it survives, can be described in just this way, in terms of its neumatic content and transformation. Two unaccompanied works for solo voice, *The Letter* and *Psalm 137,* were published in *New Music* 26/3 (1953), the same issue that contained Crawford's *Diaphonic Suite No. 1.* Both begin with, make extensive use of, either exactly or in transformation, and return to, a single neume, <–1, –3>, or its conversions.

61 Seeger illustrates this possibility with a music example that transforms the first two measures of Schubert's Symphony No. 9 into the motto from Strauss's *Till Eulenspiegel* in just seven steps!

62 Recall that accidentals affect only the notes before which they occur; they are not effective throughout the measure. The fourth note of the example is thus A♮.

63 In adopting this procedure, I am observing not only the spirit of Seeger's approach, with its emphasis on "progression" rather than object, but also the explicit analytical practice of David Lewin in *Generalized Musical Intervals and Transformations* and *Musical Form and Transformation: 4 Analytic Essays* (New Haven: Yale University Press, 1993).

64 My INT has its basis in Seeger's idea of "progression by complement": "The four [conversions] of the basic neume form are exact. Modified versions can be made in a variety of different ways, one of the most interesting being Progression by Complement . . . The simplest and, at present, most useful is the Octave Complement, whose operation consists in a substitution of the octave complement of each progression as it occurs." Seeger, *Tradition and Experiment*.

65 These are Seeger's "conversions," as discussed earlier.

66 This is also a transformation described by Seeger: "Each interval of the neume is expanded or contracted by a fixed amount." Seeger, *Tradition and Experiment*.

67 Recall that the operations I, R, and RI act on pitch class, not directly on interval. Inverting a motive replaces each interval, in order, with its complement. Retrograding a motive replaces each interval with its complement, but reverses their order of occurrence. Retrograde inverting a motive maintains the intervals, but reverses their order of occurrence.

68 RICH is one of several serial transformations that are described and illustrated by David Lewin in *Generalized Musical Intervals and Transformations*. Lewin defines RICH as follows: "Let us consider a series s of pitches or pitch-classes $s_1, s_2, \ldots, s_n$. We can apply to s the RI-chaining operation RICH. RICH(s) is that retrograde-inverted form of s whose first two elements are s_{n-1} and s_n, in that order" (180). In other words, the last two notes of one motive must become the first two notes of its retrograde inversion. While I will normally adhere strictly to this definition, I will occasionally use the term RICH to refer to motives that share only one note.

69 In addition to the Three Songs (1930–32), which comprise settings of "Rat Riddles" and "Prayers of Steel" as well as "In Tall Grass," Crawford produced an earlier set of Five Songs (1929), which are settings of "Home Thoughts," "Loam," "Joy," "White Moon," and "Sunsets." She also collaborated with Sandburg on his *American Songbag* (1926), providing piano accompaniments for several of the American folk songs in that collection. This early interest in folk music would later flower into the professional activities that preoccupied Crawford during the 1930s and 1940s.

70 My PIVOTs are modeled on Lewin's FLIPEND and FLIPSTART, which are his names and generalizations for the transformations Jonathan Bernard calls "unfolding" and "infolding" in his study of Varèse. See Lewin, *Generalized Musical Intervals and Transformations*, 189, and Bernard, *The Music of Edgard Varèse* (New Haven: Yale University Press, 1987), 73–82.

71 Inversion is commonly described as a compound operation, TnI, where I means "invert around C" and Tn means "transpose by some interval n." In this book, I will normally use instead Lewin's convention of describing inversion as I_u^v, which means "invert around an axis of symmetry defined by pitch classes u and v," or "invert around that axis that maps u and v onto each other." Pitch classes u and v may be any pitch classes and they may be the same pitch class. See Lewin, *Generalized Musical Intervals and Transformations*, 50–59.

72 Unlike the others, RICH applies not to a single note but to a sequence of at least four notes. On this example, I have placed the label above the note that concludes the RICH.

73 Seeger, *Tradition and Experiment*.

74 Crawford, letter to Edgard Varèse, May 22, 1948; cited in Gaume, *Memoirs, Memories, Music*, 213. This letter came in response to Varèse's request for Crawford's musical "credo" and her description of one or two of her works, information he intended to use in a course he was planning to teach. By that time, Crawford had not composed for fifteen years.

75 Moving registral frames are related to what Bernard calls "projections" in the music of Varèse. These involve the transposition in pitch space of a fixed registral boundary interval. See Bernard, *The Music of Edgard Varèse*, 48–49.

76 Similar preferences, particularly for symmetrical and nearly-symmetrical partitioning of the pitch space, shape the music of Varèse, as Bernard has shown. See ibid., 43–48.

77 As previously noted, "ip" is an abbreviation for "pitch interval," the space between two pitches counted in semitones.

78 Crawford, diary, October 29, 1928; cited in Tick, "'Spiritual Concept,'" 241.

79 Aggregate completion also plays a role in shaping this piece. D is the only pitch class absent from the entire opening section (measures 1–9), only to be introduced almost immediately when the middle section begins. D is then the last note heard in the middle section before the opening music returns to conclude the piece.

80 Crawford, letter to Varèse, May 22, 1948; cited in Gaume, *Memoirs, Memories, Music*, 213.

81 Seeger, *Tradition and Experiment*.

82 Crawford's explanation of her system of markings may be found on the first page of her manuscript for each of the *Diaphonic Suites*. It is disappointing that these markings, entered so meticulously in the manuscript and so crucial to Crawford's conception of the form of the Suites, are preserved in the published scores only in the case of *Diaphonic Suite No. 1*.

83 This physical layout is apparent in the manuscripts for all four Suites and in the publication of *Diaphonic Suite No. 1* in *New Music*. It unfortunately is omitted in the later publication of the Suites by Continuo Music Press. A similar notational system, using double bars and musical rhymes to delineate phrases, characterizes two of Seeger's few surviving compositions, *The Letter* and *Psalm 137*, both for solo voice. These works were also published in *New Music* 26/3, the same issue that contained Crawford's *Diaphonic Suite No. 1*.

84 The formal organization of this movement is discussed in detail in Judith Tick, "Dissonant Counterpoint Revisited," 405–22.

85 This quotation is from Crawford's performing notes, which accompany the published score.

86 Seeger, *Tradition and Experiment*.

87 In my Examples 2.52 and 2.53, and in the accompanying discussion, I refer to the clarinet notes as they are written, not as they sound.

88 Judith Tick, "'Spirit of me . . . Dear rollicking far-gazing straddler of two worlds': The 'Autobiography' of Ruth Crawford Seeger," paper presented at Gender and Music Conference, King's College, University of London, July 1991. Crawford burned the score in 1932, but a manuscript in the possession of Vivian Fine survived. It resurfaced in 1980 and is now published and recorded.

89 The nature and function of ostinati in Crawford's music, their relationship to her brand of melodic serialism, and the striking resemblance between the ostinato from the Violin Sonata and that of the Suite for Wind Quintet, will be discussed in detail below.

90 Whole-tone scales play a significant role in the structure of Crawford's music, and will be discussed in detail below.

91 On her compositional manuscript, Crawford conveniently labels each melody with a roman numeral, and identifies any relevant transposition, inversion, or retrograde. Tick describes and analyzes the manuscript in "Dissonant Counterpoint Revisited."

92 Seeger, *Tradition and Experiment*.

93 The retrograde symmetry of this piece is discussed in detail in Mark Nelson, "In Pursuit of Charles Seeger's Heterophonic Ideal: Three Palindromic Works by Ruth Crawford," *The Musical Quarterly* 72/4 (1986), 458–75.

94 Crawford, letter to Seeger, April 4, 1931; cited in Gaume, *Memoirs, Memories, Music*, 155.

95 In an earlier, unpublished version of this movement (catalogued as item 1k in the Ruth Crawford Seeger Collection at the Library of Congress), the two parts were in a rhythmically free canon, but at T_2, not T_0, and the second half was the inversion rather than the retrograde of the first.

96 Seeger, *Tradition and Experiment*.

97 There are a few "wrong notes" in the score, that is, notes that would not be predicted by this scheme: m. 56, cello, a cautionary accidental would clarify that the last note in the measure is F♯; m. 64, oboe, G should be E, but G is clearly indicated in Crawford's manuscript; m. 68, cello, F should be A, but F is clearly indicated in Crawford's manuscript; m. 92, oboe, a cautionary accidental would clarify that the last note in the measure is G♯.

98 If G–A–G♯–B–C–F–C♯ is P_0, the prime ordering that begins G, which is designated 0, then G–F–F♯–E♭–D–A–C♯ is I_0, the inverted ordering that begins on G. It maintains the intervallic ordering of P_0, but replaces each interval with its complement. R_0 refers to the retrograde of P_0, thus C♯–F–C–B–G♯–A–G, and RI_0 to the retrograde of I_0, thus C♯–A–D–E♭–F♯–F–G. Notice that R and RI forms *end* on the pitch class defined by their subscript number while P and I forms begin there. Notice also that, in this discussion, G=0, G♯=1, A=2, etc.

99 Cited in Tick, *An American Woman's Life in Music*, Chapter 7.

100 If two notes are related by Tn (transposition), n is an interval, and is equal to the value of the difference between the two notes. If two notes are related by In (inversion), n is an index, and is equal to the value of the sum of the two notes. Notice that I have momentarily abandoned Lewin's notation for inversion in order to accommodate traditional twelve-tone nomenclature. In a further accommodation to twelve-tone nomenclature, I have assigned integer 0 to pitch class G in Examples 2.65 and 2.66.

101 There are a small number of deviations from the serial plan in the published score. Some of these are simple misprints, with the correct note indicated clearly in Crawford's manuscripts: in measure 65, D should precede D♭; in measure 77, the last note of the measure should be G♭, not B♭. Others are more difficult to account for, because the "wrong" note is clearly indicated in Crawford's manuscripts: in m. 15, the third note should be B, not C; in m. 50, the fourth note should be A, not G; in m. 66, the sixth note should be G, not A; and in m. 78, the second note should be B, not A. These latter instances not only violate the serial plan, but generally create the kinds of pitch repetitions in close proximity that are avoided by Crawford in the rest of this piece, and throughout all of her compositions. Are they intentional deviations, what she referred to in the fourth movement of the String Quartet as

"loose threads in the persian rug," or are they mistakes that should be corrected? I see no apparent reason for the deviations, and good reason to dislike them. As a result, I would recommend correcting them for a performance, although there can be no unambiguous solution to this problem.

102 The rhythmic series, and its interaction with the pitch series, will be discussed in detail below.

103 Crawford, letter to Varèse, May 22, 1948; cited in Gaume, *Ruth Crawford Seeger*, 213.

104 "As far as I know, Ruth knew next to nothing of Ives except a few of the compositions that happened to be played in New York at the time she was there, the end of '29 to the end of '35." Seeger, in Wilding-White, "Remembering Ruth Crawford Seeger," 445.

105 Seeger's use of the term differs sharply from its current use in the field of ethno-musicology. There, it refers to "the simultaneous statement, especially in improvised performance, of two or more different versions of what is essentially the same melody (as distinct from polyphony). It often takes the form of a melody combined with an ornamented version of itself, the former sung and the latter played on an instrument." *The New Harvard Dictionary of Music*, ed. Don Randal (Cambridge, Mass.: Harvard University Press, 1986), 377.

106 Charles Seeger, "Ruth Crawford," in Cowell, *American Composers on American Music*, 111.

107 Seeger, "On Dissonant Counterpoint," 28.

108 Seeger, *Tradition and Experiment*.

109 Crawford, letter to Seeger, February 22, 1931; cited in Tick, "Dissonant Counterpoint Revisited," 407. The reader should recall once again that in the String Quartet, and most other works, accidentals affect only those notes they immediately precede.

110 Tick, "Dissonant Counterpoint Revisited," describes Crawford's system of analytical notations.

111 There are two whole-tone collections: WT_0 (C–D–E–F$\sharp$–G$\sharp$–A$\sharp$), so named because it contains pitch class C, commonly designated with the integer 0; and WT_1 (C$\sharp$–D$\sharp$–F–G–A–B), so named because it contains C$\sharp$, pitch class 1. The role of the whole-tone collections in Crawford's music will be discussed below.

112 Seeger describes his dissonant species counterpoint briefly in "On Dissonant Counterpoint," 26.

113 The analysis of tonal music, following Schenker, finds a similar relationship between strict and free composition, between species and prolonged counterpoint: "A significant – if indirect – connection exists between the progressions of each species and the voice leading of composition. Counterpoint, as manifested in composition, is the elaboration of basic progressions presented in Fux's method. This connection was first pointed out by Heinrich Schenker . . . The relation of species counterpoint to the voice leading of composition resembles the connection between a fundamental scientific or philosophical concept and its manifold elaborations and developments." Felix Salzer and Carl Schachter, *Counterpoint in Composition* (New York: McGraw-Hill, 1969), xviii.

114 Adolf Weidig, *Harmonic Material and Its Uses: A Textbook for Teachers, Students, and Music Lovers* (Chicago: Clayton F. Summy Co., 1923), 421–23.

115 Seeger, "Ruth Crawford," 110.

116 Crawford, spoken remarks at Composers' Forum-Laboratory, April 6, 1938; cited in Gaume, *Memoirs, Memories, Music*, 202.

117 Arnold Schoenberg, "Composition with Twelve Tones," in *Style and Idea*, ed. Leonard Stein, trans. Leo Black (Berkeley: University of California Press, 1984), 220.

118 Vivian Fine, Crawford's most important composition student, has observed, "Ruth's music before Charlie [Charles Seeger] was influenced by Scriabin, mainly in the chords, the fourths, augmented fourth plus perfect fourth" (interview November 29, 1984, cited in Judith Tick, "Ruth Crawford's 'Spiritual Concept'"). The influence of Scriabin on Crawford will be considered in Chapter Four, but for now we should observe that the combination of a perfect fourth with an augmented fourth always produces a member of set class (016), and that this is indeed a characteristic harmony for Crawford, both before and after "Charlie."

119 The final chord contains nine notes, excluding only B♭, B, and E. This complementary trichord, like so many of the registral trichords in the final chord, is a member of set class (016).

120 Unordered collections of pitch classes will often be presented, as here, in "normal form," that is, in their most compressed repesentation. Normal forms will be written within square brackets, with the pitch classes separated by commas.

121 For a discussion of "predominantly whole-tone sets" in the music of Scriabin, see James Baker, *The Music of Alexander Scriabin* (New Haven: Yale University Press, 1986), 124–28.

122 Crawford, letter to Seeger, October 26, 1930; cited in Gaume, *Memoirs, Memories, Music*, 160. It is not clear which part Crawford considers the "second part," because, for me at least, neither describes any obvious tonality.

123 The basic description of atonal voice leading, and the particular representation of it, are derived from Henry Klumpenhouwer, "A Generalized Model of Voice-Leading for Atonal Music" (Ph.D. dissertation, Harvard University, 1991). Chords under scrutiny are circled in the score and their notes are written, using letter names, directly beneath the score, usually in registral order, but occasionally in score order. The operation that connects the chords is identified. Where the operation is inversion, I will use Lewin's convention, I_u^v, where v and u are pitch classes mapped onto each other under that particular I. Each note in the first chord is connected via a horizontal or near-horizontal line to the note in the second chord onto which it is mapped by the operation in question.

124 I am assuming that the highest note in the second cello chord of m. 7 is B♭, following the convention in the *Diaphonic Suites* that accidentals remain in effect throughout the measure – see, for example, mm. 4 and 5 in the bassoon melody, where an accidental is removed only by an explicit natural sign, and mm. 3 and 6, where an accidental, in these instances a D♯, is clearly retained throughout the measure. In Crawford's first complete manuscript, the B♭ was explicitly altered to B♮, but this alteration did not survive in subsequent drafts or in the published score. It is not clear whether its failure to survive was the result of a change of mind, or inadvertence.

125 The set types are 1) (0145); 2) (0134); 3) (0146); 4) (0236); 5) (0246). The third chord is one of the all-interval tetrachords.

126 Within each stanza, the accompanying chord is stated numerous times, and is constantly respaced and projected throughout the available register. The first chord, for example, is heard in seventeen different registral orderings. It is always partitioned into two trichords, one in each hand, and, of the ten possible ways of partitioning a six-note chord into two trichords, fully eight are realized. The registral permutations are neither systematic nor exhaustive, but seem to be motivated by a general interest in achieving maximum variety. Because of the extremely varied registral orderings, the chords are simply written in a convenient way in the example, not with reference to their actual registral disposition.

127 My analysis assumes the correction of two misprints in the score. In m. 56, E replaces D for a single chord in the published score. A brief change of this kind would be unique in the piece and is thus probably incorrect, even though it is supported by two separate manuscripts in the composer's hand, and I have reinstated the D. In m. 78, the chord should contain a B♭ and a D♮, not a B♮ and a D♭ – a flat sign simply got misplaced.

128 There are three anomalies, where the expected pattern x is unaccountably replaced by pattern z (mm. 43, 54, and 69).

129 Rita Mead, *Henry Cowell's New Music 1925–1936*, 426.

130 Milton Babbitt, personal communication – this is an expression he uses frequently in his teaching.

131 Seeger's comments in dissonating the rhythms of a melody may be found throughout *Tradition and Experiment in the New Music*, of which the following is a typical example: "Within the limit of the single neume rhythmic dissonance is obtained chiefly through: (1) syncopation, (2) unusual meter (5, 7, 10, 11, etc.), [and] (3) uneven divisions of measure and beat."

132 Ibid.

133 See Elizabeth West Marvin, "The Perception of Rhythm in Non-Tonal Music," 61–78.

134 The perception of pitch and duration contours differs somewhat. One knows right at the attack point of some note whether it is higher or lower than the previous notes, but one may not know until the release point whether it was longer or shorter. My notation, however, will be the same in both cases, with the relevant + or – sign positioned directly between the two notes being compared.

135 This is a possibility acknowledged and encouraged by Seeger, as we saw in Example 2.15 and the surrounding discussion.

136 As before, the rhythms and dynamics are scaled from 0 for the shortest or softest up to n for the longest or loudest.

137 Crawford's most dramatic attempt to structure the dynamics of her music comes in the third movement of the String Quartet, to be discussed in detail in Chapter Three.

3 Six analyses

1 *The Complete Poems of Carl Sandburg*, rev. edn (New York: Harcourt Brace Jovanovich, 1970), 416.

2 Charles Seeger, "Ruth Crawford," 110–111.

3 Crawford, "General Notes," published with the score of "Rat Riddles," *New Music Orchestra Series* (1933).

4 Note that mm. 65–68 are excluded from the example. That part of the rat's gnomic utterance is motivically distinct from the rest of the melody, although linked to it in other ways, as we shall see.

5 The tritone has a similar function in the series for *Diaphonic Suite No. 1*, third movement, and "Chinaman, Laundryman," where it is the interval between the last note and the first.

6 As before, "ip" is an abbreviation for "pitch interval," that is, the number of semitones in an interval without an octave modulus. The expression "T_n^p" designates "pitch transposition," that is, the transposition of each note in a line or collection by some number of semitones, without an octave modulus.

7 The prime forms of the chords are as follows: 1)(01234); 2) (01234); 3) (01268); 4) (01367); 5) (01234); 6) (01236); 7) (01568); 8) (02357); 9) (01235); 10) (01256); 11) (01347); 12) (01245).

8 *The Complete Poems of Carl Sandburg*, 109–10.

9 Seeger, "Ruth Crawford," 113.

10 I have in mind particularly the "time-point system" developed by Milton Babbitt, about which I will have more to say below.

11 As is frequently Crawford's practice, the transpositions are not always exact. The "wrong notes" are usually one semitone or, at most, two away from the note predicted by the underlying scheme. In addition, the rotations also contain occasional "wrong notes," also one or two semitones away from their expected location. A small number of new deviations are introduced in the second half of the piece, which is otherwise an exact repetition of the first. Occasionally, as in the first rotation of T_{11}, the wrong notes create additional statements of Motive M1 that would not be present otherwise. In some cases, the deviations are apparently intended "to avoid the 'hitting of unisons' between the parts" (Seeger, "Ruth Crawford," 113). In many cases, however, there is no obvious explanation for them.

12 All represent set class (01236).

13 The chart in Example 3.21 is modeled on Seeger's chart in "Ruth Crawford," 112.

14 The series itself is an exact transposition, but in the rotations, notes are occasionally moved one or two semitones out of position, reordered, or omitted entirely.

15 I have omitted the rests between the melodic fragments and the octave doublings in both winds and strings.

16 The first sophisticated analytical study of the piece, particularly its fourth movement, is included in George Perle, "Atonality and the Twelve-Tone System in the United States," *The Score*, July 1960, 51–61. An important recent study is Margaret Thomas, "The String Quartet of Ruth Crawford: Analysis with a View toward Charles Seeger's Theory of Dissonant Counterpoint" (M.A. thesis, University of Washington, 1991).

17 Crawford, spoken remarks at Composers' Forum-Laboratory, April 6, 1938; cited in Gaume, *Memoirs, Memories, Music*, 204.

18 As we shall see, Crawford follows a similar procedure in the first movement of the Suite for Wind Quintet, where a melodic ostinato leaves a variety of harmonies in its wake.

19 A misprint in the score – the second violin in m. 35 should remain on B throughout the measure – has been corrected for this and all examples.

20 The first four notes are an exact transposition of the first four notes of the vocal melody in "Rat Riddles."

21 Many of the contour-related segments also identify members of the same set class. Set class (0124) is particularly well represented among the bracketed segments and is a basic harmony of the passage, as will be discussed in more detail below.

22 For an original and important discussion of the instrumentation and registration of this movement, see Ellie Hisama, "The Question of Climax in Ruth Crawford's String Quartet, third movement," in *Musical Pluralism: Aspects of Structure and Aesthetics in Music since 1945*, ed. Elizabeth West Marvin and Richard Hermann (Rochester: University of Rochester Press, 1995). Hisama measures what she calls the "degree of twist" of each harmony, that is, the degree of its departure from the norm of first violin as registral soprano, second violin as alto, viola as tenor, and cello as bass. She concludes that the level of voice-twisting activity increases and decreases throughout the movement, but that the high point of twist does not coincide with the registral and dynamic climax of the movement. This lack of coincidence is further evidence of Crawford's interest in heterophonic form, in creating a multiplicity of competing structures within a single work.

23 These comments are found in an analysis of this movement Crawford supplied to Varèse at his request for use in a course he was planning to teach at Columbia University. Crawford's analysis was included with a letter to Varèse dated May 29, 1948. Crawford described the music in similar terms in addressing the Composers' Forum-Laboratory on April 6, 1938: "This movement is built on a counterpoint of dynamics. The crescendi and diminuendi should be exactly timed, and no instrument should reach the high or low point at the same time as any other." (Remarks cited in Gaume, *Memoirs, Memories, Music*, 204.)

24 Wherever possible, I have imagined each pattern as beginning on the downbeat of a measure. A description of the dynamic high points that did not observe that restriction might look considerably different.

25 The large-scale structure of this melody will be described later when we consider the harmonic progression, which this melody essentially animates and arpeggiates. Margaret Thomas identifies and discusses this melody in somewhat different terms in "The String Quartet of Ruth Crawford."

26 See Thomas, "The String Quartet of Ruth Crawford," for a discussion of the harmonic progression in terms of Jonathan Bernard's "unfolding" and "infolding" as described in *The Music of Edgard Varèse*, 73–118.

27 Crawford designates the opposing parts as Voices 1 and 2 in her analysis of the movement supplied to Varèse along with her letter of May 29, 1948. The reader should recall once again that in the String Quartet accidentals affect only those notes they immediately precede.

28 Ibid.

29 Ibid.

30 There is a second occurrence of Motive M1, wrapping around from the last two notes, D♭–C, to the first, D.

31 There is a single note in the first half of the piece (m. 24), and another in the analogous spot in the second (m. 93), that are missing from the rotational plan. In her analysis of the movement, Crawford refers to these glitches as "a loose thread in the persian rug."

32 "Since duration is a measure of distance between time points, as interval is a measure of distance between pitch points, we begin by interpreting interval as duration. Then, pitch number is interpretable as the point of initiation of a temporal event, that is, as a time-point number. If this number is to be further interpretable as a representative of an equivalence class of time points and the durational interval with regard to the first such element, it is necessary merely to imbed it in a metrical unit, a measure in the usual musical metrical sense, so that a recurrence of succession of time points is achieved, while the notion of meter is made an essential part of the systematic structure. The equivalence relation is statable as 'occurring at the same time point with relation to the measure.' The 'ascending' ordered 'chromatic scale' of twelve time points, then, is a measure divided into twelve equally spaced time points, with the metrical signature probably determined by the internal structure of the time-point set, and with the measure now corresponding in function to the octave in the pitch-class system. A time-point set, then, is a serial ordering of time points . . ." Milton Babbitt, "Twelve-Tone Rhythmic Structure and the Electronic Medium," *Perspectives of New Music* 1/1 (1962), 49–79; reprinted in *Perspectives on Contemporary Music Theory*, ed. Benjamin Boretz and Edward T. Cone (New York: Norton, 1972), 162.

33 Judith Tick, "'Spirit of me.'" Crawford had burned her manuscript of the Violin Sonata, although unbeknownst to her, a copy had survived in the possession of Vivian Fine, who later arranged for its publication. For Crawford, then, the Sonata was truly dead, and lived on only in the ostinato of the Suite for Wind Quintet.

34 The dissolution of the theme into a relatively amorphous chromatic mass is analogous to Schoenberg's concept of liquidation: "*Liquidation* consists in gradually eliminating characteristic features, until only uncharacteristic ones remain, which no longer demand a continuation. Often only residues remain, which have little in common with the basic motive." *Fundamentals of Musical Composition*, ed. Gerald Strang (New York: St. Martin's Press, 1967), 58.

35 In the preceding discussion, I have intentionally omitted the final seven notes of the first half, which are set apart from the others by rhythm and dynamics. Like the others, this final statement differs by one single note from its immediate predecessor. In this case, the new note is the final sustained C with which it, and the entire first half of the movement, end. This additional statement would, if that C were an A$\sharp$, be pitch-class identical to T_4 of the original. T_4, of course, is the level at which the third principal statement of the ostinato occurs, in m. 61.

36 There is an additional striking family resemblance to the first movement of the *Diaphonic Suite No. 3*, for two clarinets. In the first movement, the second clarinet part, although not serialized, moves in the steady, even pulsations that characterize the later serial melodies. Except for one small glitch, its first ten notes are the exact transposition, at T_2, of the series for the String Quartet, fourth movement.

37 There is a fourth occurrence if the last two notes, C$\sharp$–C, are understood to "wrap around" to the first note, D.

38 The series thus has fancy properties from a twelve-tone point of view, in that it is derived from (0123), one of the all-combinatorial tetrachords. Neither systematic derivation nor combinatoriality, however, is at all a part of Crawford's compositional approach.

39 Example 3.60 is intentionally designed to mimic the examples in Richard Cohn's important article, "Inversional Symmetry and Transpositional Combination in Bartók," *Music Theory Spectrum* 10 (1988), 19–42. Cohn would describe Crawford's series as the recursive application of the operation of transpositional combination: (2 * 1) * 4.

40 The last tetrachord has been unrotated, as before, to reveal whole-tone dyads.

41 Two notes, A and G♯, are missing from the third rotation in measure 35. I cannot account for their absence in any satisfactory way, and will have to consider them two more "loose threads in the persian rug."

42 In Section B, the retrograde of T_2 begins with the second rotation and ends with the first. The rotations themselves thus occur in a rotated order. The melody is shared by the bassoon and the clarinet. Sections C1 and C2 involve incomplete rotations, beginning in both cases in the middle of the fifth rotation and ending, as in Section B, with the first. In Section C2, furthermore, the tenth rotation is heard twice, the first time missing its last note. The rotations in Section C1 are shared by the bassoon and horn, and in Section C2 by the bassoon and clarinet. The bassoon thus plays a serial melody in all of the sections of the movement, joined by the flute in the A sections, by the clarinet in Sections B and C2, and by the horn in Section C1. Only the oboe does not participate.

43 This view of the structure of the series differs from that expressed in Example 3.59 only in beginning with the wrap-around dyad C–D. Both construct the series in relation to its whole-tone dyads.

44 As Milton Babbitt has cautioned in a somewhat different context, music that is relentlessly heterophonic runs the risk of creating a situation in which "harmonic structure in all dimensions is proclaimed to be irrelevant, unnecessary, and perhaps, undesirable, . . . so a principle, or non-principle, of harmony by fortuity reigns." "Some Aspects of Twelve-Tone Composition," *The Score and I.M.A. Magazine* 12 (1955), 55.

45 With a few slight changes, the second C section is the pitch-class transposition, at T_7, of the first, so the following commentary, focusing on the first C section, will apply to both, with allowances for changes in instrumentation and register.

4 Crawford's music in its contexts

1 The factual elements in the following biographical sketch are based on the following sources: Matilda Gaume, "Ruth Crawford Seeger: Her Life and Works" and *Ruth Crawford Seeger: Memoirs, Memories, Music*; Ann Pescatello, *Charles Seeger: A Life in American Music* (Pittsburgh: University of Pittsburgh Press, 1992); and Judith Tick, "Ruth Crawford's 'Spiritual Concept': The Sound-Ideals of an Early American Modernist," 221–61.

2 Weidig's approach can be gleaned from his textbook, *Harmonic Material*.

3 Adolf Weidig, *Harmonic Material*, 417.

4 Ruth Crawford, letter to Nicolas Slonimsky, Jan 29, 1933; cited in Gaume, *Memoirs, Memories, Music*, 35.

5 In the words of Alfred Frankenstein, a well-known music critic and a friend and neighbor of Crawford in Chicago: new music activity "was largely confined to very small groups like Madam Herz and her circle." Cited in Rita Mead, *Henry Cowell's New Music 1925–1936*, 108.

6 Crawford, undated letter, addressee unknown, cited in Gaume, "Life and Works," 11.

7 Crawford, diary, November 9, 1928, cited in Tick, "'Spiritual Concept,'" 233–34.

8 The Eastern mystical and Theosophical leanings of Herz and Rudhyar, and their impact on Crawford's thought and music, are discussed in detail in Tick, "'Spiritual Concept.'"

9 These include the Prelude No. 6, "Andante Mystico," two passages in the first movement of the Violin Sonata, and the third movement of the Violin Sonata, marked "mystic, intense."

10 Tick, "'Spiritual Concept,'" 234.

11 Crawford, letter to Seeger, January 18, 1931; cited in Tick, "Ruth Crawford's '' 'Spiritual Concept,'" 235.

12 These included a performance of three of the Piano Preludes at a League of Composers Concert at Town Hall in New York (December 1925); a performance of the Violin Sonata at a League of Composers concert in New York (February 1927); a performance by Richard Buhlig of Preludes 6–9 at a Copland–Sessions concert in New York (May 1928); and a second performance of the Violin Sonata at the first concert of the Chicago chapter of the International Society of Contemporary Music (February 1928).

13 Henry Cowell, "Charles Seeger," 119.

14 Crawford, letter to Nicolas Slonimsky, January 29, 1935; reprinted in Carol Neuls-Bates, ed., *Women in Music: An Anthology of Source Readings from the Middle Ages to the Present* (New York: Harper and Row, 1982), 305–306.

15 Seeger, taped interview with Matilda Gaume, London, July, 1967; cited in Gaume, *Memoirs, Memories, Music*, 64.

16 Crawford, letter to Nicolas Slonimsky, January 29, 1933; cited in Gaume, *Memoirs, Memories, Music*, 65.

17 Crawford, undated letter, addressee unknown, cited in Gaume, "Life and Works," 18.

18 "I am deluging my soul with all the Strawinsky I can get from the library. Because I realize I am swallowing opinions second hand. Berating neo-classicism when I know few examples of it. Strawinsky's Sonata, 1924, gives a sad example. Tho there are parts which I like. This gives me the impression which many amateurs express when they characterize modern music as music with wrong notes. Here Strawinsky has achieved a combination of Bach and Chopin, with each hand full of mistakes. It seems needlessly ugly." Crawford, diary, February 27, 1930, cited in Gaume, *Memoirs, Memories, Music*, 198.

19 Gaume, *Memoirs, Memories, Music*, 65.

20 Weiss's account of his studies with Schoenberg may be found in his article "The Lyceum of Schoenberg," 99–107.

21 Steven Gilbert makes this point in "'The Ultra-Modern Idiom,'" 290.
22 "Whatever happens in a piece of music is nothing but the endless reshaping of a basic shape." Arnold Schoenberg, "Linear Counterpoint," in *Style and Idea*, 290.
23 For a discussion of these issues, see Joseph N. Straus, *Remaking the Past: Musical Modernism and the Influence of the Tonal Tradition* (Cambridge, Mass.: Harvard University Press, 1990) and two articles by Peter Burkholder: "Museum Pieces," *Journal of Musicology* 2/2 (1983), 115–34 and "Brahms and Twentieth-Century Classical Music," *19th Century Music* 8/1 (1984), 75–83.
24 David K. Dunaway, "Charles Seeger and Carl Sands: The Composers' Collective Years," 159–68; Barbara Zuck, *A History of Musical Americanism*, 103–38.
25 Carl Sandburg, *The American Songbag* (New York: Harcourt Brace Jovanovich, 1927).
26 Her publications during this period include: *American Folk Songs for Children* (Garden City: Doubleday, 1948); *Animal Folk Songs for Children* (Garden City: Doubleday, 1950); and *American Folk Songs for Christmas* (Garden City: Doubleday, 1950). She also transcribed and arranged thousands of recordings of folk music from field recordings for the American Folk Song Archive in the Library of Congress. She collaborated with John and Alan Lomax on *Our Singing Country* (New York: Macmillan, 1941) and *Folk Song U.S.A* (Duell, Solan and Pearce, 1947) and with George Korson on *Coal Dust on the Fiddle* (Philadelphia: University of Pennsylvania Press, 1943) and *Anthology of Pennsylvania Folklore* (Philadelphia: University of Pennsylvania Press, 1949).
27 This expression is quoted without reference in Judith Tick, "'Spirit of me.'"
28 Comment by Charles Seeger in Ray Wilding-White, "Remembering Ruth Crawford Seeger," 443.
29 Seeger, interview with Matilda Gaume, London, July 1967; cited in Gaume, "Her Life and Works," 22.
30 Seeger, taped interview with Matilda Gaume, London, July 28, 1967; cited in Gaume, *Memoirs, Memories, Music*, 85.
31 The term and concept are Sandra Gilbert's and Susan Gubar's in their important study, *The Madwoman in the Attic: The Woman Writer and the Nineteenth-Century Literary Imagination* (New Haven: Yale University Press, 1979): "The 'anxiety of influence' that a male poet experiences is felt by a female poet as an even more primary 'anxiety of authorship' – a radical fear that she cannot create, that because she can never become a 'precursor' the act of writing will isolate or destroy her" (48–49). For a consideration of this concept in relation to women composers, see Marcia J. Citron, *Gender and the Musical Canon* (Cambridge: Cambridge University Press, 1993), 54–70.
32 Crawford, diary entry, August 5, 1929; cited in Gaume, *Memoirs, Memories, Music*, 59.
33 It is interesting to note, parenthetically, that other modernist composers, including Ruggles, Varèse, and, a bit farther afield, Schoenberg, also stopped composing for long periods. A comparative study of this issue might be extremely revealing, both about the composers and, possibly, about the nature of musical modernism.
34 Crawford, letter to Edgard Varèse, May 22, 1948.
35 Henry Cowell, "Trends in American Music," in *American Composers on American Music*, 3–4.
36 For general discussions of the ultra-modern movement, see Steven Gilbert, "'The Ultra-Modern Idiom,'" 282–314; David Nicholls, *American Experimental Music*,

1890–1940 (Cambridge: Cambridge University Press, 1990); and Gilbert Chase, *America's Music: From the Pilgrims to the Present*: "Before the term avant-garde became fashionable, critics and proponents called the movement it designated 'ultramodern.' It had its heyday in the 1920s and 1930s, coinciding curiously with the Jazz Age and the Great Depression" (449). "The ultramodern movement was promoted by organized group action, as represented notably by the International Composers' Guild (1921–27) and the Pan American Association of Composers (1928–34) . . . The leading promoters and organizers of these associations were Edgard Varèse and Henry Cowell, the former from France, the latter from California, both meeting on common ground in New York City" (454).

37 Carl Ruggles, interview with Marilyn J. Ziffrin; cited in Ziffrin, *Carl Ruggles: Composer, Painter, and Storyteller* (Urbana and Chicago: University of Illinois Press, 1994), 71.

38 The essay appeared in *American Composers on American Music*, ed. Henry Cowell, along with essays on Ives, Varèse, and Seeger by Cowell, and one on Crawford by Seeger. Virtually the entire ultra-modern movement is represented in this volume, as subjects, authors, or both.

39 Deane L. Root, "The Pan American Association of Composers (1928–1934)," *Yearbook for Inter-American Musical Research* 8 (1972), 49–70.

40 According to Rita Mead, "Cowell met Rudhyar at Halcyon, a famous theosophical community in Northern California." See *Henry Cowell's New Music 1925–1936*, 20–21. On the role of Theosophy in the music of Crawford and Rudhyar, see Judith Tick, "'Spiritual Concept.'"

41 For an exhaustive description of Henry Cowell's enterprises, see Mead, *Henry Cowell's New Music 1925–1936*. My discussion is based on this account.

42 Ibid., 32.

43 "This group came to rely almost solely on *New Music* for the dissemination of its creative efforts." Gilbert, "'The Ultra-Modern Idiom,'" 284.

44 The works and the volume, number, and date of their publication are as follows: Four Preludes (2/1, Oct. 1928), *Piano Study in Mixed Accents* (6/1, Oct. 1932), String Quartet (14/2, Jan. 1941), *Diaphonic Suite No. 1* (for Flute or Oboe) (1930) (26/3, April 1953).

45 The Three Songs appeared in 1933 as No. 5 in the series.

46 It appeared in 1934 as Recording No. 1011A–B.

47 Letter from Cowell to Ives, November 14, 1933; cited in Mead, *Henry Cowell's New Music 1925–1936*, 257. For Ives's skeptical reply, see note 74 below.

48 Ultra-modern music may have represented the most successful such declaration, but it was neither the first nor the last in American music. See Barbara Zuck, *A History of Musical Americanism*.

49 Cowell, "Trends in American Music," 12–13.

50 Henry Cowell, *New Musical Resources*, 41–42. Seeger also pointed out this feature of Ruggles's melodies, and in remarkably similar terms: "The determining feature or principle of the melodic line is that of non-repetition of tone (either the same tone or any octave of it) until the tenth progression. This applies rigidly to the leading melody and characterizes the other parts to a surprising extent." (Charles Seeger, "Carl Ruggles," in *American Composers on American Music*, 23–24.)

51 André Jolivet, *Entretiens*, "Deuxieme Entretien" (1961), 3; cited in Bridget Conrad, "The Terror of Silence and the Magical Power of Music: The Musical Language of Jolivet in Relation to Varèse and Messiaen" (Ph.D. dissertation, Graduate School and University Center, City University of New York, 1993), 94. Jolivet studied with Varèse during Varèse's brief return to France in 1928–33.

52 Cowell, *New Musical Resources*, 38–39.

53 Ibid., 117–39.

54 Ibid., 115–16.

55 For a history of this concept, and its meaning in Schoenberg's thought, see Robert Falck, "Emancipation of the Dissonance," *Journal of the Arnold Schoenberg Institute* 6/1 (1982), 106–11.

56 Edgard Varèse, "The Liberation of Sound," *Perspectives of New Music* 5 (1966), 14.

57 Seeger, "Carl Ruggles," 23.

58 Seeger, "On Dissonant Counterpoint," 28.

59 Carter's music is shaped, of course, by a variety of influences, but the central importance for him of the ultra-moderns has not been fully appreciated. Anne Shreffler treats this issue in a thorough, sensitive way in her unpublished paper, "The Yankee Orpheus: Elliott Carter and his America."

60 David Nicholls, *American Experimental Music, 1890–1940*, 34.

61 Nicholls cites Ives's Trio, *From the Steeples and the Mountains*, and *Three-Page Sonata*, and Cowell's *Quartet Romantic* as examples of "total polyphony."

62 Cowell, *New Musical Resources*, xvii.

63 An observation by Taylor Greer, in his recent critical commentary on Seeger's *Tradition and Experiment in the New Music*, is relevant here: "It is curious that despite the treatise's inaccessibility, the next generation of experimental composers, such as Messiaen, Boulez, Stockhausen, and Babbitt, showed a strong kinship with Seeger in that they aspired toward a similar aesthetic ideal. Their zeal in applying serial procedures to elements other than pitch, fulfilled the spirit if not the letter of Seeger's prophecies of a new balanced style. Naturally there are enormous differences between organizing dynamics, durations, or accents as loosely correlated neume-analogues and as an ordered set of objects to be manipulated: the latter requires a mathematical precision that Seeger no doubt would have eschewed. Nevertheless, it is hard to deny that over twenty years after he conceived it, Seeger's dream of a balance among musical functions was at least partially realized in Europe as well as America." "Critical Commentary on *Tradition and Experiment in the New Music*," in *Studies in Musicology II* (Charles Seeger), ed. Ann Pescatello (Berkeley: University of California Press, 1994).

64 The discussion that follows is based on: Adrienne Fried Block and Nancy Stewart, "Women in American Music, 1800–1918," in *Women and Music: A History*, ed. Karin Pendle (Bloomington, Indiana: Indiana University Press, 1991), 142–72; Judith Tick, *American Women Composers before 1870* (Ann Arbor: UMI Research Press, 1983), and "Charles Ives and Gender Ideology," in *Musicology and Difference*, ed. Ruth Solie (Berkeley: University of California Press, 1993), 83–106.

65 For an important study of the role of women, including Blanche Walton, as promoters and patrons of modern music, see Carol Oja, "Women Patrons and Crusaders for Modernist Music: New York in the 1920s," in *Women Activists in American Music*, ed. Ralph Locke and Cyrilla Barr (Berkeley: University of California Press, 1994).

66 Sandra M. Gilbert and Susan Gubar, *No Man's Land: The Place of the Woman Writer in the Twentieth Century*, vol. 1: *The War of the Words* (New Haven: Yale University Press, 1988), 168. See pages 165–226 for a full discussion of this concept.

67 Catherine Parsons Smith, "'A Distinguishing Virility': On Feminism and Modernism in American Art Music," in *Cecilia Reclaimed: Feminist Perspectives on Gender and Music*, ed. Susan C. Cook and Judy S. Tsou (Urbana: University of Illinois Press, 1994). This article persuasively applies Gilbert and Gubar's ideas about literary modernism to musical modernism.

68 Bauer is best known today as the author of books about music, particularly *Twentieth-Century Music: How It Developed, How to Listen to It* (New York: G.P. Putnam's Sons, 1933; repr. New York: Da Capo Press, 1978). Her music deserves to be studied, as it will be, both on its own terms and in relation to Crawford's, in an important dissertation-in-progress: Ellie Hisama, "Gender, Modernism, and American Music: A Study of Selected Compositions by Marion Bauer and Ruth Crawford Seeger" (Graduate Center, City University of New York, forthcoming).

69 Sandra M. Gilbert and Susan Gubar, *The War of the Words*, xii.

70 Ives's rhetoric is discussed in Catherine Parsons Smith, "'A Distinguishing Virility,'" and Judith Tick, "Charles Ives and Gender Ideology." Tick points out that many of Ives's comments that appear misogynistic are actually directed at European art music and its commercial exploitation in the United States, not at women. Furthermore, much of it is as homophobic as it is misogynistic. Nonetheless, it would be an understatement to say that Ives did not have much confidence in women as composers. "Whatever his purpose, Ives's language contributed to an antiwoman atmosphere among musical modernists that was highly destructive to women's creativity, although it was also enabling for some men." (Smith, "On Feminism and Modernism.")

71 Frank R. Rossiter, *Charles Ives and His America* (New York: Liveright, 1975), 42.

72 "An important aspect of Ives's assertion of his masculinity against a feminized musical culture was his strong liking for musical dissonance . . . Ives erected in his mind a dichotomy between manly dissonant music and effeminate 'easy-on-the-ears' music." Rossiter, *Charles Ives and His America*, 36.

73 Cowell, "Trends in American Music," 12–13.

74 Cowell had asked Ives to provide funding for a recording series, and proposed including Crawford's String Quartet on the first disk. Ives initially declined, writing: "I know nothing about [Henry] Brant's or Crawford's music – except what you, [Adolph] Weiss, Nic[olas] S[lonimsky], Carl R[uggles], [John] Becker, & others have told me – which is that 'in time & a nice tide' they may get mansized (even Miss C.)." Cowell vigorously defended Crawford's Quartet, and the recording went forward as he had planned. This story, and the relevant documents, are cited in Mead, *Henry Cowell's New Music 1925–1936*, 256–57.

75 Ray Wilding-White, "Remembering Ruth Crawford Seeger," 445.

76 The same unnerving reversibility, this time with reference to the tonic and other triads, was dramatically illustrated by two papers presented at a recent conference, Feminist Theory & Music II: A Continuing Dialogue (Rochester, New York, June 1993). In the first paper, "Musical Voyeurism and the Feminine Tonic in Rameau's *Pigmalion*," Brian Hyer argued that "The tonic, like Pigmalion's Galatea, is gendered

feminine, a notion consistent with the rhetoric of Rameau's discourse, where the tonic, '*la tonique*,' is feminine in gender. For Rameau, the dominant desires the tonic, as does the listener . . . so that the tonic, like Galatea, becomes a thing to gaze at." In Hyer's view, then, the dominant is male, and the tonic is female. In the second paper, "Engendering the Triad in Eighteenth-Century Music Theory," Rebecca Green argued just the opposite, namely that the tonic triad, when major, functions "as an autonomous, perfect, creation of nature with the authority to govern large spans of musical material." The tonic is thus the male authority, governing the other triads in the manner of a *pater familias*.

77 Judith Tick, "'Spirit of me.'"

78 This is the view taken by Ellie Hisama in "Experiencing Ruth Crawford's String Quartet, fourth movement," paper presented at the 1992 meeting in Ithaca, New York, of the Music Theory Society of New York State.

79 The quotation is from Sandra M. Gilbert and Susan Gubar, *The Madwoman in the Attic*, xi. See also Elaine Showalter, *A Literature of Their Own: British Women Novelists from Brontë to Lessing* (Princeton: Princeton University Press, 1977) and *The Gender of Modernism: A Critical Anthology*, ed. Bonnie Kime Scott (Bloomington: Indiana University Press, 1990).

List of works

Five Preludes for Piano (1924–25)

Sonata for Violin and Piano (1925–26)

Music for Small Orchestra (1926)
    (flute, clarinet in A, bassoon, four violins, two cellos, piano)

Suite No. 1 for Five Wind Instruments and Piano (1927; rev. 1929)
    (flute, oboe, clarinet in A, bassoon, horn in F, piano)

Four Preludes for Piano, Nos. 6–9 (1927–28)

Five Songs to poems by Carl Sandburg (1929)
    (contralto and piano)
    "Home Thoughts"
    "White Moon"
    "Joy"
    "Loam"
    "Sunsets"

Suite No. 2 for Four Strings and Piano (1929)
    (two violins, viola, cello, piano)

Four Diaphonic Suites (1930)
    No. 1 (flute or oboe)
    No. 2 (bassoon and cello or two cellos)
    No. 3 (two clarinets in B♭)
    No. 4 (oboe and cello)

Piano Study in Mixed Accents (1930)

Three Chants (1930)
    No. 1 "To an Unkind God" (female chorus)
    No. 2 "To an Angel" (SATB chorus and soprano solo)
    No. 3 "To a Kind God" (female chorus and soprano and alto solos)

List of works

Three Songs to poems by Carl Sandburg (1930–32)
    (contralto, oboe, piano, percussion, and optional orchestra)
    "Rat Riddles"
    "In Tall Grass"
    "Prayers of Steel"

String Quartet (1931)
    (two violins, viola, cello)

Two Ricercare to poems by H. T. Tsiang (1932)
    (voice and piano)
    "Chinaman, Laundryman"
    "Sacco, Vanzetti"

Rissolty, Rossolty (1939)
    (orchestra)

Suite for Wind Quintet (1952)
    (flute, oboe, clarinet in B♭, horn in F, bassoon)

Bibliography

Babbitt, Milton. "Some Aspects of Twelve-Tone Composition," *The Score and I.M.A. Magazine* 12 (1955), 53–61

Milton Babbitt: Words About Music, ed. Stephen Dembski and Joseph N. Straus. Madison, Wis.: University of Wisconsin Press, 1987

Baker, James M. *The Music of Alexander Scriabin*. New Haven: Yale University Press, 1986

Bauer, Marion. *Twentieth Century Music*. New York: G.P. Putnam's Sons, 1933; repr. New York: Da Capo Press, 1978

Bernard, Jonathan. *The Music of Edgard Varèse*. New Haven: Yale University Press, 1987

Block, Adrienne Fried, and Stewart, Nancy. "Women in American Music, 1800–1918," in Pendle, *Women and Music: A History*, 142–72

Bowers, Jane, and Tick, Judith. *Women Making Music* (Urbana: University of Illinois Press, 1986)

Burkholder, Peter. "Museum Pieces," *Journal of Musicology* 2/2 (1983), 115–34

"Brahms and Twentieth-Century Classical Music," *19th Century Music* 8/1 (1984), 75–83

Chase, Gilbert. *America's Music: From the Pilgrims to the Present*, rev. 3rd edn. Urbana: University of Illinois Press, 1987

Citron, Marcia J. *Gender and the Musical Canon*. Cambridge: Cambridge University Press, 1993

Cowell, Henry. *New Musical Resources*. New York: Alfred Knopf, 1930; repr. edn. New York: Something Else Press, 1969

"Trends in American Music," in Cowell, Henry, ed., *American Composers on American Music: A Symposium*. Palo Alto: Stanford University Press, 1933; repr. New York: Frederick Ungar Publishing, 1962, 3–13

(ed.) *American Composers on American Music: A Symposium*. Palo Alto: Stanford University Press, 1933; repr. New York: Frederick Ungar Publishing, 1962

Cox, Renee. "Recovering Jouissance: An Introduction to Feminist Musical Aesthetics," in Pendle, *Women and Music: A History*, 331–40

Drinker, Sophie. *Music and Women: The Story of Women in Their Relation to Music*. New York: Coward-McCann, 1948

Dunaway, David K. "Charles Seeger and Carl Sands: The Composers' Collective Years," *Ethnomusicology* 24/2 (May 1980), 159–68

Edwards, J. Michele, and Lassetter, Leslie. "North America Since 1920," in Pendle, *Women and Music: A History*, 211–57

Forte, Allen. *The Structure of Atonal Music.* New Haven: Yale University Press, 1973

Friedmann, Michael. "A Methodology for the Discussion of Contour: Its Application to Schoenberg's Music," *Journal of Music Theory* 29/2 (1985), 223–48

Gaume, Matilda. "Ruth Crawford: A Promising Young Composer in New York, 1929–30," *American Music* 5/1 (Spring 1987), 74–84

"Ruth Crawford Seeger," *The New Grove Dictionary of Music*, ed. Stanley Sadie (New York: Macmillan, 1986)

"Ruth Crawford Seeger: Her Life and Works" (Ph.D. dissertation: Indiana University, 1973)

Ruth Crawford Seeger: Memoirs, Memories, Music (Metuchen, N.J.: Scarecrow Press, 1987)

Gilbert, Sandra M., and Gubar, Susan. *No Man's Land: The Place of the Woman Writer in the Twentieth Century.* Vol. 1, *The War of the Words* (1988); vol. 2, *Sexchanges* (1989). New Haven: Yale University Press, 1988–89

The Madwoman in the Attic: The Woman Writer and the Nineteenth-Century Literary Imagination. New Haven: Yale University Press, 1979

Gilbert, Steven. "The 'Twelve-Tone System' of Carl Ruggles—a Study of the Evocations for Piano," *Journal of Music Theory* 14/1 (1970), 68–91

"'The Ultra-Modern Idiom': A Survey of *New Music*," *Perspectives of New Music* 12/1–2 (1973–74), 282–314

Greer, Taylor. "Critical Commentary on *Tradition and Experiment in the New Music*," in *Studies in Musicology II* (Charles Seeger), ed. Ann Pescatello. Berkeley: University of California Press, 1994

Hamm, Charles. *Music in the New World.* New York: W. W. Norton, 1983

Hisama, Ellie. "Experiencing Ruth Crawford's String Quartet, fourth movement." Paper presented at the 1992 meeting in Ithaca, New York, of the Music Theory Society of New York State

"Gender, Modernism, and American Music: A Study of Selected Compositions by Marion Bauer and Ruth Crawford Seeger". Ph.D. dissertation, Graduate Center, City University of New York, forthcoming

"The Question of Climax in Ruth Crawford's String Quartet, third movement," in Elizabeth West Marvin and Richard Hermann, eds, *Musical Pluralism: Aspects of Structure and Aesthetic in Music since 1945.* Rochester: University of Rochester Press, 1995

Hitchcock, H. Wiley. *Music in the United States: A Historical Introduction*, 3rd edn. Englewood Cliffs, N.J.: Prentice-Hall, 1988

Jepson, Barbara. "Ruth Crawford Seeger: A Study in Mixed Accents," *Feminist Art Journal*, Spring 1977, 13–16

Klumpenhouwer, Henry. "A Generalized Model of Voice-Leading for Atonal Music." Ph.D. dissertation, Harvard University, 1991

Lerner, Gerda. "Placing Women in History: Definitions and Challenges," *Feminist Studies* 3/2 (Fall 1975), 5–14

Lewin, David. *Generalized Musical Intervals and Transformations.* New Haven: Yale University Press, 1987

Musical Form and Transformation: 4 Analytic Essays. New Haven: Yale University Press, 1993

Lott, R. Allen. "'New Music for New Ears': The International Composers' Guild," *Journal of the American Musicological Society* 36 (1982), 266–86

Marvin, Elizabeth West. "The Perception of Rhythm in Non-Tonal Music: Rhythmic Contours in the Music of Edgard Varèse," *Music Theory Spectrum* 13/1 (1991), 61–78

Marvin, Elizabeth West and Laprade, Paul. "Relating Musical Contours: Extensions of a Theory for Contour," *Journal of Music Theory* 31/2 (1987), 225–67

Mead, Rita. *Henry Cowell's New Music 1925–1936: The Society, the Music Editions, and the Recordings*. Ann Arbor: UMI Research Press, 1981

Mellers, Wilfrid. *Music in a New Found Land: Themes and Developments in the History of American Music*. New York: Alfred A. Knopf, 1965

Meyer, Felix. "'Thoughtful Bricklaying': Zu einigen Werker der americanischen 'Ultramodernistin' Ruth Crawford," in Christoph Ballmes and Thomas Gastmann, eds, *Festschrift Ernst Lichtenhahn*. Winterthur: Amadeus, 1994, 167–92

Morris, Robert. *Composition with Pitch-Classes*. New Haven: Yale University Press, 1987

Nelson, Mark. "In Pursuit of Charles Seeger's Heterophonic Ideal: Three Palindromic Works by Ruth Crawford," *The Musical Quarterly* 72/4 (1986), 458–75

Neuls-Bates, Carol, ed. *Women in Music: An Anthology of Source Readings from the Middle Ages to the Present*. New York: Harper and Row, 1982

Nicholls, David. *American Experimental Music, 1890–1940*. Cambridge: Cambridge University Press, 1990

Oja, Carol. "The Copland-Sessions Concerts and Their Reception in the Contemporary Press," *The Musical Quarterly*, 65 (1979), 212–29

"Women Patrons and Crusaders for Modernist Music: New York in the 1920s," in Ralph Locke and Cyrilla Barr, eds, *Women Activists in American Music*. Berkeley: University of California Press, 1994

Pendle, Karin, ed. *Women and Music: A History*. Bloomington, Ind.: Indiana University Press, 1991

Perle, George. "Atonality and the Twelve-Tone System in the United States," *The Score*, July 1960, 51–61

Serial Composition and Atonality. 6th edn Berkeley: University of California Press, 1991

Pescatello, Ann. *Charles Seeger: A Life in American Music*. Pittsburgh: University of Pittsburgh Press, 1992

Polansky, Larry. "Envisioning Ruth Crawford Seeger's *Piano Study in Mixed Accents*." Paper presented at national conference of the American Musicological Society and the Society for Music Theory, Montreal, November 1993

Rahn, John. *Basic Atonal Theory*. New York: Longman, 1980

Root, Deane. "The Pan American Association of Composers (1928–34)," *Yearbook for Inter-American Musical Research* 8 (1972), 49–70

Rossiter, Frank. *Charles Ives and His America*. New York: Liveright, 1975

Rudhyar, Dane. "The Dissonant in Art," in *Art as Release of Power*. Carmel, Cal.: Hamsa Publications, 1930, 1–22

"The Mystic's Living Tone," *Modern Music* 7/3 (1929–30), 32–36

"The Relativity of Our Musical Conceptions," *The Musical Quarterly* 8 (1922), 108–18

"The Rise of the Musical Proletariat," *The Musical Quarterly* 6 (1920), 500–509

Scott, Bonnie Kime, ed. *The Gender of Modernism*. Bloomington, Ind.: Indiana University Press, 1990

Seeger, Charles. "Carl Ruggles," in Cowell, *American Composers on American Music: A Symposium*, 14–35

"On Dissonant Counterpoint," *Modern Music* 7 (1930), 25–31

"On Proletarian Music," *Modern Music* 11 (1934), 121–27

"On Style and Manner in Modern Composition," *Musical Quarterly* 9 (1923), 423–31

"Ruth Crawford," in Cowell, *Symposium*, 110–118

Tradition and Experiment in the New Music, in *Studies in Musicology II*, ed. Ann Pescatello (Berkeley: University of California Press, 1994)

Shreffler, Anne. "The Yankee Orpheus: Elliott Carter and his America." Unpublished paper

Smith, Catherine Parsons. "'A Distinguishing Virility': On Feminism and Modernism in American Art Music," in Susan C. Cook and Judy S. Tsou, eds, *Cecilia: Exploring Gender and Music*. Urbana: University of Illinois Press, 1994

Straus, Joseph N. *Remaking the Past: Musical Modernism and the Influence of the Tonal Tradition*. Cambridge, Mass.: Harvard University Press, 1990

Thomas, Margaret. "The String Quartet of Ruth Crawford: Analysis with a View toward Charles Seeger's Theory of Dissonant Counterpoint." (M.A. thesis, University of Washington, 1991)

Tick, Judith. "Charles Ives and the 'Masculine' Ideal," in Ruth Solie, ed., *Musicology and Difference*. Berkeley: University of California Press, 1993, 83–106

"Dissonant Counterpoint Revisited: The First Movement of Ruth Crawford's String Quartet 1931," in Richard Crawford, R. Allen Lott, and Carol Oja, eds, *A Celebration of American Music: Words and Music in Honor of H. Wiley Hitchcock*, Ann Arbor: University of Michigan Press, 1990, 405–22

Ruth Crawford Seeger: An American Woman's Life in Music. Oxford: Oxford University Press, 1995

"Ruth Crawford's 'Spiritual Concept': The Sound-Ideals of an Early American Modernist," *Journal of the American Musicological Society* 44/2 (1991), 221–61

"'Spirit of me . . . Dear rollicking far-gazing straddler of two worlds': The 'Autobiography' of Ruth Crawford Seeger." Paper presented at Gender and Music Conference, King's College, University of London, July 1991

Tischler, Barbara. *An American Music: The Search for an American Musical Identity*. New York: Oxford University Press, 1986

Varèse, Edgard. "The Liberation of Sound," *Perspectives of New Music* 5 (1966), 11–19

Weidig, Adolf. *Harmonic Material and Its Uses: A Treatise for Teachers, Students, and Music Lovers*. Chicago: Clayton F. Summy Co., 1923

Weisgall, Hugo. "The Music of Henry Cowell," *The Musical Quarterly* 45 (1959), 484–507

Weiss, Adolph. "The Lyceum of Schoenberg," *Modern Music* 9/3 (March–April 1932), 99–107

Whittall, Arnold. "Experience, Thought and Musicology," *Musical Times* 134 (1993), No. 1804, 318–20

Wilding-White, Ray. "Remembering Ruth Crawford Seeger: An Interview with Charles and Peggy Seeger," American Music 6/4 (1988), 442–54

Ziffrin, Marilyn. *Carl Ruggles: Composer, Painter, and Storyteller*. Urbana and Chicago: University of Illinois Press, 1994

Zuck, Barbara A. *A History of Musical Americanism*. Ann Arbor: UMI Research Press, 1980

Index

Albrechtsberger, Johann Georg, 4

Babbitt, Milton, 2, 219, 243 n.32
  time-points, 178
Bartók, Béla, 210
Bauer, Marion, 221
Beach, Amy, 220, 221, 225
Beethoven, Ludwig van, 4
Berg, Alban, 210
Blitzstein, Marc, 9
Boulanger, Nadia, 4

Cage, John, 219
Carter, Elliott, 218–19
Composers' Collective, 9, 211, 214
Copland, Aaron, 4, 9, 214
Cowell, Henry, 1, 2, 3, 9, 15, 86, 207,
    208–10, 211, 214–15, 219, 220, 221
  New Music project, 214–15
  New Musical Resources, 3, 219
  on ultra-modernism, 217
  Quartet Euphometric, 219
  Quartet Romantic, 219
Crawford, Ruth
and music by women, 220–26
life, 206–13
  decision to stop composing, 211–13
style
  and form, 123
  counterpoint, 80–93
    heterophony, 80–82, 218; principal
      means of coordinating, 82
    shared motivic content, 82–86
    intervals formed between parts, 85–91
    inversional pivoting, 91–93
  dynamics, 126–30
  harmony, 93–115
    integration of melody and harmony,
      94–95
    whole-tone affiliations, 96–97
    symmetrical harmonies, 97–100
    harmonic progression, 100–15

inversional symmetry, 46–48
large-scale designs, 53–67
  verse form, 53–57
  phrase-neume (motive projection), 57–59
  transpositional projection, 60–67
melody, 5–45, 78–79
  non-repetition and equal distribution of
    notes, 5–8
  chromatic completion, 8–16
  non-repetition and equal distribution of
    intervals, 16–17
  dissonation, 17–20
  neumes, 20–25; transformations, 34–40
  Motive M1, 26–34
  melodic process, 41–45; techniques of
    generating melodies, 41–45;
    ASSERT, 41; OPEN, 41;
    CENTER, 41–42; FILL, 42;
    ADJOIN, 42; RICH (RI-chains),
    42–44, 48; PIVOT (inversional
    centers), 44–45
motivic projection, 57–59
precompositional plans, 67–79
  retrograde symmetry, 67–73
  rotational serialism, 73–76
  ostinato, 76–79
register, 48–53
rhythm, 115–26
  precompositional plans and patterns,
    115–23
  rhythmic contours, 123–26
works
Diaphonic Suites (1930), 1, 3, 210, 215, 236
    n.82–83
  verse form in, 54–56
  No. 1, 7–8, 54–56, 117, 152
    Motive M1 in, 28–30
    rhythmic contours in, 125–26
    first movement: registral frame, 48–50;
      RI-chains in, 42–43; melodic
      transformations in, 44–45
    second movement, 19

257